OPERATIONAL PROCEDL

CW01476948

Stuart E. Smith

STUDY GUIDE SERIES for EASA examinations

British Library Cataloguing in Publication Data.
A catalogue record for this book is pending from the British Library.

First published in the United Kingdom by Cranfield Aviation Training School Limited. 2002

Further volumes in this series are:
Aircraft General Knowledge: Airframes / Systems / Powerplant / Electrics / Emergency Equipment
Aviation Law & ATC Procedures
Flight Planning & Monitoring
General Navigation
Human Performance & Limitations
Instruments & Electronics
Mass & Balance
Meteorology
Performance
Principles of Flight
Radio Navigation
VFR & IFR Communications

Series editor: Dr Stuart E. Smith

CRANFIELD AVIATION TRAINING SCHOOL LTD. PART-FCL GBR.ATO-0136
CATS INNOVATION CENTRE, LUTON, Bedfordshire LU2 8DL U.K.

www.catsaviation.com
Operational Procedures

THEORETICAL KNOWLEDGE SYLLABUS AND LEARNING OBJECTIVES

Syllabus reference	Syllabus details and associated Learning Objectives	Aeroplane		Helicopter			
		ATPL	CPL	ATPL/ IR	ATPL	CPL	IR
070 00 00 00	**OPERATIONAL PROCEDURES**						
071 01 00 00	**GENERAL REQUIREMENTS**						
071 01 01 00	**ICAO Annex 6**						
071 01 01 01	**Definitions**						
LO	Alternate aerodrome: take-off alternate, en route alternate, ETOPS en route alternate, destination alternate (ICAO Annex 6, Part I, Chapter 1).	X	X				
LO	Alternate heliport (ICAO Annex 6, Part III, Section 1, Chapter 1).			X	X	X	
LO	Flight time — aeroplanes (ICAO Annex 6, Part I, Chapter 1).	X	X				
LO	Flight time — helicopters (ICAO Annex 6, Part III, Section 1, Chapter 1).			X	X	X	
071 01 01 02	**Applicability**						
LO	State that Part I shall be applicable to the operation of aeroplanes by operators authorised to conduct international commercial air transport operations (ICAO Annex 6, Part I, Chapter 2).	X	X				
LO	State that Part III shall be applicable to all helicopters engaged in international commercial air transport operations or in international general aviation operations, except it is not applicable to helicopters engaged in aerial work (ICAO Annex 6, Part III, Section 1, Chapter 2).			X	X	X	
071 01 01 03	**General**						
LO	State compliance with laws, regulations and procedures (ICAO Annex 6, Part I, Chapter 3.1/Part III, Section 2, Chapter 1.1).	X	X	X	X	X	
LO	State accident prevention and flight safety programme (ICAO Annex6, Part I, Chapter 3.2).	X	X				
LO	State flight safety documents system (ICAO Annex 6, Part I, Chapter 3.3).	X	X				
LO	State maintenance release (ICAO Annex 6, Part I, Chapter 8.8/Part III, Section 2, Chapter 6.7).	X	X	X	X	X	
LO	List and describe the lights to be displayed by aircraft (ICAO Annex 6, Part I, Appendix 1).	X	X				
071 01 02 00	**Operational requirements**						
071 01 02 01	**Applicability**						
LO	State the operational regulations applicable to commercial air transportation.	X	X	X	X	X	
LO	Nature of operations and exceptions.	X	X	X	X	X	
071 01 02 02	**General**						
LO	State that a commercial air transportation flight must meet the applicable operational requirements.	X	X	X	X	X	
LO	Flight Manual limitations — Flight through the Height Velocity (HV) envelope.			X	X	X	
LO	Define 'Helicopter Emergency Medical Service'.			X	X	X	
LO	Operations over a hostile environment — Applicability.			X	X	X	
LO	Local area operations — Approval.			X	X	X	

CRANFIELD AVIATION TRAINING SCHOOL LTD. PART-FCL GBR.ATO-0136
CATS INNOVATION CENTRE, LUTON, Bedfordshire LU2 8DL U.K.

www.catsaviation.com

Operational Procedures

vii

LO	State the requirements about language used for crew communication and operations manual.	x	x	x	x	x	
LO	Explain the relation between MMEL and MEL.	x	x	x	x	x	
LO	State the operator's requirements regarding a management system.	x	x	x	x	x	
LO	State the operator's requirements regarding accident prevention and flight safety programme.	x	x	x	x	x	
LO	State the operator's responsibility regarding the distinction between cabin crew members and additional crew members.	x	x				
LO	State the operations limitations regarding ditching requirements.	x	x				
LO	State the regulations concerning the carriage of persons on an aircraft.	x	x	x	x	x	
LO	State the crew members' responsibilities in the execution of their duties, and define the commander's authority.	x	x	x	x	x	
LO	State the operator's and commander's responsibilities regarding admission to the flight deck and carriage of unauthorised persons or cargo.	x	x	x	x	x	
LO	State the operator's responsibility concerning portable electronic devices.	x	x	x	x	x	
LO	State the operator's responsibilities regarding admission in an aircraft of a person under the influence of drug or alcohol.	x	x	x	x	x	
LO	State the regulations concerning endangering safety.	x	x	x	x	x	
LO	List the documents to be carried on each flight.	x	x	x	x	x	
LO	State the operator's responsibility regarding manuals to be carried.	x	x	x	x	x	
LO	List the additional information and forms to be carried on board.	x	x	x	x	x	
LO	List the items of information to be retained on the ground by the operator.	x	x	x	x	x	
LO	State the operator's responsibility regarding inspections.	x	x	x	x	x	
LO	State the responsibility of the operator and of the commander regarding the production of and access to records and documents.	x	x	x	x	x	
LO	State the operator's responsibility regarding the preservation of documentation and recordings, including recorders recordings.	x	x	x	x	x	
LO	Define the terms used in leasing and state the responsibility and requirements of each party in various cases.	x	x	x	x	x	
071 01 02 03	**Operator certification and supervision**						
LO	State the requirement to be satisfied for the issue of an Air Operator's Certificate (AOC).	x	x	x	x	x	
LO	State the rules applicable to air operator certification.	x	x	x	x	x	
LO	State the conditions to be met for the issue or revalidation of an AOC.	x	x	x	x	x	
LO	Explain the contents and conditions of the AOC.	x	x	x	x	x	
071 01 02 04	**Operational procedures (except long-range flight preparation)**						
LO	Define the terms used for operational procedures.	x	x				
LO	State the operator's responsibilities regarding Operations Manual.	x	x	x	x	x	
LO	State the operator's responsibilities regarding competence of operations personnel.	x	x	x	x	x	

	LO						
LO	State the operator's responsibilities regarding establishment of procedures.	x	x	x	x	x	
LO	State the operator's responsibilities regarding use of air traffic services.	x	x	x	x	x	
LO	State the operator's responsibilities regarding authorization of aerodromes/ heliports by the operator.	x	x	x	x	x	
LO	Explain which elements must be considered by the operator when specifying aerodrome/heliport operating minima.	x	x	x	x	x	
LO	State the operator's responsibilities regarding departure and approach procedures.	x	x	x	x	x	
LO	State the parameters to be considered in noise-abatement procedures.	x	x				
LO	State the elements to be considered regarding routes and areas of operation.	x	x	x	x	x	
LO	State the additional specific navigation- performance requirements.	x	x	x	x	x	
LO	State the maximum distance from an adequate aerodrome for two-engine aeroplanes without an ETOPS approval.	x	x				
LO	State the requirement for alternate-airport accessibility check for ETOPS operations.	x	x				
LO	List the factors to be considered when establishing minimum flight altitude.	x	x	x	x	x	
LO	Describe the components of the fuel policy.	x	x	x	x	x	
LO	State the requirements for carrying persons with reduced mobility.	x	x	x	x	x	
LO	State the operator's responsibilities for the carriage of inadmissible passengers, deportees or persons in custody.	x	x	x	x	x	
LO	State the requirements for the stowage of baggage and cargo in the passenger cabin.	x	x	x	x	x	
LO	State the requirements regarding passenger seating and emergency evacuation.	x	x	x	x	x	
LO	Detail the procedures for a passenger briefing in respect of emergency equipment and exits.	x	x	x	x	x	
LO	State the flight preparation forms to be completed before flight.	x	x	x	x	x	
LO	State the commander's responsibilities during flight preparation.	x	x	x	x	x	
LO	State the rules for aerodromes/heliports selection (including ETOPS configuration).	x	x	x	x	x	
LO	Explain the planning minima for IFR flights.	x		x			
LO	State the rules for refueling / defuelling.	x	x	x	x	x	
LO	State 'crew members at station' policy.	x	x	x	x	x	
LO	State the use of seats, safety belts and harnesses.	x	x	x	x	x	
LO	State securing of passenger cabin and galley requirements.	x	x	x	x	x	
LO	State the commander's responsibility regarding smoking on board.	x	x	x	x	x	
LO	State under which conditions a commander can commence or continue a flight regarding meteorological conditions.	x	x	x	x	x	
LO	State the commander's responsibility regarding ice and other contaminants.	x	x	x	x	x	
LO	State the commander's responsibility regarding fuel to be carried and in-flight fuel management.	x	x	x	x	x	

CRANFIELD AVIATION TRAINING SCHOOL LTD. PART-FCL GBR.ATO-0136
CATS INNOVATION CENTRE, LUTON, Bedfordshire LU2 8DL U.K.
www.catsaviation.com
Operational Procedures

ix

LO	State the requirements regarding the use of supplemental oxygen.	x	x	x	x	x	
LO	State the ground-proximity detection reactions.	x	x	x	x	x	
LO	Explain the requirements for use of ACAS.	x	x	x	x	x	
LO	State the commander's responsibility regarding approach and landing.	x	x	x	x	x	
LO	State the circumstances under which a report shall be submitted.	x	x	x	x	x	
071 01 02 05	**All-weather operations**						
LO	State the operator's responsibility regarding aerodrome/heliport operating minima.	x		x			
LO	List the parameters to be considered in establishing the aerodrome operating minima.	x		x			
LO	Define the criteria to be taken into consideration for the classification of aeroplanes.	x					
LO	Define the following terms: 'circling', 'low-visibility procedures', 'low-visibility take-off', 'visual approach'.	x		x			
LO	Define the following terms: 'flight control system', 'fail-passive flight control system', 'fail-operational flight control system', 'fail-operational hybrid landing system'.	x					
LO	Define the following terms: 'final approach and take-off area'.			x			
LO	State the general operating rules for low-visibility operations.	x		x			
LO	Low-visibility operations — aerodrome/heliport considerations.	x		x			
LO	State the training and qualification requirements for flight crew to conduct low-visibility operations.	x		x			
LO	State the operating procedures for low-visibility operations.	x		x			
LO	State the operator's and commander's responsibilities regarding minimum equipment for low-visibility operations.	x		x			
LO	VFR operating minima.	x		x			
LO	Aerodrome operating minima: state under which conditions the commander can commence take-off.	x		x			
LO	Aerodrome operating minima: state that take-off minima are expressed as visibility or RVR.	x		x			
LO	Aerodrome operating minima: state the take-off RVR value depending on the facilities.	x		x			
LO	Aerodrome operating minima: state the system minima for non-precision approach.	x		x			
LO	Aerodrome operating minima: state under which conditions a pilot can continue the approach below MDA/H or DA/H.	x		x			
LO	Aerodrome operating minima: state the lowest minima for precision approach category 1 (including single-pilot operations).	x		x			
LO	Aerodrome operating minima: state the lowest minima for precision approach category 2 operations.	x		x			
LO	Aerodrome operating minima: state the lowest minima for precision approach category 3 operations.	x					
LO	Aerodrome operating minima: state the lowest minima for circling and visual approach.	x		x			

LO	Aerodrome operating minima: state the RVR value and cloud ceiling depending on the facilities (class 1, 2 and 3).			X		
LO	Aerodrome operating minima: state under which conditions an airborne radar approach can be performed and state the relevant minima.			X		
071 01 02 06	**Instruments and equipment**					
LO	State which items do not require an equipment approval.	X	X	X	X	X
LO	State the requirements regarding spare- fuses availability.	X	X			
LO	State the requirements regarding operating lights.	X	X	X	X	X
LO	State the requirements regarding windshield wipers.	X	X			
LO	List the equipment for operations requiring a radio communication.			X	X	X
LO	List the equipment for operations requiring a radio-navigation system.			X	X	X
LO	List the minimum equipment required for day and night VFR flights.	X	X	X	X	X
LO	List the minimum equipment required for IFR flights.	X		X		
LO	State the required equipment for single-pilot operation under IFR.	X		X		
LO	State the requirements for an altitude alert system.	X	X			
LO	State the requirements for radio altimeters.			X	X	X
LO	State the requirements for GPWS/TAWS.	X	X			
LO	State the requirements for ACAS.	X	X			
LO	State the conditions under which an aircraft must be fitted with a weather radar.	X	X	X	X	X
LO	State the requirements for operations in icing conditions.	X	X	X	X	X
LO	State the conditions under which a crew member interphone system and public address system are mandatory.	X	X	X	X	X
LO	State the circumstances under which a cockpit voice recorder is compulsory.	X	X	X	X	X
LO	State the rules regarding the location, construction, installation and operation of cockpit voice recorders.	X	X	X	X	X
LO	State the circumstances under which a flight data recorder is compulsory.	X	X	X	X	X
LO	State the rules regarding the location, construction, installation and operation of flight data recorders.	X	X	X	X	X
LO	State the requirements about seats, seat safety belts, harnesses and child-restraint devices.	X	X	X	X	X
LO	State the requirements about 'Fasten seat belt' and 'No smoking' signs.	X	X	X	X	X
LO	State the requirements regarding internal doors and curtains.	X	X			
LO	State the requirements regarding first-aid kits.	X	X	X	X	X
LO	State the requirements regarding emergency medical kits and first-aid oxygen.	X	X			
LO	Detail the rules regarding the carriage and use of supplemental oxygen for passengers and crew.	X	X	X	X	X
LO	Detail the rules regarding crew-protective breathing equipment.	X	X			

LO	Describe the minimum number, type and location of handheld fire extinguishers.	x	x	x	x	x	
LO	Describe the minimum number and location of crash axes and crowbars.	x	x				
LO	Specify the colours and markings used to indicate break-in points.	x	x	x	x	x	
LO	State the requirements for means of emergency evacuation.	x	x				
LO	State the requirements for megaphones.	x	x	x	x	x	
LO	State the requirements for emergency lighting.	x	x	x	x	x	
LO	State the requirements for an emergency locator transmitter.	x	x	x	x	x	
LO	State the requirements for life jackets, life rafts, survival kits and ELTs.	x	x	x	x	x	
LO	State the requirements for crew survival suit.			x	x	x	
LO	State the requirements for survival equipment.	x	x	x	x	x	
LO	State the additional requirements for helicopters operating to or from heli-decks located in a hostile sea area.			x	x	x	
LO	State the requirements for emergency flotation equipment.			x	x	x	
071 01 02 07	**Communication and navigation equipment**						
LO	Explain the general requirements for communication and navigation equipment.	x	x	x	x	x	
LO	State that the radio-communication equipment must provide communications on 121.5 MHz.	x	x	x	x	x	
LO	State the requirements regarding the provision of an audio selector panel.	x	x	x	x	x	
LO	List the requirements for radio equipment when flying under VFR by reference to visual landmarks.	x	x	x	x	x	
LO	List the requirements for communications and navigation equipment when operating under IFR or under VFR over routes not navigated by reference to visual landmarks.	x	x	x	x	x	
LO	State the equipment required to operate within RVSM airspace.	x	x				
071 01 02 09	**Flight crew**						
LO	State the requirement regarding crew composition and in-flight relief.	x	x	x	x	x	
LO	State the requirement for conversion training and checking.	x	x	x	x	x	
LO	State the requirement for differences training and familiarisation training.	x	x	x	x	x	
LO	State the conditions for upgrade from co-pilot to commander.	x	x	x	x	x	
LO	State the minimum qualification requirements to operate as a commander.	x	x	x	x	x	
LO	State the requirement for recurrent training and checking.	x	x	x	x	x	
LO	State the requirement for a pilot to operate on either pilot's seat.	x	x	x	x	x	
LO	State the minimum recent experience for the commander and the co-pilot.	x	x	x	x	x	
LO	Specify the route and aerodrome/heliport qualification required for a commander or a pilot flying.	x	x	x	x	x	
LO	State the requirement to operate on more than one type or variant.	x	x	x	x	x	
LO	State that when a flight crew member operates both helicopters and aeroplanes, the operations are limited to one type of each.	x	x				

LO	State the training records requirement.	x	x	x	x	x	
071 01 02 10	**Cabin crew/crew members other than flight crew**						
LO	State who is regarded as a cabin crew member.	x	x	x	x	x	
LO	Detail the requirements regarding cabin crew members.	x	x	x	x	x	
LO	State the acceptability criteria.	x	x	x	x	x	
LO	State the requirements regarding senior cabin crew members.	x	x	x	x	x	
LO	State the conditions to operate on more than one type or variant.	x	x	x	x	x	
071 01 02 11	**Manuals, logs and records**						
LO	Explain the general rules for the operations manual.	x	x	x	x	x	
LO	Explain the structure and subject headings of the operations manual.	x	x	x	x	x	
LO	State the requirements for a journey logbook.	x	x	x	x	x	
LO	Describe the requirements regarding the operational flight plan.	x	x	x	x	x	
LO	State therequirements for document storage periods.	x	x	x	x	x	
071 01 02 12	**Flight and duty-time limitations and rest requirements**						
LO	Explain the definitions used for flight-time regulation.	x	x				
LO	State the flight and duty limitations.	x	x				
LO	State the requirements regarding the maximum daily flight-duty period.	x	x				
LO	State the requirements regarding rest periods.	x	x				
LO	Explain the possible extension of flight-duty period due to in-flight rest.	x	x				
LO	Explain the captain's discretion in case of unforeseen circumstances in actual flight operations.	x	x				
LO	Explain the regulation regarding standby.	x	X				
LO	State the requirements regarding flight-duty, duty and rest-period records.	x	x				
071 01 02 13	**Transport of dangerous goods by air**						
LO	Explain the terminology relevant to dangerous goods.	x	x	x	x	X	
LO	Explain the scope of the regulation.	x	x	x	x	x	
LO	Explain the limitations on the transport of dangerous goods.	x	x	x	x	x	
LO	State the requirements for the acceptance of dangerous goods.	x	x	x	x	x	
LO	State the requirements regarding inspection for damage, leakage or contamination.	x	x	x	x	x	
LO	Explain the loading restrictions.	x	x	x	x	x	
LO	State the requirement for provision of information to the crew.	x	x	x	x	x	
LO	Explain the requirements for dangerous goods incident and accident reports.	x	x	x	x	x	
071 01 03 00	**Long-range flights**						
071 01 03 01	**Flight management**						
LO	Navigation-planning procedures: — describe the operator's responsibilities concerning ETOPS routes; — list the factors to be considered by the commander before commencing the flight.	x					

LO	Selection of a route:	x						
	— describe the meaning of the term 'adequate aerodrome';							
	— describe the limitations on extended- range operations with two-engine aeroplanes with and without ETOPS approval.							
LO	Selection of cruising altitude (MNPSA Manual Chapter 4):	x						
	— specify the appropriate cruising levels for normal long-range IFR flights and for those operating on the North Atlantic Operational Track Structure.							
LO	Selection of alternate aerodrome:	x						
	— state the circumstances in which a take-off alternate must be selected;							
	— state the maximum flight distance of a take-off alternate for: two-engine aeroplane, ETOPS-approved aeroplane, three or four-engine aeroplane;							
	— state the factors to be considered in the selection of a take-off alternate;							
	— state when a destination alternate need not be selected;							
	— state when two destination alternates must be selected;							
	— state the factors to be considered in the selection of a destination alternate aerodrome;							
	— state the factors to be considered in the selection of an en route alternate aerodrome.							
LO	Minimum time routes:	x						
	— define, construct and interpret minimum time route (route giving the shortest flight time from departure to destination adhering to all ATC and airspace restrictions).							
071 01 03 02	**Transoceanic and polar flight**							

			X					
LO	(ICAO Doc 7030)							

LO | (ICAO Doc 7030)

— Describe the possible indications of navigation- system degradation.

— Describe by what emergency means course and INS can be cross-checked in the case of: three navigation systems, two navigation systems.

— Interpret VOR, NDB, VOR/DME information to calculate aircraft position and aircraft course.

— Describe the general ICAO procedures applicable in North Atlantic airspace (NAT) if the aircraft is unable to continue the flight in accordance with its air traffic control clearance.

— Describe the ICAO procedures applicable in North Atlantic Airspace (NAT) in case of radio- communication failure.

— Describe the recommended initial action if an aircraft is unable to obtain a revised air traffic control clearance.

— Describe the subsequent action for: aircraft able to maintain assigned flight level, and aircraft unable to maintain assigned flight level.

— Describe determination of tracks and courses for random routes in NAT.

— Specify the method by which planned tracks are defined (by latitude and longitude) in the NAT region: when operating predominately in an east–west direction south of 70°N, when operating predominately in an east–west direction north of 70°N.

— State the maximum flight time recommended between significant points.

— Specify the method by which planned tracks are defined for flights operating predominantly in a north–south direction.

— Describe how the desired route must be specified in the air traffic control flight plan.

CRANFIELD AVIATION TRAINING SCHOOL LTD. PART-FCL GBR.ATO-0136
CATS INNOVATION CENTRE, LUTON, Bedfordshire LU2 8DL U.K.

www.catsaviation.com

Operational Procedures

XV

LO	Polar navigation	x						
	Terrestrial magnetism characteristics in polar zones							
	— Explain why magnetic compasses become unreliable or useless in polar zones.							
	— State in which area VORs are referenced to the true north.							
	Specific problems of polar navigation							
	— Describe the general problems of polar navigation.							
	— Describe what precautions can be taken when operating in the area of compass unreliability as a contingency against INS failure.							
	— Describe how grid navigation can be used in conjunction with a Directional Gyro (DG) in polar areas.							
	— Use polar stereographic chart and grid coordinates to solve polar navigation problems.							
	— Use polar stereographic chart and grid coordinates to calculate navigation data.							
	— Use INS information to solve polar navigation problems.							
	— Define, calculate: transport precession, Earth- rate (astronomic) precession, convergence factor.							
	— Describe the effect of using a free gyro to follow a given course.							
	— Describe the effect of using a gyro compass with hourly rate corrector unit to follow a given course.							
	— Convert grid navigation data into true navigation data, into magnetic navigation data, and into compass navigation data.							
	— Justify the selection of a different 'north' reference at a given position.							
	— Calculate the effects of gyro drift due to the Earth's rotation (15 degrees / h × sin Lm).							
071 01 03 03	**MNPS airspace**							
LO	Geographical limits: — state the lateral dimensions (in general terms) and vertical limits of MNPS airspace (ICAO Doc 7030 NAT/RAC-2 3.2.1);	x						
	— state that operators must ensure that crew Follow NATMNPSA Operations Manual procedures (ICAO Doc 7030 NAT/RAC-2 3.2.3).							
LO	Define the following acronyms: MNPS, MNPSA, OCA, OTS, PRM, PTS, RVSM, LRNS, MASPS, SLOP, WATRS (MNPSA Manual, Glossary of Terms).	x						
LO	Aircraft system requirements (MNPSA Manual, Chapter 1): — navigation requirements for unrestricted MNPS airspace operations; — routes for use by aircraft not equipped with two LRNSs: routes for aircraft with only one LRNS, routes for aircraft with short-range navigation equipment only; — performance monitoring.	x						
LO	Organised Track System (MNPSA Manual, Chapter 2): — construction of the Organised Track System (OTS); — NAT track message; — OTS changeover periods.	x						

LO	Other routes and route structures within or adjacent to NAT MNPS airspace (MNPSA Manual, Chapter 3): — other routes within NAT MNPS airspace; — route structures adjacent to NAT MNPS airspace: North American routes (NARs), Canadian domestic track systems, routes between North America and the Caribbean area.	x						
LO	Flight planning (MNPSA Manual, Chapter 4): — all flights should plan to operate on great-circle tracks joining successive significant waypoints; — during the hours of validity of the OTS, operators are encouraged to flight plan as follows: in accordance with the OTS or along a route to join or leave an outer track of the OTS or on a random route to remain clear of the OTS; — flight levels available on OTS tracks during OTS periods; — flight levels on random tracks or outside OTS periods (appropriate direction levels).	x						
LO	Oceanic ATC Clearances (MNPSA Manual, Chapter 5): — it is recommended that pilots should request their Oceanic Clearance at least 40 minutes prior to the oceanic entry point ETA; — pilots should notify the Oceanic Area control Centre (OAC) of the maximum acceptable flight level possible at the boundary; — at some airports, which are situated close to oceanic boundaries, the Oceanic Clearance must be obtained before departure; — if an aircraft, which would normally be RVSM and/or MNPS approved, encounters, whilst en route to the NAT Oceanic Airspace, a critical in-flight equipment failure, or at dispatch is unable to meet the MEL requirements for RVSM or MNPS approval on the flight, then the pilot must advise ATC at initial contact when requesting Oceanic Clearance; — After obtaining and reading back the clearance, the pilot should monitor the forward estimate for oceanic entry, and if this changes by 3 minutes or more, should pass a revised estimate to ATC; — the pilot should pay particular attention when the issued clearance differs from the flight plan, as a significant proportion of navigation errors investigated in the NAT involve an aircraft which has followed its flight plan rather than its differing clearance; — if the entry point of the oceanic route on which the flight is cleared differs from that originally requested and/or the oceanic flight level differs from the current flight level, the pilot is responsible for requesting and obtaining the necessary domestic re-clearance; — there are three elements to an Oceanic Clearance: route, Mach number and flight level. These elements serve to provide for the three basic elements of separation: lateral, longitudinal and vertical.	x						

			x					
	LO	Communications and position-reporting procedures (MNPSA Manual, Chapter 6) *HF voice communications* — Pilots communicate with OACs via aeradio stations staffed by communicators who have no executive ATC authority. Messages are relayed, from the ground station to the air traffic controllers in the relevant OAC for action. — Frequencies from the lower HF bands tend to be used for communications during night-time and those from the higher bands during daytime. — When initiating contact with an aeradio station, the pilot should state the HF frequency in use. *SATCOM voice communications* Since oceanic traffic typically communicates with ATC through aeradio facilities, a SATCOM call made due to unforeseen inability to communicate by other means should be made to such a facility rather than the ATC centre, unless the urgency of the communication dictates otherwise. An air-to-air VHF frequency has been established for worldwide use when aircraft are out of range of VHF ground stations which utilise the same or adjacent frequencies. This frequency (123.45 MHz) is intended for pilot-to-pilot exchanges of operationally significant information. Standard position report message type. Some aircraft flying in the NAT are required to report MET observations of wind speed and direction plus outside-air temperature. Any turbulence encountered should be included in these reports. General guidance for aircraft operating in, or proposing to operate in, the NAT region, which experience a communications failure: general provisions, onboard HF equipment failure, poor HF propagation conditions, loss of HF communications prior to entry into the NAT, loss of HF communications after entering the NAT. All turbine-engine aeroplanes having a maximum certified take-off mass exceeding 5 700 kg or authorised to carry more than 19 passengers are required to carry and operate ACAS II in the NAT region.	x					
	LO	Application of Mach number technique (MNPSA Manual, Chapter 7): — practical experience has shown that when two or more turbojet aircraft, operating along the same route at the same flight level, maintain the same Mach number, they are more likely to maintain a constant time interval between each other than when using other methods; — pilots must ensure that any required corrections to the indicated Mach number are taken into account when complying with the true Mach number specified in the ATC clearance; — after leaving oceanic airspace, pilots must maintain their assigned Mach number in domestic controlled airspace unless and until the appropriate ATC unit authorises a change.	x					

			x					
LO	MNPS flight operation & navigation procedures (MNPSA Manual, Chapter 8):		x					
	— the pre-flight procedures for any NAT MNPS flight must include a UTC time check and resynchronisation of the aircraft master clock;							
	— state the use of the Master Document;							
	— state the requirements for position plotting;							
	— PRE-FLIGHT PROCEDURES: alignment of IRS, Satellite Navigation Availability Prediction Programme for flights using GNSS LRNS, loading of initial waypoints, flight plan check;							
	— IN-FLIGHT PROCEDURES: ATC Oceanic Clearance, entering the MNPS airspace and reaching an oceanic waypoint, routine monitoring;							
	— Strategic Lateral Offset Procedure (SLOP): state that along a route or track there will be three positions that an aircraft may fly: centre line or one or two miles right.							
LO	RVSM flight in MNPS airspace (MNPSA Manual, Chapter 9):		x					
	— state the altimeter cross-check to be performed before MNPS airspace entry;							
	— state the altimeter cross-check to be performed into the MNPS airspace;							
	— in NAT MNPS airspace, pilots always have to report to ATC immediately on reaching any new cruising level;							
	— crews should report when a 300' or more deviation occurs.							
LO	Navigation system degradation or failure (MNPSA Manual, Chapter 10) For this part, consider aircraft equipped with only two operational LRNSs. State the requirements for the following situations:		x					
	— one system fails before take-off;							
	— one system fails before the OCA boundary is reached;							
	— one system fails after the OCA boundary is crossed;							
	— the remaining system fails after entering MNPS airspace.							
LO	Special procedures for in-flight contingencies (MNPSA Manual, Chapter 11) *General*		x					
	— Until a revised clearance is obtained, the specified NAT in-flight contingency procedures should be carefully followed.							
	— The general concept of these NAT in-flight contingency procedures is, whenever operationally feasible, to offset from the assigned route by 15 NM and climb or descend to a level which differs from those normally used by 500' if below FL410 or by 1 000' if above FL410.							
	— State the factors which may affect the direction of turn: direction to an alternate airport, terrain clearance, levels allocated on adjacent routes or tracks and any known SLOP offsets adopted by other nearby traffic.							
	Deviations around severe weather							
	— State that if the deviation is to be greater than 10 NM, the assigned flight level must be changed by ± 300' depending on the followed track and the direction of the deviation (Table 1).							
071 01 03 04	**ETOPS**							
LO	State that ETOPS approval is part of an AOC.		x					

	LO	State that prior to conducting an ETOPS flight, an operator shall ensure that a suitable ETOPS en route alternate is available, within either the approved diversion time or a diversion time based on the MEL-generated serviceability status of the aeroplane, whichever is shorter.	x				
	LO	State the requirements for take-off alternate.	x				
	LO	State the planning minima for ETOPS en route alternate.	x				
071 02 00 00		**SPECIAL OPERATIONAL PROCEDURES AND HAZARDS (GENERAL ASPECTS)**					
071 02 01 00		**Operations Manual**					
071 02 01 01		**Operating procedures**					
	LO	State that all non-type-related operational policies, instructions and procedures needed for a safe operation are included in Part A of the Operations Manual.	x	x	x	x	x
	LO	State that the following items are included into Part A: de-icing and anti-icing on the ground, adverse and potentially hazardous atmospheric conditions, wake turbulence, incapacitation of crew members, use of the minimum equipment and configuration deviation list(s), security, handling of accidents and occurrences.	x	x	x	x	x
	LO	State that the following items are included into Part A: altitude alerting system procedures, ground proximity warning system procedures, policy and procedures for the use of TCAS/ACAS.	x	x			
	LO	State that the following items are included into Part A: rotor downwash.			x	x	x
	LO	Define the following terms: 'commencement of flight', 'inoperative', 'MEL', 'MMEL', rectification interval.	x	x	x	x	x
	LO	Define the 'limits of MEL applicability'.	x	x	x	x	x
	LO	Identify the responsibilities of the operator and the authority with regard to MEL and MMEL.	x	x	x	x	x
	LO	State the responsibilities of the crew members with regard to MEL.	x	x	x	x	x
	LO	State the responsibilities of the commander with regard to MEL.	x	x	x	x	x
071 02 01 02		**Aeroplane/helicopter operating matters — type- related**					
	LO	State that all type-related instructions and procedures needed for a safe operation are included in Part B of the Operations Manual. They will take account of any differences between types, variants or individual aircraft used by the operator.	x	x	x	x	x
	LO	State that the following items are included into Part B: abnormal and emergency procedures, configuration deviation list, minimum equipment list, emergency evacuation procedures.	x	x			
	LO	State that the following items are included into Part B: emergency procedures, configuration deviation list, minimum equipment list, emergency evacuation procedures.			x	x	x
071 02 02 00		**Icing conditions**					
071 02 02 01		**On ground de-icing/anti-icing procedures, types of de- icing/anti-icing fluids**					
	LO	Define the following terms: 'anti-icing', 'de-icing', 'one- step de-icing/anti-icing', 'two-step de-icing/anti-icing', 'holdover time'. (ICAO Doc 9640 Glossary)	x	x			
	LO	Define the following weather conditions: 'drizzle', 'fog', 'freezing fog', 'freezing drizzle', 'freezing rain', 'frost', 'rain', 'rime', 'slush', 'snow', 'dry snow', 'wet snow'. (ICAO Doc 9640 Glossary)	x	x	x	x	x

CRANFIELD AVIATION TRAINING SCHOOL LTD. PART-FCL GBR.ATO-0136
CATS INNOVATION CENTRE, LUTON, Bedfordshire LU2 8DL U.K.

www.catsaviation.com
Operational Procedures

xx

LO	Describe 'The clean aircraft concept' as presented in the relevant chapter of ICAO Doc 9640. (ICAO Doc 9640, Chapter 2)	x	x				
LO	List the types of de-icing/anti-icing fluids available. (ICAO Doc 9640, Chapter 4)	x	x	x	x	x	
LO	State the procedure to be followed when an aeroplane has exceeded the holdover time. (ICAO Doc 9640, Chapter 4)	x	x				
LO	Interpret the fluid holdover time tables and list the factors which can reduce the fluid protection time. (ICAO Doc 9640, Chapter 5 + Attachment tables)	x	x				
LO	State that the pre-take-off check, which is the responsibility of the pilot-in-command, ensures that the critical surfaces of the aeroplane are free of ice, snow, slush or frost just prior to take-off. This check shall be accomplished as close to the time of take-off as possible and is normally made from within the aeroplane by visually checking the wings. (ICAO Doc 9640, Chapter 6)	x	x				
LO	State that an aircraft has to be treated symmetrically. (ICAO Doc 9640, Chapter 11)	x	x				
LO	State that an operator shall establish procedures to be followed when ground de-icing and anti-icing and related inspections of the aeroplane(s) are necessary.	x	x	x	x	x	
LO	State that a commander shall not commence take-off unless the external surfaces are clear of any deposit which might adversely affect the performance and/or controllability of the aircraft except as permitted in the Flight Manual.	x	x	x	x	x	
071 02 02 02	**Procedure to apply in case of performance deterioration, on ground/in flight**						
LO	State that the effects of icing are wide-ranging, unpredictable and dependent upon individual aeroplane design. The magnitude of these effects is dependent upon many variables, but the effects can be both significant and dangerous. (ICAO Doc 9640, Chapter 1)	x	x	x	x	x	
LO	State that in icing conditions, for a given speed and a given angle of attack, wing lift can be reduced by as much as 30 % and drag increased by up to 40 %. State that these changes in lift and drag will significantly increase stall speed, reduce controllability and alter flight characteristics. (ICAO Doc 9640, Chapter 1)	x	x	x	x	x	
LO	State that ice on critical surfaces and on the airframe may also break away during take-off and be ingested into engines, possibly damaging fan and compressor blades. (ICAO Doc 9640, Chapter 1)	x	x	x	x	x	
LO	State that ice forming on pitot tubes and static ports or on angle-of-attack vanes may give false altitude, airspeed, angle-of-attack and engine-power information for air-data systems. (ICAO Doc 9640, Chapter 1)	x	x	x	x	x	
LO	State that ice, frost and snow formed on the critical surfaces on the ground can have a totally different effect on aircraft flight characteristics than ice formed in flight. (ICAO Doc 9640, Chapter 1)	x	x	x	x	x	
LO	State that flight in known icing conditions is subject to limitations found in Part B of the Operations Manual.	x	x	x	x	x	
LO	State where procedures and performances regarding flight in expected or actual icing conditions are located.	x	x	x	x	x	

071 02 03 00	**Bird-strike risk and avoidance**						
LO	State that presence of birds constituting a potential hazard to aircraft operations is part of the pre-flight information. (ICAO Annex 15, Chapter 8)	x	x	x	x	x	
LO	State that information concerning the presence of birds observed by aircrews is made available to the Aeronautical Information Service for such distribution as the circumstances necessitate. (ICAO Annex 15, Chapter 8)	x	x	x	x	x	
LO	State that AIP ENR 5.6 contains information regarding bird migrations. (ICAO Annex 15, Appendix 1)	x	x	x	x	x	
LO	State significant data regarding bird strikes contained in ICAO Doc 9137. (ICAO Doc 9137, Part 3, 1.1.6)	x	x	x	x	x	
LO	List incompatible land use around airports. (ICAO Doc 9137, Part 3, 10.4)	x	x	x	x	x	
LO	Define the commander's responsibilities regarding the reporting of bird hazards and bird strikes.	x	x	x	x	x	
071 02 04 00	**Noise abatement**						
071 02 04 01	**Noise-abatement procedures**						
LO	Define the operator responsibilities regarding establishment of noise-abatement procedures.	x	x	x	x	x	
LO	State the main purpose of NADP 1 and NADP 2. (ICAO Doc 8168, Volume 1, Part V, 3.1.1)	x	x	x	x	x	
LO	State that the pilot-in-command has the authority to decide not to execute a noise-abatement departure procedure if conditions preclude the safe execution of the procedure. (ICAO Doc 8168, Volume 1, Part V, 3.2.1.3)	x	x	x	x	x	
071 02 04 02	**Influence of the flight procedure (departure, cruise, approach)**						
LO	List the main parameters for NADP 1 and NADP 2 (i.e. speeds, heights, etc.). (ICAO Doc 8168, Volume 1, Part V, Appendix to Chapter 3)	x	x				
LO	State that a runway lead-in lighting system should be provided where it is desired to provide visual guidance along a specific approach path for purposes of noise abatement. (ICAO Annex 14, Volume 1, 5.3.7.1/Volume 2, 5.3.4.1)	x	x	x	x	x	
LO	State that detailed information about noise-abatement procedures is to be found in AD 2 and 3 of the AIP. (ICAO Annex 15, Appendix 1)	x	x	x	x	x	
071 02 04 03	**Influence by the pilot (power setting, low drag)**						
LO	List the adverse operating conditions under which noise-abatement procedures in the form of reduced- power take-off should not be required. (ICAO Doc 8168, Volume 1, Part V, 3.2.2)	x	x				
LO	List the adverse operating conditions under which noise-abatement procedures during approach should not be required. (ICAO Doc 8168, Volume 1, Part V, 3.4.4)	x	x				
LO	State the rule regarding the use of reverse thrust on landing. (ICAO Doc 8168, Volume 1, Part V, 3.5)	x	x				
071 02 04 04	**Influence by the pilot (power setting, track of helicopter)**						
LO	List the adverse operating conditions under which noise-abatement procedures in the form of reduced- power take-off should not be required. (ICAO Doc 8168, Volume 1, Part V, 3.2.2)			x	x	x	
071 02 05 00	**Fire and smoke**						
071 02 05 01	**Carburettor fire**						

CRANFIELD AVIATION TRAINING SCHOOL LTD. PART-FCL GBR.ATO-0136

CATS INNOVATION CENTRE, LUTON, Bedfordshire LU2 8DL U.K.

CATS

www.catsaviation.com

Operational Procedures

xxii

LO	List the actions to be taken in the event of a carburettor fire.	x	x				
071 02 05 02	**Engine fire**						
LO	List the actions to be taken in the event of an engine fire.	x	x				
071 02 05 03	**Fire in the cabin, cockpit, cargo compartment**						
LO	Identify the different types of extinguishants and the type of fire on which each one may be used.	x	x				
LO	Describe the precautions to be considered in the application of fire extinguishant.	x	x				
LO	Identify the appropriate handheld extinguishers to be used in the cockpit, the passenger cabin and toilets, and in the cargo compartments.	x	x				
071 02 05 04	**Smoke in the cockpit and cabin**						
LO	List the actions to be taken in the event of smoke in the cockpit or in the cabin.	x	x				
071 02 05 05	**Actions in case of overheated brakes**						
LO	Describe the problems and safety precautions following overheated brakes after landing or a rejected take-off.	x	x				
071 02 06 00	**Decompression of pressurised cabin**						
071 02 06 01	**Slow decompression**						
LO	Indicate how to detect a slow decompression or an automatic pressurisation system failure.	x	x				
LO	Describe the actions required following a slow decompression.	x	x				
071 02 06 02	**Rapid and explosive decompression**						
LO	Indicate how to detect a rapid or an explosive decompression.	x	x				
071 02 06 03	**Dangers and action to be taken**						
LO	Describe the actions required following a rapid or explosive decompression.	x	x				
LO	Describe the effects on aircraft occupants of a slow decompression and a rapid or explosive decompression.	x	x				
071 02 07 00	**Wind shear and microburst**						
071 02 07 01	**Effects and recognition during departure and approach**						
LO	Define the meaning of the term 'low-level windshear'. (ICAO Circular 186, Chapter 1)	x	x	x	x	x	
LO	Define: vertical wind shear, horizontal wind shear, updraft and downdraft wind shear. (ICAO Circular 186, Chapter 2)	x	x	x	x	x	
LO	Identify the meteorological phenomena associated with wind shear. (ICAO Circular 186, Chapter 3)	x	x	x	x	x	
LO	Explain recognition of wind shear. (ICAO Circular 186, Chapter 4)	x	x	x	x	x	
071 02 07 02	**Actions to avoid and actions to take during encounter**						
LO	Describe the effects of and actions required when encountering wind shear, at take-off and approach. (ICAO Circular 186, Chapter 4)	x	x	x	x	x	
LO	Describe the precautions to be taken when wind shear is suspected, at take-off and approach. (ICAO Circular 186, Chapter 4)	x	x	x	x	x	
LO	Describe the effects of and actions required following entry into a strong downdraft wind shear. (ICAO Circular 186, Chapter 4)	x	x	x	x	x	
LO	Describe a microburst and its effects. (ICAO Circular 186, Chapter 4)	x	x	x	x	x	
071 02 08 00	**Wake turbulence**						

071 02 08 01	**Cause**						
LO	Define the term 'wake turbulence'. (ICAO Doc 4444, 4.9)	x	x	x	x	x	
LO	Describe tip vortices circulation. (ICAO Doc 9426, Part II)	x	x	x	x	x	
LO	Explain when vortex generation begins and ends. (ICAO Doc 9426, Part II)	x	x	x	x	x	
LO	Describe vortex circulation on the ground with and without crosswind. (ICAO Doc 9426, Part II)	x	x	x	x	x	
071 02 08 02	**List of relevant parameters**						
LO	List the three main factors which, when combined, give the strongest vortices (heavy, clean, slow). (ICAO Doc 9426, Part II)	x	x	x	x	x	
LO	Describe the wind conditions which are worst for wake turbulence near the ground. (ICAO Doc 9426, Part II)	x	x	x	x	x	
071 02 08 03	**Actions to be taken when crossing traffic, during take-off and landing**						
LO	Describe the actions to be taken to avoid wake turbulence, specially separations. (ICAO Doc 4444, 5)	x	x	x	x	x	
071 02 09 00	**Security (unlawful events)**						
071 02 09 01	**ICAO Annex 17**						
LO	Give the following definitions: aircraft security check, screening, security, security-restricted area, unidentified baggage. (ICAO Annex 17, 1)	x	x	x	x	x	
LO	Give the objectives of security. (ICAO Annex 17, 2.1)	x	x	x	x	x	
071 02 09 02	**Use of Secondary Surveillance Radar (SSR)**						
LO	Describe the commander's responsibilities concerning notifying the appropriate ATS unit. (ICAO Annex 17 Attachment)	x	x	x	x	x	
LO	Describe the commander's responsibilities concerning operation of SSR. (ICAO Annex 17 Attachment)	x	x	x	x	x	
LO	Describe the commander's responsibilities concerning departing from assigned track and/or cruising level. (ICAO Annex 17 Attachment)	x	x	x	x	x	
LO	Describe the commander's responsibilities concerning the action required or being requested by an ATS unit to confirm SSR code and ATS interpretation response. (ICAO Annex 17 Attachment)	x	x	x	x	x	
071 02 09 03	**Security**						
LO	State the requirements regarding training programmes.	x	x	x	x	x	
LO	State the requirements regarding reporting acts of unlawful interference.	x	x	x	x	x	
LO	State the requirements regarding aircraft search procedures.	x	x	x	x	x	
071 02 10 00	**Emergency and precautionary landings**						
071 02 10 01	**Definition**						
LO	Define 'ditching', 'precautionary landing', 'emergency landing'.	x	x	x	x	x	
LO	Describe a ditching procedure.	x	x	x	x	x	
LO	Describe a precautionary landing.	x	x	x	x	x	
LO	Explain the factors to be considered when deciding to make a precautionary/emergency landing or ditching.	x	x	x	x	x	
071 02 10 02	**Cause**						
LO	List some reasons that may require a ditching, a precautionary landing or an emergency landing.	x	x	x	x	x	
071 02 10 03	**Passenger information**						

CRANFIELD AVIATION TRAINING SCHOOL LTD. PART-FCL GBR.ATO-0136
CATS INNOVATION CENTRE, LUTON, Bedfordshire LU2 8DL U.K.

CATS

www.catsaviation.com

Operational Procedures

xxiv

LO	Describe the passenger briefing to be given before conducting a precautionary/emergency landing or ditching (including evacuation).	x	x	x	x	x	
071 02 10 04	**Action after landing**						
LO	Describe the actions and responsibilities of crew members after landing.	x	x	x	x	x	
071 02 10 05	**Evacuation**						
LO	State that the aircraft must be stopped and the engine shut down before launching an emergency evacuation.	x	x	x	x	x	
LO	State that evacuation procedures are to be found in Part B of the Operations Manual.	x	x	x	x	x	
LO	State the CS-25 requirements regarding evacuation procedures. (CS 25.803 + Appendix J)	x	x				
071 02 11 00	**Fuel jettisoning**						
071 02 11 01	**Safety aspects**						
LO	State that an aircraft may need to jettison fuel so as to reduce its landing mass in order to effect a safe landing. (ICAO Doc 4444, 15.5.3)	x	x				
LO	State that when an aircraft operating within controlled airspace needs to jettison fuel, the flight crew shall coordinate with ATC the following: route to be flown which, if possible, should be clear of cities and towns, preferably over water and away from areas where thunderstorms have been reported or are expected; the level to be used, which should be not less than 1800 m (6000'); and the duration of fuel jettisoning. (ICAO Doc 4444, 15.5.3)	x	x				
LO	State that flaps and slats may adversely affect fuel jettisoning. (CS 25.1001)	x	x				
071 02 11 02	**Requirements**						
LO	State that a fuel-jettisoning system must be installed on each aeroplane unless it is shown that the aeroplane meets some CS-25 climb requirements. (CS 25.1001)	x	x				
LO	State that a fuel-jettisoning system must be capable of jettisoning enough fuel within 15 minutes. (CS 25.1001)	x	x				
071 02 12 00	**Transport of dangerous goods**						
071 02 12 01	**ICAO Annex 18**						
LO	Give the following definitions: dangerous goods, dangerous goods accident, dangerous goods incident, exemption, incompatible, packaging, UN number. (ICAO Annex 18, Chapter 1)	x	x	x	x	x	
LO	State that detailed provisions for dangerous goods transportation are contained in the Technical Instructions for the Safe Transport of Dangerous Goods by Air (Doc 9284). (ICAO Annex 18, Chapter 2, 2.2.1)	x	x	x	x	x	
LO	State that in case of an in-flight emergency, the pilot-in- command must inform the ATC of dangerous goods transportation. (ICAO Annex 18, Chapter 9, 9.5)	x	x	x	x	x	
071 02 12 02	**Technical Instructions (ICAO Doc 9284)**						
LO	Explain the principle of compatibility and segregation. (ICAO Doc 9284)	x	x	x	x	x	
LO	Explain the special requirements for the loading of radioactive materials. (ICAO Doc 9284)	x	x	x	x	x	
LO	Explain the use of the dangerous goods list. (ICAO Doc 9284)	x	x	x	x	x	
LO	Identify the labels. (ICAO Doc 9284)	x	x	x	x	x	
071 02 12 03	**Transport of dangerous goods by air**						
LO	State that dangerous goods transportation is subject to operator approval.	x	x	x	x	x	

LO	Identify articles and substances, which would otherwise be classed as dangerous goods, which are excluded from the provisions.	x	x	x	x	x	
LO	State that some articles and substances may be forbidden for air transportation.	x	x	x	x	x	
LO	State that packing must comply with the Technical Instructions specifications.	x	x	x	x	x	
LO	List the labelling and marking requirements.	x	x	x	x	x	
LO	List the Dangerous Goods Transport Document requirements.	x	x	x	x	x	
LO	List the Acceptance of Dangerous Goods requirements.	x	x	x	x	x	
LO	Explain the need for an inspection prior to loading on an aircraft.	x	x	x	x	x	
LO	State that some dangerous goods are designated for carriage only on cargo aircraft.	x	x	x	x	x	
LO	State that accidents or incidents involving dangerous goods are to be reported.	x	x	x	x	x	
LO	State that mis-declared or undeclared dangerous goods found in baggage are to be reported.	x	x	x	x	x	
071 02 13 00	**Contaminated runways**						
071 02 13 01	**Kinds of contamination**						
LO	Define a 'contaminated runway', a 'damp runway', a 'wet runway', and a 'dry runway'.	x	x				
LO	List the different types of contamination: damp, wet or water patches, rime or frost-covered, dry snow, wet snow, slush, ice, compacted or rolled snow, frozen ruts or ridges. (ICAO Annex 15, Appendix 2)	x	x				
LO	Give the definitions of the various types of snow. (ICAO Annex 15, Appendix 2)	x	x				
071 02 13 02	**Estimated surface friction, friction coefficient**						
LO	Identify the difference between friction coefficient and estimated surface friction. (ICAO Annex 15, Appendix 2)	x	x				
LO	State that when friction coefficient is 0.40 or higher, the expected braking action is good. (ICAO Annex 15, Appendix 2)	x	x				
071 02 13 03	**Hydroplaning principles and effects**						
LO	Define the different types of hydroplaning. (NASA TM-85652/Tire friction performance/ pp. 6 to 9)	x	x				
LO	Compute the two dynamic hydroplaning speeds using the following formulas: Spin-down speed (rotating tire) (kt) = 9 square root (pressure in PSI) Spin-up speed (non-rotating tire) (kt) = 7.7 square root (pressure in PSI). (NASA TM-85652/Tire friction performance /p. 8)	x	x				
LO	State that it is the spin-up speed rather than the spin-down speed which represents the actual tire situation for aircraft touchdown on flooded runways. (NASA TM-85652/Tire friction performance/p. 8)	x	x				
071 02 13 04	**Procedures**						
LO	State that some wind limitations may apply in case of contaminated runways. Those limitations are to be found in Part B of the Operations Manual — Limitations.	x	x				
LO	State that the procedures associated with take-off and landing on contaminated runways are to be found in Part B of the Operations Manual — Normal procedures.	x	x				

CRANFIELD AVIATION TRAINING SCHOOL LTD. PART-FCL GBR.ATO-0136
CATS INNOVATION CENTRE, LUTON, Bedfordshire LU2 8DL U.K.

www.catsaviation.com

Operational Procedures

xxvi

LO	State that the performances associated with contaminated runways are to be found in Part B of the Operations Manual — Performance.	x	x				
071 02 13 05	**SNOWTAM**						
LO	Interpret from a SNOWTAM the contamination and braking action on a runway.	x	x				
071 02 14 00	**Rotor downwash**						
071 02 14 01	**Describe downwash**						
LO	Describe the downwash.			x	x	x	
071 02 14 02	**Effects**						
LO	Explain the effects on: soil erosion, water dispersal and spray, recirculation, damage to property, loose articles.			x	x	x	
071 02 15 00	**Operation influence by meteorological conditions (Helicopter)**						
071 02 15 01	**White-out/sand/dust**						
LO	Give the definition of 'white-out'.			x	x	x	
LO	Describe loss of spatial orientation.			x	x	x	
LO	Describe take-off and landing techniques.			x	x	x	
071 02 15 02	**Strong winds**						
LO	Describe blade sailing.			x	x	x	
LO	Describe wind operating envelopes.			x	x	x	
LO	Describe vertical speed problems.			x	x	x	
071 02 15 03	**Mountain environment**						
LO	Describe constraints associated with mountain environment.			x	x	x	
071 03 00 00	**EMERGENCY PROCEDURES (HELICOPTER)**						
071 03 01 00	**Influence of technical problems**						
071 03 01 01	**Engine failure**						
LO	Describe techniques for failure in: hover, climb, cruise, approach.			x	x	x	
071 03 01 02	**Fire in cabin/cockpit/engine**						
LO	Describe the basic actions when encountering fire in the cabin, cockpit or engine.			x	x	x	
071 03 01 03	**Tail/rotor/directional control failure**						
LO	Describe the basic actions following loss of tail rotor.			x	x	x	
LO	Describe the basic actions following loss of directional control.			x	x	x	
071 03 01 04	**Ground resonance**						
LO	Describe recovery actions.			x	x	x	
071 03 01 05	**Blade stall**						
LO	Describe cause and recovery actions when encountering retreating blade stall.			x	x	x	
071 03 01 06	**Settling with power (vortex ring)**						
LO	Describe prerequisite conditions and recovery actions.			x	x	x	
071 03 01 07	**Overpitch**						
LO	Describe recovery actions.			x	x	x	
071 03 01 08	**Overspeed: rotor/engine**						
LO	Describe overspeed control.			x	x	x	
071 03 01 09	**Dynamic rollover**						
LO	Describe potential conditions and recovery action.			x	x	x	
071 03 01 10	**Mast bumping**						
LO	Describe conditions 'conducive to' and 'avoidance of' effect.			x	x	x	

CHAPTER 1

Introduction to Operational Procedures

1.1   Before ICAO

Before the Second World War, two international conventions regulated aerial navigation. The Convention Relating to the Regulation of Aerial Navigation, often called the Paris Convention, was adopted in1919. Its permanent body was the International Commission for Air Navigation (ICAN). The Convention was ratified by 37 States of which four (Bolivia, Chile, Iran and Panama) denounced it; thus it was in force in 33 States in 1940. The Havana Convention of 1928 was ratified by 11 states but was without permanent office.

1.2   The International Civil Aviation Organization

Between November 1 and December 7 1944, 54 nations met in Chicago at the invitation of the United States to 'make arrangements for the immediate establishment of provisional world air routes and services'. A new convention was adopted – the Chicago Convention. This was the charter of a new body – the International Civil Aviation Organization (ICAO).

The Chicago Conference in the Grand Ballroom of the Stevens Hotel, Chicago (www.icao.int)

1.3   The European Aviation Safety Agency

The European Aviation Safety Agency (EASA) is an agency of the European Union governed by European public law. EASA was set up in 2002 by a Council and Parliament regulation (Regulation (EC) 1592/2002) and was given specific regulatory and executive tasks in the field of civil aviation safety and environmental protection. There are 32 EASA member states – those in the EU and Switzerland, Iceland, Norway and Liechtenstein. EASA's headquarters are in Cologne.

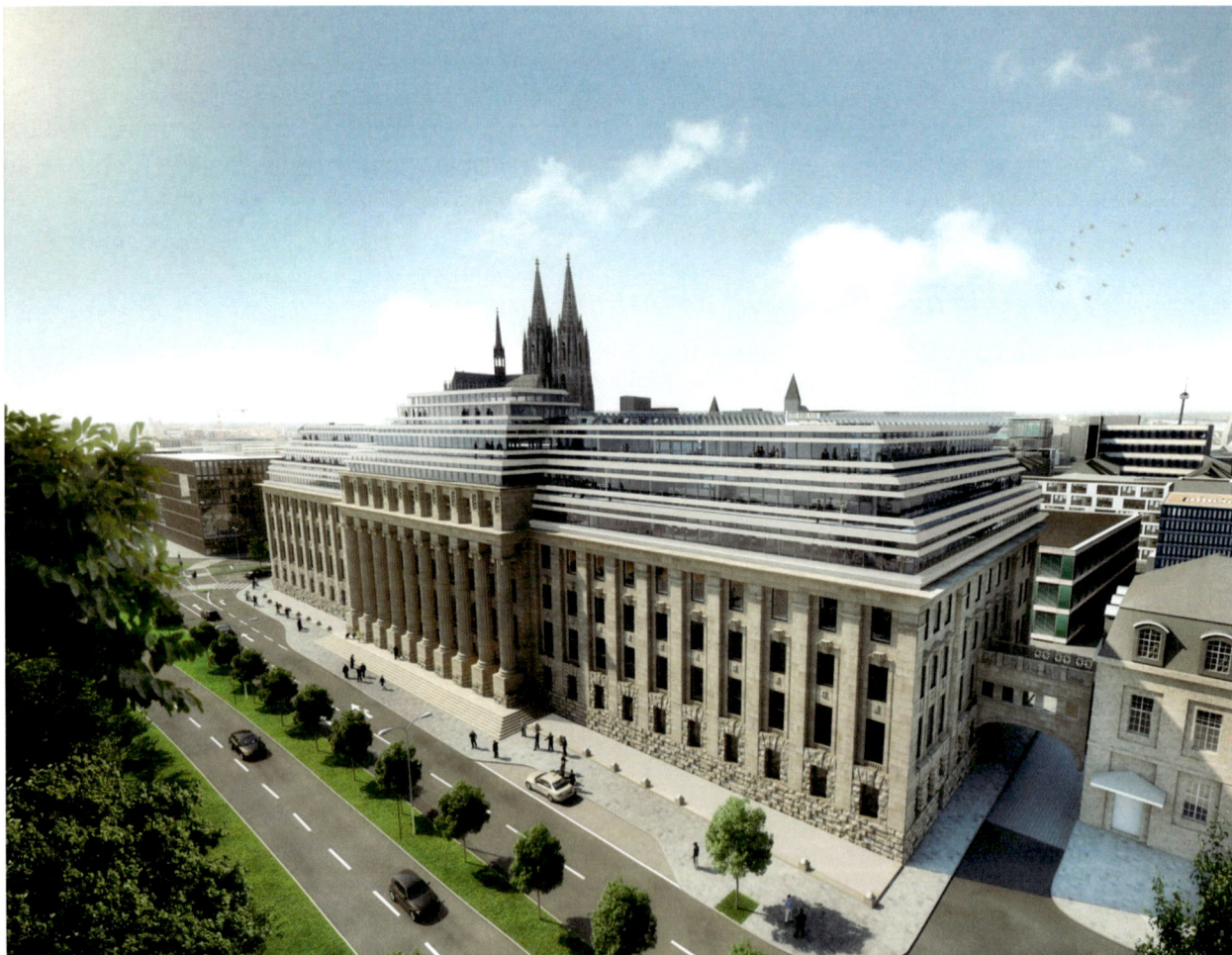

EASA's headquarters in Cologne

Before the establishment of EASA, the civil aviation authorities of certain European countries (the Joint Aviation Authorities (JAA)) agreed common requirements referred to as the Joint Aviation Requirements (JAR) to 'harmonise' standards. ICAO Annex 6 was selected to provide the basic structure of JAR-OPS, the JAR for air operator certification. The content of Annex 6 was added to where necessary by making use of existing European regulations and the Federal Aviation Requirements of the United States.

Although the European Commission had been closely associated with the JAA process, the transition to the EASA system and decision-making based on the European Community method is described by EASA as a significant improvement in the execution of certification and rulemaking tasks.

CHAPTER 2

ICAO Annex 6 Requirements

2.1 Annex 6 to the Convention on International Civil Aviation

Standards and Recommended Practices (SARP) for the Operation of Aircraft — International Commercial Air Transport were first adopted by ICAO's Council on 10 December 1948 and designated as Annex 6 to the Convention (an annex is an addition to a document). These SARPs were based on recommendations of the Operations Division at its first session in April 1946.

Regarding Annex 6, ICAO states:

'The essence of Annex 6, simply put, is that the operation of aircraft engaged in international air transport must be as standardized as possible to ensure the highest levels of safety and efficiency.'

Annex 6 was amended at further meetings in the decades that followed the 1940s. Amendment 152 was adopted by the Council on 23 January 1969. The then adoption by the Council of Part II International General Aviation — Aeroplanes, and later of Part III International Operations — Helicopters, led to Annex 6 comprising:

Part I International Commercial Air Transport — Aeroplanes
Part II International General Aviation — Aeroplanes
Part III International Operations — Helicopters

2.1.1   Applicability

The Standards and Recommended Practices of Annex 6, Part 1 are applicable to the operation of aeroplanes by operators authorised to conduct international commercial air transport operations.

2.1.2   Operator's Responsibilities

An operator shall ensure that all employees when abroad know that they must comply with the laws, regulations and procedures of those States in which operations are conducted. The operator shall ensure that its pilots are familiar with the laws, regulations and procedures, pertinent to the performance of their duties with regard to the operational areas, the aerodromes to be used and the air navigation facilities related thereto. The operator shall also ensure that other members of the flight crew are familiar with these laws, regulations and procedures with regard to the performance of their respective duties in the operation of the aeroplane. The operator or a designated representative shall have responsibility for operational control. The operator must ensure that its pilots in command have available on board the aeroplane all the essential information concerning the Search and Rescue services in those areas over which the aeroplane will be flown. This information may be made available by means of an operations manual or other appropriate means. The operator must establish and maintain an accident prevention and flight safety programme.

2.1.3   Pilot's Actions in the Event of an Emergency Violation of Local Regulations

If an emergency situation, which endangers the safety of the aeroplane or persons, necessitates the taking of an action that involves a violation of local regulations or procedures, the pilot-in-command shall notify the appropriate local authority without delay. If required by the state in which the incident occurs, the pilot in command shall submit a report on any such violation to the appropriate authority in that state or country. In that event the pilot in command shall also submit a copy of the report to the State of the Operator as soon as possible and normally within 10 days

2.2   *Flight Operations*

2.2.1   *Air Operator Certificate (AOC)*

An operator shall not carry out commercial air transport operations unless in possession of a valid air operator certificate (or equivalent document) issued by the State of the Operator. This document authorises the operator to conduct commercial air transport operations in accordance with the condition and limitations specified therein.

The issue of an AOC by the State of the Operator is dependent on the operator demonstrating an adequate organisation, method of control and supervision of flight operations, training programme and maintenance arrangements consistent with the nature and extent of the operations specified. The continued validity of the AOC is dependent on the operator maintaining the above requirements under the supervision of the State of the Operator.

The AOC shall contain at least the following information:
- the operator's identification and location
- date of issue and period of validity
- description of the types of operations authorised
- the types of aircraft authorised
- the authorised area of operation, or routes.

2.2.2   *Qualifications for taxiing aircraft*

Occasions do arise (e.g. with regard to maintenance requirements), when it becomes necessary for persons other than qualified pilots to taxi aircraft. In such cases Annex 6 states that an aeroplane shall not be taxied on the movement area of an aerodrome unless the person at the controls:
- has been duly authorised by the operator or a designated agent;
- is fully competent to taxi the aeroplane;
- is qualified to use the radio
- has received instruction from a competent person in respect of aerodrome layout, routes, signs, marking, lights, air traffic control (ATC) signals and instructions, phraseology and procedures and is able to conform to the operational standards required for safe aeroplane movement at the aerodrome.

2.2.3   *Minimum Flight Altitudes*

An operator shall be permitted to establish minimum flight altitudes for those routes flown. Those minima shall not be less than those established by the States flown over or those prescribed by another responsible State.

An operator may establish minimum flight altitudes for operations conducted over routes for which minimum flight altitudes have not been established by the State flown over or by the responsible State. These minimum flight altitudes must not be established at a level lower than the minimum level for IFR flights. The method by which minimum flight altitudes are determined for these routes must be included in the operations manual.

ICAO also recommends that the method for establishing the minimum flight altitudes should be approved by the State of the Operator and that the State of the Operator should approve such method only after careful consideration of the probable effects of the following factors on the safety of the operation in question:
- the accuracy and reliability with which the position of the aeroplane can be determined;
- the inaccuracies in the indications of the altimeters used;
- the characteristics of the terrain (e.g. sudden changes in the elevation);
- the probability of encountering unfavourable meteorological conditions (e.g. severe turbulence and descending air currents);
- possible inaccuracies in aeronautical charts; and
- airspace restrictions.

2.2.4   Aerodrome Operating Minima

The State of the Operator requires each operator to establish minimum conditions of takeoff and landing for each aerodrome to be used in operations (i.e. aerodrome operating minima). The method of determining these minima must also be approved by the State of the Operator. Due to the fact that the weather generally will be variable throughout the year at each of these airfields, aerodrome operating minima criteria must be established for each approach aid for each runway. The operator, when establishing such minima, must not instigate minima (e.g. values of ceiling and visibility) lower than those established by the State in which the aerodrome is located except when specifically approved by the State. The State of the Operator shall require that, in establishing the airport operating minima, which apply to any particular operation, full account shall be taken of:

- the type, performance and handling characteristics of the aeroplane;
- the composition of the flight crew, their competence and experience;
- the dimensions and characteristics of the runways, which may be selected for use;
- the adequacy and performance of the available visual and non-visual ground aids;
- the equipment available on the aeroplane for the purpose of navigation and / or control of the flight path during the approach to landing and the missed approach;
- the obstacles in the approach and missed approach areas and the obstacle clearance attitude / height for the instrument approach procedures;
- the means used to determine and report meteorological conditions; and
- the obstacles in the climb-out areas and necessary clearance margins.

2.2.5   Passenger Briefing

An operator shall ensure that passengers are made familiar with the location and use of:

- seat belts;
- emergency exits;
- life jackets, if the carriage of life jackets is prescribed;
- oxygen dispensing equipment, if the provision of oxygen for the use of passengers is prescribed; and
- other emergency equipment provided for individual use, including passenger emergency briefing cards.

The operator shall inform the passengers of the location and general manner of use of the principal emergency equipment carried for collective use.

The briefing must be done on the ground.

In the event of an emergency during flight, passengers must be instructed in such emergency action that may be appropriate to the circumstances

2.2.6   Flight Preparation

A flight may not be commenced until flight preparation forms have been completed which certify that the pilot-in-command is satisfied that:

- the aeroplane is airworthy (as annotated by the maintenance department in the Technical Logbook for that particular aeroplane);
- the instruments and equipment legally required for the particular type of operation to be flown, are installed and are sufficient for the flight;
- a maintenance release has been issued in respect of the aeroplane;
- the mass of the aeroplane and centre of gravity location are within prescribed limits;
- any load carried is properly distributed and safely secured;
- a check has been completed indicating that the aeroplane performance operating limitations can be complied with for the flight to be undertaken; and
- an operational fight plan has been prepared in accordance with the rules set out and applicable to the operation

Completed flight preparation forms must be kept by the operator for a period of at least 3 months.

2.2.7   Operational Flight Plan

An operational flight plan shall be completed for every intended flight and shall be approved and signed by the pilot in command and, where applicable, by the flight operations officer / flight dispatcher.

A copy of the operational flight plan shall be kept on file with the operator or a designated agent or if this is not possible, it shall be left with the aerodrome authority or on record in a suitable place at the point of departure

In the event of an accident or incident happening to the aeroplane after departure, if the on-board copy of the operational flight plan is destroyed, the copy left behind on the ground will provide valuable information with regard to some of the important flight operational aspects of the proposed flight.

Unless specified in the operations manual, the operational flight plan must include the minimum flight altitudes for the route to be flown and the aerodrome operating minima for the aerodromes to be used and the alternates specified.

2.2.8   Alternate Aerodromes

2.2.8.1 Takeoff Alternate

A takeoff alternate aerodrome shall be selected and specified in the operational flight plan if the weather conditions at the aerodrome of departure are at or below the applicable aerodrome operating landing minima or it would not be possible to return to the aerodrome of departure for other reasons. This takeoff alternate aerodrome shall be located within the following distance from the aerodrome of departure:

Number of aircraft engines	Distance
2	equivalent to a flight time of 1 h at single-engine cruise speed
3 or more	equivalent to a flight time of 2 h at the one-engine inoperative engine cruise speed

To be selected as a takeoff alternate the available weather forecast information must indicate that, at the estimated time of use, the conditions will be at or above the aerodrome operating minima for that operation.

2.2.8.2 En-route Alternate

En-route alternate aerodromes required for extended range operations by aeroplanes with 2 turbine engines must be selected and specified in the operational and air traffic services (ATS) flight plans.

2.2.8.3 Destination Alternate

For flights conducted under IFR, at least one destination alternate aerodrome must be specified in the operational and ATS flight plans unless:

- the duration of the flight and the meteorological conditions prevailing are such that there is a reasonable certainty that, at the estimated time of arrival at the aerodrome of intended landing, and for a reasonable period before and after such time, the approach and landing may be made under visual meteorological conditions; or
- the aerodrome of intended landing is isolated and there is no suitable destination alternate

2.2.9   Weather conditions for VFR / IFR

A flight to be conducted in accordance with the visual flight rules (VFR) shall not be commenced unless current meteorological reports, or a combination of current reports and forecasts indicate that the meteorological conditions along the route, or that part of the route to be flown under the visual flight rules will, at the appropriate time, be such as to render compliance with these rules possible.

A flight to be conducted in accordance with instrument flight rules (IFR) shall not be commenced unless information is available which indicates that conditions at the aerodrome of intended landing (or where a destination alternate is required, at least one destination alternate) will, at the estimated time of arrival, be at or above the aerodrome operating minima.

It is the practice in some States to declare, for flight planning purposes, higher minima for an aerodrome when nominated as a destination alternate than for the same aerodrome when planned as that of intended landing.

2.2.10 *Fuel and Oil Requirements*

A flight shall not be commenced unless, taking into account both the meteorological conditions and any delays that are expected in flight, the aeroplane carries sufficient fuel and oil to ensure that it can safely complete the flight. In addition, a reserve shall be carried to provide for contingencies.

2.2.10.1 *Propeller-driven Aeroplanes*

The fuel and oil carried in order to comply with the provisions of Annex 6 shall, in the case of propeller-driven aeroplanes, be at least the amount sufficient to allow the aeroplane:

2.2.10.1.1 *Destination Alternate required*

When a destination alternate aerodrome is required, either:
a) to fly to the aerodrome to which the flight is planned, thence to the most critical (in terms of fuel consumption) alternate aerodrome specified in the operational and ATS flight plans and thereafter for a period of 45 minutes; or
b) to fly to the alternate aerodrome via any predetermined point and thereafter for 45 min, provided that this shall not be less than the amount required to fly to the aerodrome to which the flight is planned and thereafter for:
1) 45 min plus 15% of the flight time planned to be spent at the cruising level(s), or
2) 2 h,
whichever is less.

2.2.10.1.2 *Destination Alternate not required*

When a destination alternate aerodrome is not required:
a) to fly to the aerodrome to which the flight is planned and thereafter for a period of 45 min; or
b) to fly to the aerodrome to which the flight is planned and thereafter for:
1) 45 min plus 15% of the flight time planned to be spent at the cruising level(s), or
2) 2 h,
whichever is less.

2.2.10.2 *Turbo-jet Aeroplanes*

The fuel and oil carried in the case of turbo-jet aeroplanes shall be at least the amount sufficient to allow the aeroplane:

2.2.10.2.1 *Destination Alternate required*

When a destination alternate aerodrome is required, either:
a) to fly to and execute an approach and a missed approach, at the aerodrome to which the flight is planned and thereafter:
1) to fly to the alternate aerodrome specified in the operational flight plan and ATS flight plans; and then
2) to fly for 30 min at holding speed at 450 m (1500') above the alternate aerodrome under standard temperature conditions and approach and land; and
3) to have an additional amount of fuel sufficient to provide for the increased consumption on the occurrence of any of the potential contingencies specified by the operator to the satisfaction of the State of the operator; or
b) to fly to the alternate aerodrome via any predetermined point and thereafter for 30 min at 450 m (1500') above the alternate aerodrome due provision having been made for an additional amount of fuel sufficient to

provide for the increased consumption on the occurrence of any of the potential contingencies specified by the operator to the satisfaction of the State of the Operator; provided that fuel shall not be less than the amount of fuel required to fly to the aerodrome to which the flight is planned and thereafter for two hours at normal cruise consumption.

2.2.10.2.2   *Destination Alternate not required*

When a destination alternate aerodrome is not required:

a) To fly to the aerodrome to which the flight is planned and additionally:

1) to fly, under standard temperature conditions, 30 min at holding speed at 450 m (1500') above the aerodrome to which the flight is planned; and

2) to have an additional amount of fuel, sufficient to provide for the increased consumption on the occurrence of any of the potential contingencies specified by the operator to the satisfaction of the State of the operator;

b) to fly to the aerodrome to which the flight is planned and thereafter for a period of two hours at normal cruise consumption.

Note that in computing the stated fuel and oil requirements at least the following shall be considered:

- meteorological conditions forecast;
- expected air traffic control routings and traffic delays;
- for IFR flight, one instrument approach at the destination aerodrome, including a missed approach;
- the procedures prescribed in the operations manual for loss of pressurisation, where applicable, or failure of one power unit while en route; and
- any other conditions that may delay the landing of the aeroplane or increase fuel and/or oil consumption.

2.2.11   *Refuelling with Passengers on Board*

An aeroplane shall not be refuelled when passengers are embarking, on board or disembarking unless it is properly attended by qualified personnel ready to initiate and direct an evacuation of the aeroplane by the most practical and expeditious means available should an unforeseen occurrence make such an evacuation necessary.

> When refuelling with passengers embarking, on board or disembarking, two-way communication shall be maintained by the aeroplane's inter-communication system or other suitable means, between the ground crew supervising the refuelling and the qualified personnel on board the aeroplane

2.2.12   *Oxygen Requirements*

A flight to be operated at flight altitudes at which the atmospheric pressure in personnel compartments will be less than 700 hPa (i.e. altitude greater than 10000') shall not be commenced unless sufficient stored breathing oxygen is carried to supply:

- all crew members and 10% of the passengers for any period in excess of 30 min that the pressure in compartments occupied by them will be between 700 hPa and 620 hPa (10000' – 13000'); and
- the crew and passengers for any period that the atmospheric pressure in compartments occupied by them will be less than 620 hPa (altitude greater than 13000').

A flight to be operated with a pressurised aeroplane shall not be commenced unless a sufficient quantity of stored breathing oxygen is carried to supply all the crew members and a proportion of the passengers as is appropriate to the circumstances of the flight being undertaken, in the event of loss of pressurisation, for any period that the atmospheric pressure in any compartment occupied by them would be less than 700 hPa (altitude greater than 10000').

All flight crew members of pressurised aeroplanes operating above an altitude where the atmospheric pressure is less than 376 hPa (altitude greater than 25000') shall have available at the flight duty station a quick-donning type of oxygen mask, which will readily supply oxygen upon demand.

In the event that an aeroplane is operated at flight altitudes at which the atmospheric pressure is less than 376 hPa, (7600 m / 25000') or, the aeroplane is operated at flight altitudes at which the atmospheric pressure is more than 376 hPa but cannot descend safely within four minutes to a flight altitude at which the atmospheric pressure is equal to 620 hPa: the rules require that there shall be no less than a 10-min supply of oxygen available for the occupants of the passenger compartment.

2.3 In-flight Procedures

2.3.1 Compliance / non-compliance with Aerodrome Operating Minima

A flight shall not be continued towards the aerodrome of intended landing, unless the latest available information indicates that at the expected time of arrival, a landing can be made at that aerodrome, or at least one destination alternate aerodrome, in compliance with the aerodrome operating minima established.

Except in the case of an emergency, an aeroplane shall not continue its approach to land at any aerodrome beyond a point at which the limits of the operating minima specified for that aerodrome would be infringed.

2.3.2 Aeroplane Flight Crew

Irrespective of the number of pilots rostered for each flight, which may be as many as five depending upon the stage length (e.g. London to Hong Kong), the operator must designate one of the pilot crewmembers to act as pilot-in-command. This will normally be the most experienced and, in terms of company employment, the most senior.

2.3.2.1 Crew Members at Duty Stations

2.3.2.1.1 Takeoff and Landing

It is generally accepted that the critical phases of flight are those of the takeoff and landing. Consequently all required flight deck crewmembers shall be at their stations.

2.3.2.1.2 En-Route

During the en-route phase all flight crewmembers required to be on flight deck duty shall remain at their stations except when their absence is necessary for the performance of duties in connection with regard to the operation of the aeroplane or for physiological reasons.

2.3.2.1.3 Seat Belts

For safety reasons all flight crew members shall keep their seat belts fastened when at their stations.

2.3.2.1.4 Safety Harness

Any flight crew member occupying a pilot's seat shall keep the safety harness fastened during the takeoff and landing phases. All other flight crew members shall also keep their safety harness fastened during the takeoff and landing phases unless the shoulder straps interfere with the performance of their duties, in which case the shoulder straps may be unfastened but the seat belt itself must remain fastened. Note that a safety harness includes shoulder straps and a seat belt which may be used independently.

2.3.2.2 In-flight changes to ATS flight plan

Where operational instructions involve a change in the ATS flight plan such change shall, where practicable, be co-ordinated with the appropriate ATS unit before transmission to the aeroplane. Where prior co-ordination has not been possible, the pilot must obtain an appropriate clearance from an ATS unit, if applicable, before making a change in flight plan.

CRANFIELD AVIATION TRAINING SCHOOL LTD. PART-FCL GBR.ATO-0136
CATS INNOVATION CENTRE, LUTON, Bedfordshire LU2 8DL U.K.   www.catsaviation.com

2-7

Operational Procedures

2.3.2.3 Duties of the Pilot-in-Command

The pilot-in-command shall be responsible for the operation and safety of the aeroplane and for the safety of all persons on board during flight time, which is considered to begin when the aeroplane first starts to move away from the boarding area and ends when the engines are shut down at the end of the flight. The pilot-in-command shall ensure that checklists specified in the operations manual are complied with in detail. The pilot-in-command shall be responsible for notifying the nearest appropriate authority by the quickest available means of any accident involving the aeroplane, resulting in serious injury or death of any person or substantial damage to the aeroplane or property. The pilot-in-command shall be responsible for reporting all known or suspected defects in the aeroplane, to the operator, at the termination of the flight. These reports are normally provided to maintenance department – directly or via the flight operations / flight dispatch department. The pilot-in-command shall be responsible for the journey log book or the general declaration containing the information regarding:

- Aeroplane nationality and registration
- Date of flight
- Names of each crewmember and position
- Places of departure and arrival
- Scheduled time of departure
- Scheduled en-route block and arrival time
- Nature of flight
- Signature of pilot-in-command

2.3.2.4 Duties of Flight Operations Officer

A flight operations officer shall:
- assist the pilot-in-command in flight preparation and provide the relevant information required;
- assist the pilot-in-command in preparing the operational and ATS flight plans, sign when applicable and file the ATS flight plan with the appropriate ATS unit;
- furnish the pilot-in-command whilst in flight with information which may be necessary for the safe conduct of the flight;
- in the event of an emergency, initiate such procedures as may be outlined in the operations manual.

2.4 Aeroplane Performance and Operating Limitations

Aeroplanes shall be operated in accordance with a comprehensive and detailed code of performance established by the State of Registry in compliance with the applicable standards. Single-engined aeroplanes shall only be operated in conditions of weather and light, and over such routes and diversions that permit a safe forced landing to be executed in the event of engine failure. An aeroplane shall be operated in compliance with the terms of its certificate of airworthiness and within the approved operating limitations that are contained in the Aeroplane Flight Manual (AFM). The State of Registry shall take precautions to ensure that an acceptable level of safety is maintained (e.g. by making regular inspections or audits). A flight shall not be commenced unless the performance information provided in the flight manual indicates that the requirements regarding the aeroplane, ambient weather conditions, aerodrome characteristics, including elevation plus the runway conditions, length and gradient can be complied with for the flight to be undertaken. In fulfilling these requirements, account shall be taken of all factors that significantly affect the performance of the aeroplane. These factors will include such elements as:

- mass
- operating procedures
- the pressure-altitude appropriate to the elevation of the aerodrome
- temperature
- wind
- runway gradient and condition of runway, i.e. presence of slush, water and / or ice, for landplanes, water surface condition for seaplanes.

Such factors shall be taken into account directly as operational parameters or indirectly by means of allowances or margins, which may be provided in the scheduling of performance data or in the comprehensive and detailed code of performance in accordance with which the aeroplane is being operated.

2.4.1   Takeoff

In the event of a critical power-unit failing at any point in the takeoff, the aeroplane shall be able, either:
• to discontinue the takeoff and stop within the accelerate/stop distance available, or;
• to continue the takeoff and clear all obstacles along the flight path by an adequate margin, until the aeroplane is in a position to comply with the requirements for en-route performance.
In determining the length of the runway available, account shall be taken of the loss, if any, of runway length due to alignment of the aeroplane prior to takeoff. Account shall also be taken of charting accuracy when assessing compliance with the laid down performance criteria.

2.4.2   En-Route Performance

2.4.2.1 One power-unit inoperative

In the event of the critical power-unit becoming inoperative at any point along the route or planned diversions, the aeroplane shall be able to continue the flight to an aerodrome at which the requirements for a safe landing can be met. During this flight it must not descend below the minimum flight altitude at any point.

2.4.2.2 Two power-units inoperative

This covers the case of aeroplanes having three or more power-units. Considering any part of a route where, if the general level of safety implied by the performance criteria is to be maintained the location of en-route alternate aerodromes and the total duration of the flight are such that the probability of a second power-unit becoming inoperative must be allowed for. In such cases the aeroplane shall be able, in the event of the second power-unit becoming inoperative, to continue the flight to an en-route alternate aerodrome and land.

2.4.2.3 Landing

The aeroplane shall, at the aerodrome of intended landing and at any alternate aerodrome, after clearing all obstacles in the approach path by a safe margin, be able to land, with assurance that it can come to a stop or, for a seaplane, to a satisfactorily low speed, within the landing distance available. Allowance shall be made for expected variations in the approach and landing techniques, if such allowance has not been made in the scheduling of performance data.

> Turboprops 0.7 x LDA
> Jets 0.6 x LDA

Note: Obstacle data shall be compiled to enable the operator to develop procedures that will comply with the rules for safe take off, en-route and landing performance in the event of engine(s) failure.

2.4.3   Aeroplane Mass Limitations

The mass of the aeroplane at the start of the takeoff shall not exceed the mass at which the takeoff, en-route and landing performance requirements are complied with, allowing for expected reductions in mass as the flight proceeds and for fuel jettisoning, if applicable.

In no case shall the mass at the start of takeoff exceed the maximum takeoff mass specified in the aeroplane flight manual for the elevation or pressure altitude of the aerodrome and any other local atmospheric conditions used in calculating this maximum takeoff mass, including relative humidity.

In no case shall the estimated mass for the expected time of landing at the aerodrome of intended landing and at any destination alternate aerodrome, exceed the maximum landing mass specified in the aeroplane flight manual for the elevation or the pressure altitude of those aerodromes and any other local atmospheric conditions used in calculating this maximum landing mass, including relative humidity.

In no case shall the mass at the start of takeoff or at the expected time of landing exceed the relevant maximum masses at which compliance has been demonstrated with regard to any applicable Noise Certification standard, by the competent authority of the State in which the aerodrome is situated, unless otherwise authorised in exceptional circumstances for a certain aerodrome or runway where there is no noise disturbance problem.

2.5   *Aeroplane Instruments, Equipment and Flight Documents*

2.5.1   *General*

In addition to the minimum equipment necessary for the issue of a certificate of airworthiness, the instruments, equipment and flight documents prescribed in the following paragraphs shall be installed or carried, as appropriate, according to the aeroplane used and to the circumstances under which the flight is to be conducted. The operator shall include in the operations manual a minimum equipment list (MEL), approved by the State of the Operator, which will enable the pilot-in-command to determine whether a flight may be commenced or continued from any intermediate stop should any instrument, equipment or systems become inoperative. The operator must also provide operations staff and flight crew with an aircraft operating manual, for each aircraft type operated, containing the normal, abnormal and emergency procedures relating to the operation of the aircraft. The manual shall include details of the aircraft systems and of the checklists to be used.

2.5.2   *Medical Kits and Fire Extinguishers*

An aeroplane must be equipped with accessible and adequate medical supplies appropriate to its passenger carrying capacity. The supplies should comprise of a first-aid kit for normal use and one or more medical kits for emergency use stowed as to be readily acceptable and near an exit. Anyone can open a first aid kit. Only authorised personnel may open a medical kit and permission must be granted by the Captain.

An aeroplane shall carry portable fire extinguishers of a type which, when discharged, will not cause dangerous contamination of the air within the aeroplane. At least one shall be located in:
- the pilot's compartment; and
- each passenger compartment that is separate from the pilot's compartment and that is not readily accessible to the flight crew.

2.5.3   *Mandatory Documents*

An aeroplane shall carry:
- the operations manual or those parts of it that pertain to flight operations;
- the aeroplane flight manual for the aeroplane, or other documents containing required performance data and any other information necessary for the operation of the aeroplane within the terms of its certificate of airworthiness; and
- current and suitable charts to cover the route of the proposed flight and any route along which it is reasonable to expect that the flight may be diverted.

2.5.4   *Break-in Points*

If areas of the fuselage on an aeroplane are suitable for outside break-in by rescue crews in an emergency, these areas should be marked according to the diagram below.

The colour of the markings shall be red or yellow and if necessary they shall be outlined in white to contrast with the background

If the corner markings are more than 2 m apart, intermediate lines 9 cm x 3 cm shall be inserted so that there are no more than 2 m between adjacent markings.

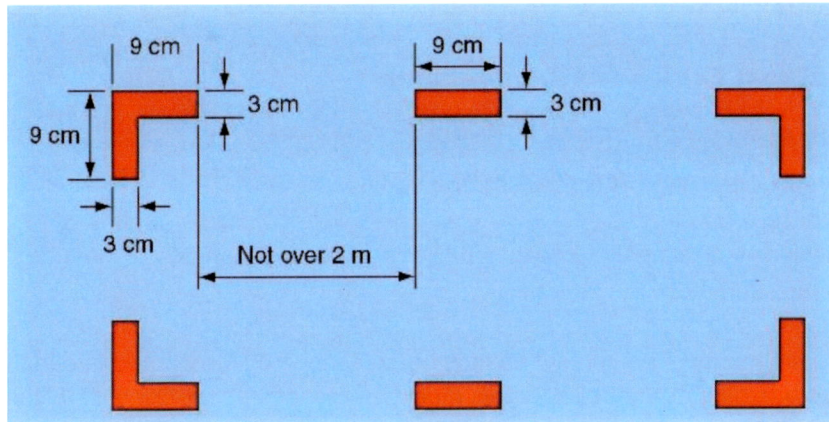

Figure 2.1 Break-in markings

2.5.5 Flight Recorders

Currently all commercial aircraft above 5700 kg are mandated to carry flight data recorders and cockpit voice recorders. The flight data recorder (FDR) traces information provided by the main flight instruments, controls and engine parameters, while the cockpit voice recorder (CVR) monitors all human voice exchanges on the flight deck throughout the flight. These two pieces of equipment are colloquially called *"the aeroplane black boxes'*.

2.5.5.1 Flight Data Recorder – Types

There arc 3 types of flight data recorder specifications depending upon the initial date of aeroplane Certificate of Airworthiness. They shall at least be able to record the parameters required to determine accurately the aeroplane flight path, speed, attitude, engine power, configuration and operation.

2.5.5.2 Duration of FDR Records

All flight data recorders shall be capable of retaining the information recorded during at least the last 25 h of their operation, except for the Type IIA flight data recorder that shall be capable of retaining the information recorded during at least the last 30 min of its operation

2.5.5.3 Retention of FDR Records

An operator shall ensure, as far as possible, that, in the event of the aeroplane becoming involved in an accident or incident, all related flight recorder data, and, if necessary, the associated flight recorders, shall be preserved and retained in safe custody for a minimum period of 60 days.

2.5.5.4 Cockpit Voice Recorder

The objective of the CVR is to provide the best possible post-accident / incident information with regard to the last conversations between the individual crewmembers themselves and with Air Traffic Control in the last seconds prior to the occurrence for at least 30 min.

2.5.5.5 Flight Recorder General Information

The objective of the FDR is to provide the best possible post-accident /incident information with regard to the flying attitude and condition of the aeroplane and its engines in the seconds prior to the occurrence.
Flight recorders are constructed, located and installed so as to provide maximum practical protection for the recordings in order that the recorded information may be preserved, recovered and transcribed.

Flight recorders are activated during ore-flight checks and shall not be switched off during flight time. To preserve flight recorder data, flight recorders shall be de-activated following an accident or incident and not re-activated until the records are retrieved.

2.5.6   *Minimum Equipment Requirements*

2.5.6.1 Visual Flight Rules (VFR)

All aeroplanes, when operated as VFR flights, shall be equipped with:
- a magnetic compass;
- an accurate timepiece indicating the time in hours, minutes and seconds;
- a sensitive pressure altimeter;
- an airspeed indicator; and
- such additional instruments or equipment as may be prescribed by the appropriate authority.

VFR flights which are operated as controlled flights must be equipped as for flights in IFR.

2.5.6.2 Instrument Flight Rules (IFR)

All aeroplanes, when operated in accordance with the instrument flight rules, or when the aeroplane cannot be maintained in a desired attitude without reference to one or more flight instruments, shall be equipped with:
- a turn and slip indicator;
- an attitude indicator (artificial horizon);
- a heading indicator (directional gyroscope);
- a means of indicating whether the power supply to the gyroscopic instrument is adequate;
- two sensitive pressure altimeters;
- a means of indicating in the flight crew compartment, the outside air temperature;
- an accurate timepiece indicating the time in hours, minutes and seconds;
- an airspeed indicating system with means of preventing malfunctioning due to either condensation or icing;
- a rate-of-climb and descent indicator; and
- such additional instruments or equipment as may be prescribed by the appropriate authority.

All aeroplanes with a maximum certificated takeoff mass of over 5700 kg must be fitted with an emergency power supply, independent of the main electrical generating system, for the purpose of illuminating and operating for at least 30 min, an attitude indicating instrument. The emergency supply must operate automatically after total failure of the main electrical system and an indication must be given on the instrument panel that the attitude indicator is on emergency supply.

2.5.6.3 All flights operated at night

All aeroplanes operated at night shall be equipped with:
- the equipment required for IFR flight;
- lights required for aircraft in flight or operating on the movement area of an aerodrome
- 2 landing lights;
- illumination for all instruments and equipment that are essential for the safe operation of the aeroplane that are used by the flight crew;
- lights in all passenger compartments; and
- an electric torch for each crew member station.

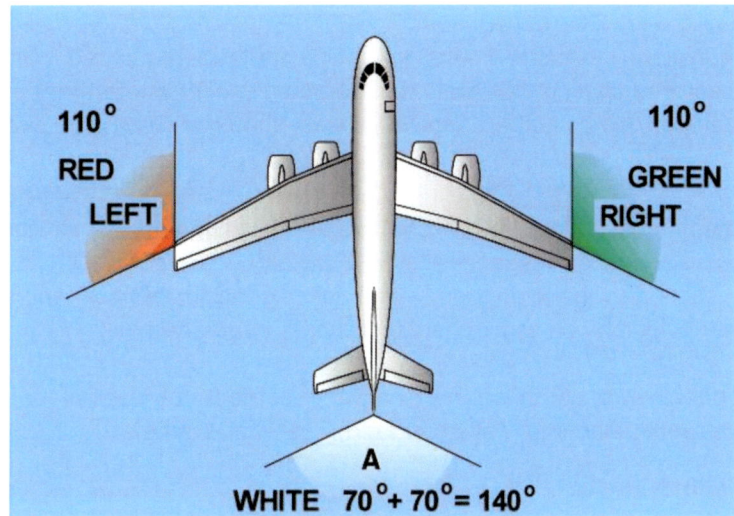

Figure 2.2 Aircraft lighting for night operations

2.5.7 All Aeroplanes on Flights over Water

2.5.7.1 Seaplanes

All seaplanes for all flights shall be equipped with:
• one life jacket, or equivalent individual floatation device, for each person on board, stowed in a position easily accessible from the seat or berth of the person for whose use it is provided:
• equipment for making the sound signals prescribed in the International Regulations for Preventing Collisions at Sea, where applicable; and
• one sea anchor (drogue).

2.5.7.2 Landplanes

Landplanes shall carry one life jacket or equivalent individual floatation device for each person on board, stowed in a position easily accessible from the seat or berth of the person for whose use it is provided:
• when flying over water and at a distance of more than 93 km (50 NM) away from the shore, in the case of engine failure on a single-engine aeroplane or of a single or more engine failure(s) in twin or multi-engine aeroplane;
• when flying en route over water beyond gliding distance from the shore, in the case of all other landplanes; and
• when taking off or landing at an aerodrome where, in the opinion of the State of the Operator, the takeoff or approach path is so disposed over water that in the event of a mishap there would be a likelihood of a ditching.

2.5.7.3 Long range over-water flights

In addition to the equipment prescribed for seaplanes and landplanes above, the following equipment must be installed in all aeroplanes when used over routes on which the aeroplane may be over water and at more than a distance corresponding to:
• 120 min at cruising speed or 740 km (400 NM), whichever is the lesser, away from land suitable for making an emergency landing in the case of aeroplanes with 2 or more engines; and
• for all other aeroplanes, 30 min at cruising speed or 185 km (100 NM) whichever is less;
unless carrying life saving equipment as specified below:
• life-saving rafts, stowed so as to facilitate their ready use in emergency and provided with such life-saving equipment including means of sustaining life as is appropriate to the flight to be undertaken and pyrotechnic equipment for making distress signals; and
• at least 2 sets of survival radio equipment (ELTs).

Each life jacket and equivalent individual floatation device shall be equipped with a means of electric illumination for the purpose of facilitating the location of persons, except where the requirement is met by the provision of individual floatation devices other than life jackets, should a ditching be likely to occur.

2.5.7.4 Flights over Designated Land Areas

Aeroplanes, when operated across land areas which have been designated by the State concerned as areas in which search and rescue would be especially difficult, shall be equipped with at least 1 survival radio equipment. Aeroplanes shall also be equipped with such signalling devices and life-saving equipment including survival equipment, as may be appropriate to the area overflown.

Note: The four areas designated as those requiring the carriage of special emergency and survival equipment are Polar – ice areas, Maritime – sea or ocean, Desert and Jungle.

2.5.7.5 High Altitude Flights

Note: Approximate altitude in the standard atmosphere corresponding to the value of absolute pressure used in this text is as follows:

Absolute pressure	Metres	Feet
700 hPa	3000	10000
620 hPa	4000	13000
376 hPa	7600	25000

An aeroplane intended to be operated at flight altitudes at which the atmospheric pressure is less than 700 hPa (above 10000') in personnel compartments, shall be equipped with oxygen storage and dispensing apparatus capable of storing and dispensing the required oxygen supplies.

An aeroplane intended to be operated at flight altitudes at which the atmospheric pressure is less than 700 hPa (above 10000') but which is provided with means of maintaining pressures greater than 700 hPa (below 10000') in personnel compartments shall be provided with oxygen storage and dispensing apparatus capable of storing and dispensing the oxygen supplies.

Pressurised aeroplanes newly introduced into service on or after 1 July 1962 and intended to be operated at flight altitudes at which the atmospheric pressure is less than 376 hPa (above 25000') shall be equipped with a device to provide positive warning to the pilot of any dangerous loss of pressurisation.

The following rule applies to aeroplanes (with an individual certificate of airworthiness first issued on or after 9th November 1998) that are intended to be operated at flight altitudes at which the atmospheric pressure is less than 376 hPa, or which, if operated at flight altitudes at which the atmospheric pressure is more than 376 hPa, cannot descend safely within 4 min to a flight altitude at which the atmospheric pressure is equal to 620 hPa. Such aeroplanes shall be provided with automatically deployable oxygen equipment to satisfy the requirements as stated. The total number of oxygen dispensing units shall exceed the number of passenger and cabin attendant seats by at least 10%.

2.5.8   Additional Equipment

Listed below are some additional items of aircraft equipment, which, depending upon the type of aeroplane and type of operation being flown may be mandatory or just optional.

2.5.8.1 Weather Radar

Pressurised aeroplanes, when carrying passengers, should be equipped with operative weather radar whenever such aeroplanes are being operated in areas where thunderstorms (or other potentially hazardous weather conditions regarded as detectable with airborne weather radar) may be expected to exist along the route either at night or under instrument meteorological conditions.

2.5.8.2 Radiation Indicator

All aeroplanes intended to be operated above 15000 m (49000'), shall carry equipment to measure and indicate continuously the dose rate of total cosmic radiation being received (i.e. the total of ionising and neutron radiation of galactic and solar origin) and the cumulative dose on each flight. The display unit of the equipment shall be readily visible to a flight crewmember.

2.5.8.3 Machmeter

All aeroplanes with speed limitations expressed in terms of Mach number shall be equipped with a Mach number indicator. This device is required in airspace where the longitudinal separation of aeroplanes in that airspace is based upon the Mach numbers of each aeroplane as advised to Air Traffic Control.

2.5.8.4 Ground Proximity Warning System (GPWS)

This applies to all turbine-engine aeroplanes having an individual certificate of airworthiness first issued on or after 1 July 1979. If such an aircraft has a maximum certificated takeoff mass in excess of 15000 kg or is authorised to carry more than 30 passengers, it shall be equipped with a ground proximity warning system.

From 1 January 1999 this requirement becomes effective for all aircraft with a certificated mass in excess of 5700 kg or authorised to carry more than 9 passengers.

A GPWS shall, automatically, provide a timely and distinctive warning to the flight crew when the aeroplane is in potentially hazardous proximity to the earth's surface. Also, a GPWS shall provide, as a minimum, warnings of the following circumstances:
- excessive descent rate;
- excessive terrain closure rate;
- excessive altitude loss after takeoff or go-around;
- unsafe terrain clearance while not in landing configuration;
- gear not locked down;
- flaps not in a landing position; and
- excessive descent below the instrument glide path.

2.6   Aeroplane Communication and Navigation Equipment

2.6.1   Communication Equipment

An aeroplane shall be provided with radio communication equipment capable of:
- conducting two-way communication for aerodrome control purposes;
- receiving meteorological information at any time during flight; and
- conducting two-way communication at any time during the flight with at least one aeronautical station and with such other aeronautical stations and on such frequencies as may be prescribed by the appropriate authority.

2.6.2   Navigation Equipment

An aeroplane shall be provided with navigation equipment that will enable it to proceed:
- in accordance with its operational flight plan;
- in accordance with prescribed Required Navigation Performance (RNP) types; and
- in accordance with the requirements of air traffic services.
Except when, if not precluded by the appropriate authority, navigation for flights under visual flight rules is carried out by visual reference to landmarks.

For flights in portions of airspace where, based on regional air navigation agreements, minimum navigation performance specifications (MNPS) are prescribed, an aeroplane shall be provide with navigation equipment which:

• continuously provides indications to the flight crew of adherence to or departure from track to the required degree of accuracy at any point along track; and

• has been authorised by the State of the Operator for MNPS operations.

The aeroplane shall be provided with sufficient navigation equipment to ensure that, in the event of the failure of one item of equipment at any stage of the flight, the remaining equipment will enable the aeroplane to navigate in accordance with the accuracy required by the operational flight plan, applicable RNP or ATS.

On flights in which it is intended to land in instrument meteorological conditions, an aeroplane shall be provided with radio equipment capable of receiving signals providing guidance to a point from which a visual landing can be effected. This equipment shall be capable of providing such guidance at each aerodrome at which it is intended to land in instrument meteorological condition and at any designated alternate aerodromes.

The equipment installation shall be such that the failure of any single unit required for either communications or navigation purposes or both will not result in the failure of another unit required for communications or navigation purposes.

2.7 Aeroplane Maintenance

A document called a Maintenance Release shall be completed and signed to certify that maintenance work has been completed satisfactorily and in accordance with procedures described in the maintenance manual.

A maintenance release shall contain a certification including:

• basic details of the maintenance carried out;
• date such maintenance was complete;
• when applicable, the identity of the approved maintenance organisation; and
• the identity of the person or persons signing the release.

This maintenance release document usually forms part of the aeroplane's Technical Log Book in which are recorded the flights operated by the aeroplane and any technical problems manifesting themselves during these flights, which subsequently require rectification after the aeroplane has arrived back on the ground.

To show acceptance that an aeroplane is fit for flight, the pilot signs the Technical Log Book. He/she will check that it has already been signed by the ground engineer, releasing the aeroplane into service and certifying that he is satisfied that the aeroplane is mechanically sound and legally ready to undertake the planned operation.

2.8 Aeroplane Flight Crew

2.8.1 Composition of the Flight Crew

The number and composition of the flight crew shall not be less than that specified in the operations manual. Considerations related to the type of aeroplane used, the type of operation involved and the duration of flight between points where flight crews are changed may affect the number of flight crew required. In such circumstances the flight crews shall include flight crewmembers, additional to the minimum numbers specified in the flight manual or other documents associated with the certificate of airworthiness.

2.8.1.1 Carriage of Flight Engineer

When a separate flight engineer's station is incorporated in the design of an aeroplane, the flight crew shall include at least one flight engineer especially assigned to that station, unless the duties associated with that station can be satisfactorily performance by another flight crew member, holding a flight engineer licence, without interference with regular duties

2.8.1.2 Carriage of a Flight Navigator

The flight crew shall include at least one member who holds a flight navigator licence in all operations where, as determined by the State of the operator, navigation necessary for the safe conduct of the flight cannot be adequately accomplished by the pilots from the pilot station.

2.8.2   Recent Experience

An operator shall not assign a pilot to act as pilot-in-command of an aeroplane unless, on the same type of aeroplane within the preceding 90 days, that pilot has made at least three takeoffs and landings

An operator shall not assign a co-pilot to serve at flight controls during takeoff and landing unless, on the same type of aeroplane within the preceding 90 days, that co-pilot has operated the flight controls as PIC or co-pilot during 3 takeoffs and landings or has demonstrated competence to act as co-pilot on a flight simulator approved for the purpose.

2.8.3   Pilot-in-command Route / Airport Qualification

An operator shall not utilise a pilot as pilot-in-command of an aeroplane on a route or route segment for which that pilot is not currently qualified until that pilot has been familiarised with the specified routes or route segments and the relevant airports concerned with these routes or route segments.

Each such pilot shall demonstrate to the operator an adequate knowledge of:
a)   the route to be flown and the aerodromes which are to be used. This shall include knowledge of:
1)   the terrain and minimum safe altitudes;
2)   the seasonal meteorological conditions;
3)   the meteorological, communication and air traffic facilities, services and procedures;
4)   the search and rescue procedures; and
5)   the navigational facilities and procedures, including any long-range navigation procedures associated with the route along which the flight is to take place; and
b)   procedures applicable to flight paths over heavily populated areas and areas of high air traffic density, obstructions, physical layout, lighting, approach aids and arrival, departure, holding and instrument approach procedures, and applicable operating minima.
Note: Approved aeroplane simulator devices may be used in these regards.

A pilot-in-command shall have made an actual approach into each aerodrome of landing on the route, accompanied by a pilot who is qualified for the aerodrome, as a member of the flight crew or as an observer on the flight deck, unless:
a)   the approach to the aerodrome is not over difficult terrain and the instrument approach procedures and aids available are similar to those with which the pilot is familiar and a margin to be approved by the State of the operator is added to the normal operating minima, or there is reasonable certainty that approach and landing can be made in visual meteorological conditions; or
b)   the descent from the initial approach altitude can be made by day in visual meteorological conditions; or
c)   the operator qualifies the pilot-in-command to land at the aerodrome concerned by means of an adequate pictorial presentation; or
d)   the aerodrome concerned is adjacent to another aerodrome at which the pilot-in-command is currently qualified to land.

The operator shall maintain a record, sufficient to satisfy the State of the Operator, of the qualification of the pilot and of the manner in which such qualification has been achieved.

An operator shall not continue to utilise a pilot as a pilot-in-command on a route unless, within the preceding 12 months, the pilot has made at least one trip between the terminal points of that route as a pilot member of the flight crew, or as a check pilot, or as an observer on the flight deck. In the event that more than 12 months elapse in which a pilot has not made such a trip on a route in close proximity and over similar terrain, prior to again serving as a pilot-in-command on that route, that pilot must be re-qualified.

2.8.4   *Proficiency Checks*

An operator shall ensure that piloting technique and the ability to execute emergency procedures is checked in such a way as to demonstrate the pilot's competence. Where the operation may be conducted under instrument flight rules, an operator shall ensure that the pilot's competence to comply with such rules is demonstrated to either a check pilot of the operator or to a representative of the State of the Operator. Such checks shall be performed twice within any period of 1 year. Any 2 such checks which are similar and which occur within a period of 4 consecutive months shall not alone satisfy this requirement.

2.9   *Manuals, Logs and Records*

2.9.1   *Operations Manual*

An operator shall provide an operations manual for the use and guidance of flight operations personnel concerned. The operations manual shall be amended or revised as is necessary to ensure that the information contained therein is kept up to date. All such amendments or revisions shall be issued to all personnel that are required to use the manual.

The State of the Operator shall establish a requirement for the operator to provide a copy of the operations manual together with all amendments and / or revisions, for review and acceptance and, where required, approval. The operator shall incorporate in the operations manual such mandatory material as the State of the Operator may require.

2.9.1.1 *Contents of the Operations Manual*

The operations manual must contain guidance on at least the following:
- Operations administrations and supervision
- Accident prevention and flight safety programme
- Personnel training
- Fatigue and flight time limitations
- Flight operations
- Aeroplane performance
- Route guides and charts
- Minimum flight altitudes
- Aerodrome operating minima
- Search and rescue
- Dangerous goods
- Navigation
- Communication
- Security
- Human factors

2.9.2   *Journey Log Book*

The aeroplane journey logbook, which is sometimes combined with, or forms a part of, the aeroplane maintenance or technical logbook, should contain the following items and corresponding roman numerals:

I.   Aeroplane nationality and registration.
II. Date
III. Names of crewmembers.
IV. Duty assignment of crewmembers.
V.   Place of departure.
VI. Place of arrival.
VII. Time of departure
VIII.Time of arrival.
IX. Hours of flight.
X.   Nature of flight (private, aerial work, scheduled or non-scheduled).
XI. Incidents, observations, if any.
XII. Signature of person in charge.

Entries should be made as soon as possible after a flight and be in ink (or indelible pencil). The completed journey log book should be retained for at least 6 months.

2.9.3   *Emergency and Survival Equipment*

Operators must at all times maintain and have available for immediate communication to rescue co-ordination centres, lists containing information on the emergency and survival equipment carried on board any of their aeroplanes engaged in international air navigation. The information shall include (as applicable) the number, colour and type of life rafts and pyrotechnics, details of emergency medical supplies, water supplies and the type and frequencies of the emergency portable radio.

2.10   *Security*

2.10.1   *Security of the Flight Crew Compartment*

In all aeroplanes that are equipped with a flight crew compartment door, this door shall be capable of being locked. It shall be lockable from within the compartment only

2.10.2   *Unlawful Interference*

Following an act of unlawful interference the pilot-in-command shall submit, without delay, a report of such an act to the designated local authority.

Self Assessment Test 01

1.   Information on the operation of aircraft is contained in:
A)   Annex 2   Rules of the Air
B)   Annex 6   Operation of Aircraft
C)   Annex 9   Facilitation
D)   Annex 14   Aerodromes

2.   Which of the following is mandatory for ICAO members:
A)   ICAO must be informed about the differences from the standards in any of the annexes to the Chicago convention
B)   ICAO must be informed of the initial issue and revalidation of flight crew licences
C)   ICAO shall approve the ticket pricing on international airline flights
D)   ICAO must be informed of a change in operators responsibility to passenger and goods transportation

3.   Which of the following documents, according to the Chicago Convention Article 29, must be carried by aircraft engaged in International Air Navigation:
A)   Crew licences, radio licences (if relevant), journey logbook
B)   Certificate of registration
C)   Certificate of airworthiness
D)   All of the above

4.   Who is responsible for the renewal or validation of a C of A (Certificate of Airworthiness):
A)   State which first approved the aircraft
B)   State of Registry
C)   State of Design
D)   Aircraft manufacturer

5.   The A.O.C (Air Operators Certificate) shall contain at least the following:
A)   Operators identification, location and authorised area of operation or routes
B)   Description of the types of operations authorised
C)   Types of aircraft authorised, period of validity and date of issue
D)   All of the above

6.   A maintenance engineer is to taxi an aircraft to the hangar for work to be carried out. Which of the following requirements must be fulfilled:
A)   The engineer has been given ATC clearance
B)   The engineer has informed the operator of the movement
C)   The engineer has been duly authorised by the operator
D)   The engineer has a partial type rating

7.   Who established the OCA/H (Obstacle Clearance Attitude height) for an approach procedure:
A)   The state
B)   The pilot in command
C)   The operator
D)   The airline flight operations department

8.   The reference datum used for the calculation of DA (Decision Altitude) for a precision approach is:
A)   Mean sea level
B)   Evaluation of highest point on landing runway
C)   Threshold elevation
D)   Elevation of highest point on aerodrome

9. The reference datum used for the calculation of MDH for a non-precision approach is:
A) The elevation of the landing runway threshold
B) Mean sea level
C) The elevation of the aerodrome
D) The elevation of the aerodrome or runway threshold if that is more than 2 m (7') below the aerodrome elevation

10. The reference datum used for the calculation of OCH for a circling approach is:
A) Mean sea level
B) Aerodrome
C) The elevation of the landing threshold
D) The elevation of the highest point on the aerodrome

11. In terms of ground personnel who is responsible for the day-to-day operations of the aircraft:
A) Flight operations / Dispatch officers
B) Scheduling controllers
C) Navigation & planning staff
D) Route planning officers

12. Which of the following items must be included in a passenger emergency briefing:
A) Seat belts and briefing cards
B) Emergency equipment and oxygen equipment if carried
C) Life jackets if carried
D) All of the above

13. The recent experience of a captain assigned to a flight on an aircraft type by an operator must not be less than:
A) 6 T/Os and 6 landings as a pilot in command on the aircraft type during the preceding 90 days
B) 3 T/Os and 3 landings as a pilot in command on the aircraft type during the preceding 30 days
C) 3 T/Os and 3 landings as a pilot in command on the aircraft type during the preceding 90 days
D) 3 T/Os and 3 landings as a pilot in command on the aircraft type during the last 6 months

14. Pilot proficiency checks are to be conducted where operations are undertaken under instrument flight rules:
A) Once within any 2 year period
B) Once every year
C) Twice with any 1 year period
D) Once every 18 months

15. The refuelling of an aircraft may be carried out if passengers are on board:
A) When passengers are properly attended by qualified personnel, ready to initiate an evacuation
B) When passengers are seated with the no smoking / fasten seatbelt signs illuminated
C) When integral aircraft stairs and emergency exits are open
D) It is not permitted at any time

16. During pre-flight planning for a twin engine aircraft a T/O alternate aerodrome:
A) Need not be selected
B) Can be within a distance of 100 NM radius of T/O aerodrome
C) Within the distance equivalent to 1 hours flight time at single engine cruise speed
D) Within the distance equivalent to 2 hours flight time at single engine cruise speed

17. Flight crew members on the flight deck shall keep their safety belts fastened:
A) Only during T/Os and landings
B) From T/O to landing
C) Only during T/O and landing or when deemed necessary by the commander for safety reasons
D) While at their stations

18. For flights carried out under the instrument flight rules may be flight planned without a landing alternative aerodrome if:
A) The weather forecast at the destination CAVOK
B) The aerodrome of intended landing is isolated and there is no suitable destination alternate aerodrome
C) Icing conditions are absent and weather is suitable
D) None of the above

19. On board a pressurised aircraft a flight should only be operated if there is an oxygen supply for crew and part of the passengers to be supplied with oxygen in case of an emergency decompression during the flight where the pressure altitude is above:
A) 12000'
B) 11000'
C) 10000'
D) 14000'

20. The landing distance for a turboprop at any alternate aerodrome as determined from the flight manual shall not exceed …….. of the landing distance available:
A) 50%
B) 70%
C) 75%
D) 80%

Self Assessment Test 01 Answers

1	B
2	A
3	D
4	B
5	D
6	C
7	A
8	A
9	D
10	B
11	A
12	D
13	C
14	C
15	A
16	C
17	D
18	B
19	C
20	B

CRANFIELD AVIATION TRAINING SCHOOL LTD. PART-FCL GBR.ATO-0136
CATS INNOVATION CENTRE, LUTON, Bedfordshire LU2 8DL U.K.

www.catsaviation.com

2-23

Operational Procedures

CHAPTER 3

IR-OPS Requirements

3.1 Technical requirements and administrative procedures related to air operations

In Europe the provisions of the Regulation on Air Operations are now published in several documents: Implementing Rules (published in the Official Journal of the European Union as Commission Regulations and subsequent amending regulations – so-called 'hard law') and associated Acceptable Means of Compliance, Guidance Material and Certification Specifications (published by EASA as Decisions – so-called 'soft law' or non-binding rules).

Commission Regulation (EU) No 965/2012 of 5 October 2012 'lays down' technical requirements and administrative procedures related to air operations, including:

'… detailed rules for commercial air transport operations with aeroplanes and helicopters, …'

and:

'… detailed rules on the conditions for issuing, maintaining, amending, limiting, suspending or revoking the certificates of operators of aircraft referred to in Article 4(1)(b) and (c) of Regulation (EC) No 216/2008 engaged in commercial air transport operations, the privileges and responsibilities of the holders of certificates as well as conditions under which operations shall be prohibited, limited or subject to certain conditions in the interest of safety.'

The Regulation is officially called IR-OPS (implementing rules – operations), but it is also called EASA OPS and EASA AIR OPS. It replaces EU-OPS (Regulation (EC) 859/2008) with regard to commercial operations of aeroplanes and JAR-OPS 3 with regard to commercial operations of helicopters. It entered into force and became applicable on 28 October 2012.

The annexes to the Regulation are:

ANNEX I Definitions for terms used in Annexes II to VIII
ANNEX II Authority Requirements for Air Operations [PART-ARO]
ANNEX III Organisation Requirements for Air Operations [PART-ORO]
ANNEX IV Commercial Air Transport Operations [Part-CAT]
ANNEX V Specific Approvals [Part-SPA]
ANNEX VI Non-Commercial Air Operations with Complex Motor-Powered Aircraft [PART-NCC]
ANNEX VII Non-Commercial Air Operations with Other-Than Complex Motor-Powered Aircraft [PART-NCO]
ANNEX VIII SPECIALISED OPERATIONS [PART-SPO]

Regulations Structure

Each Part to each implementing regulation has its own **Acceptable Means of Compliance and Guidance Material (AMC/GM)**. These AMC and GM are amended along with the amendments of the regulations. These AMC/GM are so-called 'soft law' (non-binding rules) and put down in form of EASA Decisions. A comprehensive explanation on AMC in form of questions and answers can be found on the FAQ section of the EASA website.

Furthermore, **Certification Specifications** are also related to the implementing regulations, respectively their parts. Like AMC/GM they are put down as Decisions and are non-binding.

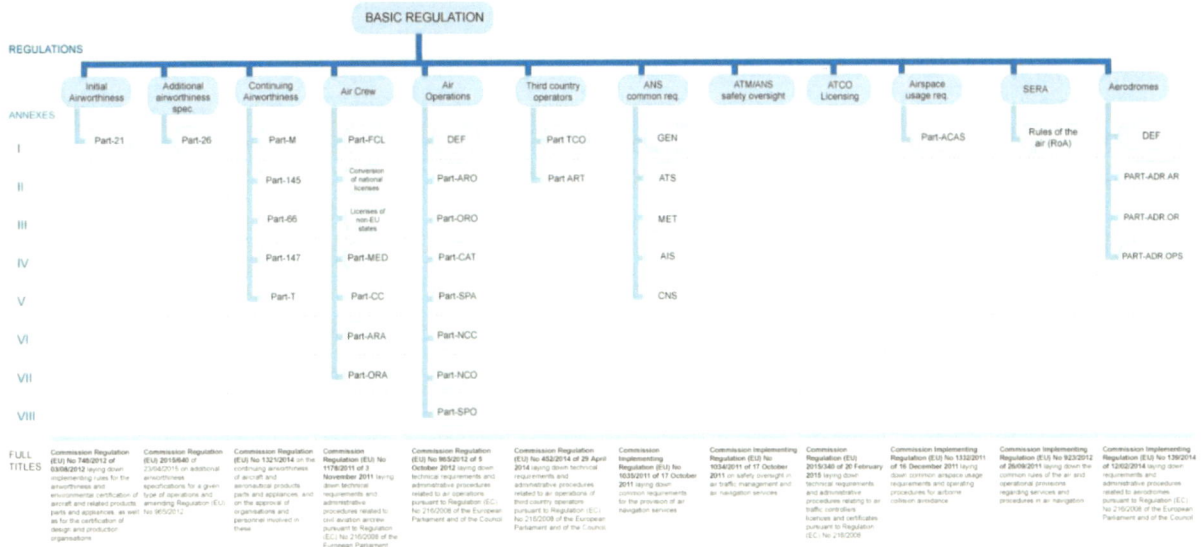

The BASIC REGULATION is Regulation (EC) No 216/2008 of 20 February 2008 on common rules in the field of civil aviation and establishing a European Aviation Safety Agency. The 'implementing' Commission Regulation (EU) No 965/2012 'Air Operations' (the fifth from the left in the figure above) is expanded in the figure below. From https://www.easa.europa.eu/regulations

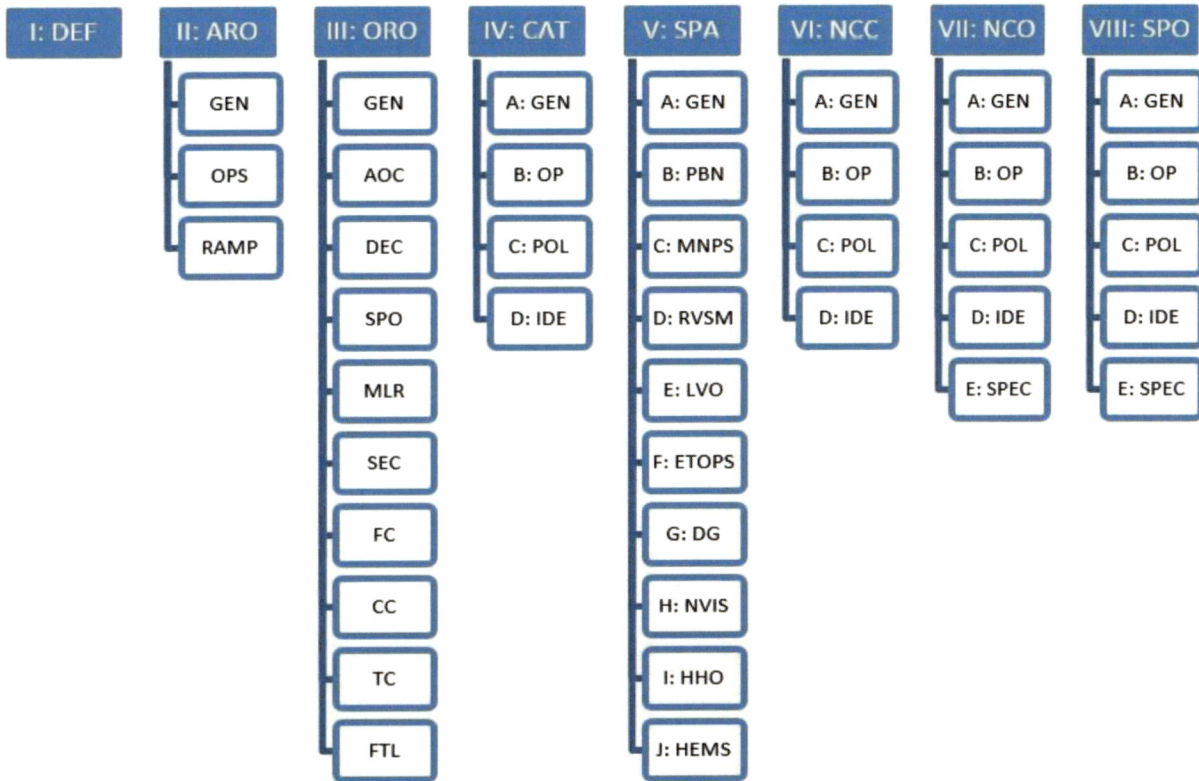

COMMISSION REGULATION (EU) No 965/2012 comprises eight annexes (parts) with related subparts.
From http://www.skybrary.aero/index.php/IR-OPS

The annexes' subparts are:

AOC air operator certificate
CC cabin crew
DEC declaration
DG dangerous goods
ETOPS extended range operations with two-engined aeroplanes
FC flight crew
FTL flight and duty time limitations
GEN general
H helicopter
HEMS helicopter emergency medical service
HHO helicopter hoist operation
IDE instruments, data and equipment
LVO low visibility operation
MAB mass and balance
MLR manuals, logs and records
MNPS minimum navigation performance specifications
MPA motor-powered aircraft
NVIS night vision imaging system
OP operational procedures
OPS operations
PBN performance-based navigation
POL aircraft performance and operating limitations
RAMP ramp inspections of aircraft of operators under the regulatory oversight of another state
RVSM reduced vertical separation minima
SEC security
SPEC specific requirements
SPO specialised operations
TC technical crew

ORO.GEN.200 Management system and ORO.FTL.120 Fatigue risk management (FRM) are notable changes in IR-OPS.

3.2   *General Requirements*

ORO.GEN.200 Management system
(a) The operator shall establish, implement and maintain a management system that includes:

(1) clearly defined lines of responsibility and accountability throughout the operator, including a direct safety accountability of the accountable manager;

(2) a description of the overall philosophies and principles of the operator with regard to safety, referred to as the safety policy;

(3) the identification of aviation safety hazards entailed by the activities of the operator, their evaluation and the management of associated risks, including taking actions to mitigate the risk and verify their effectiveness;

(4) maintaining personnel trained and competent to perform their tasks;

(5) documentation of all management system key processes, including a process for making personnel aware of their responsibilities and the procedure for amending this documentation;

(6) a function to monitor compliance of the operator with the relevant requirements. Compliance monitoring shall include a feedback system of findings to the accountable manager to ensure effective implementation of corrective actions as necessary; and

(7) any additional requirements that are prescribed in the relevant Subparts of this Annex or other applicable Annexes.

(b) The management system shall correspond to the size of the operator and the nature and complexity of its activities, taking into account the hazards and associated risks inherent in these activities.

ORO.AOC.130 Flight data monitoring — aeroplanes

Since 1 January 2005 EASA and the JAA before it have required an operator to establish and maintain a flight data monitoring programme, integrated in its management system, for aeroplanes with a maximum certificated take-off mass of more than 27 000 kg. Flight Data Monitoring (FDM) is the proactive and non-punitive gathering and analysis of data recorded during routine flights to improve aviation safety.

CAT.GEN.MPA.100 Crew responsibilities

(a) The crew member shall be responsible for the proper execution of his/her duties that are:

(1) related to the safety of the aircraft and its occupants; and

(2) specified in the instructions and procedures in the operations manual.

(b) The crew member shall:

(1) report to the commander any fault, failure, malfunction or defect which the crew member believes may affect the airworthiness or safe operation of the aircraft including emergency systems, if not already reported by another crew member;

(2) report to the commander any incident that endangered, or could have endangered, the safety of the operation, if not already reported by another crew member;

(3) comply with the relevant requirements of the operator's occurrence reporting schemes;

(4) comply with all flight and duty time limitations (FTL) and rest requirements applicable to their activities;

(5) when undertaking duties for more than one operator:

(i) maintain his/her individual records regarding flight and duty times and rest periods as referred to in applicable FTL requirements; and

(ii) provide each operator with the data needed to schedule activities in accordance with the applicable FTL requirements.

(c) The crew member shall not perform duties on an aircraft:

(1) when under the influence of psychoactive substances or alcohol or when unfit due to injury, fatigue, medication, sickness or other similar causes;

(2) until a reasonable time period has elapsed after deep water diving or following blood donation;

(3) if applicable medical requirements are not fulfilled;

(4) if he/she is in any doubt of being able to accomplish his/her assigned duties; or

(5) if he/she knows or suspects that he/she is suffering from fatigue as referred to in 7.f of Annex IV to Regulation (EC) No 216/2008 or feels otherwise unfit, to the extent that the flight may be endangered.

CAT.GEN.MPA.105 Responsibilities of the commander

(a) The commander, in addition to complying with CAT.GEN.MPA.100, shall:

(1) be responsible for the safety of all crew members, passengers and cargo on board, as soon as the commander arrives on board the aircraft, until the commander leaves the aircraft at the end of the flight;

(2) be responsible for the operation and safety of the aircraft:

(i) for aeroplanes, from the moment the aeroplane is first ready to move for the purpose of taxiing prior to take-off, until the moment it finally comes to rest at the end of the flight and the engine(s) used as primary propulsion unit(s) is(are) shut down;

(ii) for helicopters, when the rotors are turning;

(3) have authority to give all commands and take any appropriate actions for the purpose of securing the safety of the aircraft and of persons and/or property carried therein in accordance with 7.c of Annex IV to Regulation (EC) No 216/2008;

(4) have authority to disembark any person, or any part of the cargo, that may represent a potential hazard to the safety of the aircraft or its occupants;

(5) not allow a person to be carried in the aircraft who appears to be under the influence of alcohol or drugs to the extent that the safety of the aircraft or its occupants is likely to be endangered;

(6) have the right to refuse transportation of inadmissible passengers, deportees or persons in custody if their carriage increases the risk to the safety of the aircraft or its occupants;

(7) ensure that all passengers are briefed on the location of emergency exits and the location and use of relevant safety and emergency equipment;

(8) ensure that all operational procedures and checklists are complied with in accordance with the operations manual;

(9) not permit any crew member to perform any activity during critical phases of flight, except duties required for the safe operation of the aircraft;

(10) ensure that flight recorders:

(i) are not disabled or switched off during flight; and

(ii) in the event of an accident or an incident that is subject to mandatory reporting:

(A) are not intentionally erased;

(B) are deactivated immediately after the flight is completed; and

(C) are reactivated only with the agreement of the investigating authority;

(11) decide on acceptance of the aircraft with unserviceabilities in accordance with the configuration deviation list (CDL) or the minimum equipment list (MEL);

(12) ensure that the pre-flight inspection has been carried out in accordance with the requirements of Annex I (Part-M) to Regulation (EC) No 2042/2003;

(13) be satisfied that relevant emergency equipment remains easily accessible for immediate use.
(b) The commander, or the pilot to whom conduct of the flight has been delegated, shall, in an emergency situation that requires immediate decision and action, take any action he/she considers necessary under the

circumstances in accordance with 7.d of Annex IV to Regulation (EC) No 216/2008. In such cases he/she may deviate from rules, operational procedures and methods in the interest of safety.

(c) Whenever an aircraft in flight has manoeuvred in response to an airborne collision avoidance system (ACAS) resolution advisory (RA), the commander shall submit an ACAS report to the competent authority.

(d) Bird hazards and strikes:

(1) Whenever a potential bird hazard is observed, the commander shall inform the air traffic service (ATS) unit as soon as flight crew workload allows.

(2) Whenever an aircraft for which the commander is responsible suffers a bird strike that results in significant damage to the aircraft or the loss or malfunction of any essential service, the commander shall submit a written bird strike report after landing to the competent authority.

CAT.GEN.MPA.110 Authority of the commander

The operator shall take all reasonable measures to ensure that all persons carried in the aircraft obey all lawful commands given by the commander for the purpose of securing the safety of the aircraft and of persons or property carried therein.

CAT.GEN.MPA.115 Personnel or crew members other than cabin crew in the passenger compartment

The operator shall ensure that personnel or crew members, other than operating cabin crew members, carrying out their duties in the passenger compartment of an aircraft:

(a) are not confused by the passengers with operating cabin crew members;

(b) do not occupy required cabin crew assigned stations;

(c) do not impede operating cabin crew members in their duties.

CAT.GEN.MPA.120 Common language

The operator shall ensure that all crew members can communicate with each other in a common language.

CAT.GEN.MPA.125 Taxiing of aeroplanes

The operator shall ensure that an aeroplane is only taxied on the movement area of an aerodrome if the person at the controls:

(a) is an appropriately qualified pilot; or

(b) has been designated by the operator and:

(1) is trained to taxi the aircraft;

(2) is trained to use the radio telephone;

(3) has received instruction in respect of aerodrome layout, routes, signs, marking, lights, air traffic control (ATC) signals and instructions, phraseology and procedures;

(4) is able to conform to the operational standards required for safe aeroplane movement at the aerodrome.

CAT.GEN.MPA.130 Rotor engagement — helicopters

A helicopter rotor shall only be turned under power for the purpose of flight with a qualified pilot at the controls.

CAT.GEN.MPA.135 Admission to the flight crew compartment

(a) The operator shall ensure that no person, other than a flight crew member assigned to a flight, is admitted to, or carried in, the flight crew compartment unless that person is:

(1) an operating crew member;

(2) a representative of the competent or inspecting authority, if required to be there for the performance of his/her official duties; or

(3) permitted by and carried in accordance with instructions contained in the operations manual.

(b) The commander shall ensure that:

(1) admission to the flight crew compartment does not cause distraction or interference with the operation of the flight; and

(2) all persons carried in the flight crew compartment are made familiar with the relevant safety procedures.
(c) The commander shall make the final decision regarding the admission to the flight crew compartment.

CAT.GEN.MPA.140 Portable electronic devices

The operator shall not permit any person to use a portable electronic device (PED) on board an aircraft that could adversely affect the performance of the aircraft's systems and equipment, and shall take all reasonable measures to prevent such use.

CAT.GEN.MPA.145 Information on emergency and survival equipment carried

The operator shall at all times have available for immediate communication to rescue coordination centres (RCCs) lists containing information on the emergency and survival equipment carried on board any of their aircraft.

CAT.GEN.MPA.150 Ditching — aeroplanes

The operator shall only operate an aeroplane with a passenger seating configuration of more than 30 on overwater flights at a distance from land suitable for making an emergency landing, greater than 120 minutes at cruising speed, or 400 NM, whichever is less, if the aeroplane complies with the ditching provisions prescribed in the applicable airworthiness code.

CAT.GEN.MPA.155 Carriage of weapons of war and munitions of war

(a) The operator shall only transport weapons of war or munitions of war by air if an approval to do so has been granted by all States whose airspace is intended to be used for the flight.

(b) Where an approval has been granted, the operator shall ensure that weapons of war and munitions of war are:

(1) stowed in the aircraft in a place that is inaccessible to passengers during flight; and

(2) in the case of firearms, unloaded.

(c) The operator shall ensure that, before a flight begins, the commander is notified of the details and location on board the aircraft of any weapons of war and munitions of war intended to be carried.

CAT.GEN.MPA.160 Carriage of sporting weapons and ammunition

(a) The operator shall take all reasonable measures to ensure that any sporting weapons intended to be carried by air are reported to the operator.

(b) The operator accepting the carriage of sporting weapons shall ensure that they are:

(1) stowed in the aircraft in a place that is inaccessible to passengers during flight; and

(2) in the case of firearms or other weapons that can contain ammunition, unloaded.

(c) Ammunition for sporting weapons may be carried in passengers' checked baggage, subject to certain limitations, in accordance with the technical instructions.

CAT.GEN.MPA.165 Method of carriage of persons

The operator shall take all measures to ensure that no person is in any part of an aircraft in flight that is not designed for the accommodation of persons unless temporary access has been granted by the commander:

(a) for the purpose of taking action necessary for the safety of the aircraft or of any person, animal or goods therein; or

(b) to a part of the aircraft in which cargo or supplies are carried, being a part that is designed to enable a person to have access thereto while the aircraft is in flight.

CAT.GEN.MPA.170 Alcohol and drugs

The operator shall take all reasonable measures to ensure that no person enters or is in an aircraft when under the influence of alcohol or drugs to the extent that the safety of the aircraft or its occupants is likely to be endangered.

CAT.GEN.MPA.175 Endangering safety

The operator shall take all reasonable measures to ensure that no person recklessly or negligently acts or omits to act so as to:

(a) endanger an aircraft or person therein; or

(b) cause or permit an aircraft to endanger any person or property.

CAT.GEN.MPA.180 Documents, manuals and information to be carried

(a) The following documents, manuals and information shall be carried on each flight, as originals or copies unless otherwise specified:

(1) the aircraft flight manual (AFM), or equivalent document(s);

(2) the original certificate of registration;

(3) the original certificate of airworthiness (CofA);

(4) the noise certificate, including an English translation, where one has been provided by the authority responsible for issuing the noise certificate;

(5) a certified true copy of the air operator certificate (AOC);

(6) the operations specifications relevant to the aircraft type, issued with the AOC;

(7) the original aircraft radio licence, if applicable;

(8) the third party liability insurance certificate(s);

(9) the journey log, or equivalent, for the aircraft;

(10) the aircraft technical log, in accordance with Annex I (Part-M) to Regulation (EC) No 2042/2003;

(11) details of the filed ATS flight plan, if applicable;

(12) current and suitable aeronautical charts for the route of the proposed flight and all routes along which it is reasonable to expect that the flight may be diverted;

(13) procedures and visual signals information for use by intercepting and intercepted aircraft;

(14) information concerning search and rescue services for the area of the intended flight, which shall be easily accessible in the flight crew compartment;

(15) the current parts of the operations manual that are relevant to the duties of the crew members, which shall be easily accessible to the crew members;

(16) the MEL;

(17) appropriate notices to airmen (NOTAMs) and aeronautical information service (AIS) briefing documentation;

(18) appropriate meteorological information;

(19) cargo and/or passenger manifests, if applicable;

(20) mass and balance documentation;

(21) the operational flight plan, if applicable;

(22) notification of special categories of passenger (SCPs) and special loads, if applicable; and

(23) any other documentation that may be pertinent to the flight or is required by the States concerned with the flight.

(b) Notwithstanding (a), for operations under visual flight rules (VFR) by day with other-than-complex motor-powered aircraft taking off and landing at the same aerodrome or operating site within 24 hours, or remaining within a local area specified in the operations manual, the following documents and information may be retained at the aerodrome or operating site instead:

(1) noise certificate;

(2) aircraft radio licence;

(3) journey log, or equivalent;

(4) aircraft technical log;

(5) NOTAMs and AIS briefing documentation;

(6) meteorological information;

(7) notification of SCPs and special loads, if applicable; and

(8) mass and balance documentation.

(c) Notwithstanding (a), in case of loss or theft of documents specified in (a)(2) to (a)(8), the operation may continue until the flight reaches its destination or a place where replacement documents can be provided.

CAT.GEN.MPA.185 Information to be retained on the ground

(a) The operator shall ensure that at least for the duration of each flight or series of flights:

(1) information relevant to the flight and appropriate for the type of operation is preserved on the ground;

(2) the information is retained until it has been duplicated at the place at which it will be stored; or, if this is impracticable

(3) the same information is carried in a fireproof container in the aircraft.

(b) The information referred to in (a) includes:

(1) a copy of the operational flight plan, where appropriate;

(2) copies of the relevant part(s) of the aircraft technical log;

(3) route-specific NOTAM documentation if specifically edited by the operator;

(4) mass and balance documentation if required; and

(5) special loads notification.

CAT.GEN.MPA.190 Provision of documentation and records

The commander shall, within a reasonable time of being requested to do so by a person authorised by an authority, provide to that person the documentation required to be carried on board.

CAT.GEN.MPA.195 Preservation, production and use of flight recorder recordings

(a) Following an accident or an incident that is subject to mandatory reporting, the operator of an aircraft shall preserve the original recorded data for a period of 60 days unless otherwise directed by the investigating authority.

(b) The operator shall conduct operational checks and evaluations of flight data recorder (FDR) recordings, cockpit voice recorder (CVR) recordings and data link recordings to ensure the continued serviceability of the recorders.

(c) The operator shall save the recordings for the period of operating time of the FDR as required by CAT.IDE.A.190 or CAT.IDE.H.190, except that, for the purpose of testing and maintaining the FDR, up to one hour of the oldest recorded material at the time of testing may be erased.

(d) The operator shall keep and maintain up-to-date documentation that presents the necessary information to convert FDR raw data into parameters expressed in engineering units.

(e) The operator shall make available any flight recorder recording that has been preserved, if so determined by the competent authority.

(f) Without prejudice to Regulation (EU) No 996/2010 of the European Parliament and of the Council (1):

(1) CVR recordings shall only be used for purposes other than for the investigation of an accident or an incident subject to mandatory reporting, if all crew members and maintenance personnel concerned consent.

(2) FDR recordings or data link recordings shall only be used for purposes other than for the investigation of an accident or an incident which is subject to mandatory reporting, if such records are:

(i) used by the operator for airworthiness or maintenance purposes only; or (ii) de-identified; or (iii) disclosed under secure procedures.

3.3 *Operator Certification and Supervision Requirements*

L 296/26   EN   Official Journal of the European Union   25.10.2012

Appendix 1

AIR OPERATOR CERTIFICATE

(Approval schedule for air operators)

Types of operation: Commercial air transport (CAT)   ☐ Passengers;   ☐ Cargo;

☐ Other ([1])..

Commercial specialised operations (SPO)   ☐ ([2])...

5	State of the operator ([3])	([5])
	Issuing authority ([4])	
AOC ([6]):	Operator name ([7])	Operational points of contact: ([9])
	Dba trading name ([8])	Contact details, at which operational management can be contacted without undue delay, are listed in .... ([12]).
	Operator address ([10]):	
	Telephone ([11]): Fax E-mail:	

This certificate certifies that .... ([13]) is authorised to perform commercial air operations, as defined in the attached operations specifications, in accordance with the operations manual, Annex IV to Regulation (EC) No 216/2008 and its Implementing Rules.

Date of issue ([14]):	Name and signature ([15]): Title:

([1]) Other type of transportation to be specified.
([2]) Specify the type of operation, e.g. agriculture, construction, photography, surveying, observation and patrol, aerial advertisement.
([3]) Replaced by the name of the State of the operator.
([4]) Replaced by the identification of the issuing competent authority.
([5]) For use of the competent authority.
([6]) Approval reference, as issued by the competent authority.
([7]) Replaced by the operator's registered name.
([8]) Operator's trading name, if different. Insert 'Dba' (for 'Doing business as') before the trading name.
([9]) The contact details include the telephone and fax numbers, including the country code, and the e-mail address (if available) at which operational management can be contacted without undue delay for issues related to flight operations, airworthiness, flight and cabin crew competency, dangerous goods and other matters as appropriate.
([10]) Operator's principal place of business address.
([11]) Operator's principal place of business telephone and fax details, including the country code. E-mail to be provided if available.
([12]) Insertion of the controlled document, carried on board, in which the contact details are listed, with the appropriate paragraph or page reference. E.g.: 'Contact details ... are listed in the operations manual, gen/basic, chapter 1, 1.1'; or ' ... are listed in the operations specifications, page 1'; or ' ... are listed in an attachment to this document'.
([13]) Operator's registered name.
([14]) Issue date of the AOC (dd-mm-yyyy).
([15]) Title, name and signature of the competent authority representative. In addition, an official stamp may be applied on the AOC.

EASA FORM 138 Issue 1

25.10.2012   EN   Official Journal of the European Union   L 296/27

Appendix II

OPERATIONS SPECIFICATIONS (subject to the approved conditions in the operations manual)				
Issuing Authority Contact Details Telephone (¹): _____ ; Fax: _____ : E-mail: _____				
AOC (²): Operator Name (³): Date (⁴): Signature: Dba trading name Operations specifications:				
Aircraft model (⁵): Registration marks (⁶):				
Commercial operations ☐				
Area of operation (⁷)				
Special limitations (⁸)				
Specific approvals:	Yes	No	Specification (⁹)	Remarks
Dangerous goods	☐	☐		
Low visibility operations Take-off			RVR (¹¹): m CAT (¹⁰) .... RVR: m DH: ft	
Approach and landing	☐	☐		
Take-off	☐	☐		
RVSM (¹²) ☐ N/A	☐	☐		
ETOPS (¹³) ☐ N/A	☐	☐	Maximum diversion time (¹⁴): min.	
Navigation specifications for PBN operations (¹⁵)	☐	☐		(¹⁶)
Minimum navigation performance specification	☐	☐		
Helicopter operations with the aid of night vision imaging systems	☐	☐		
Helicopter hoist operations	☐	☐		
Helicopter emergency medical service operations	☐	☐		
Cabin crew training (¹⁷)	☐	☐		
Issue of CC attestation (¹⁸)	☐	☐		
Continuing airworthiness	☐	☐	(¹⁹)	
Others (²⁰)				

L 296/28   EN   Official Journal of the European Union   25.10.2012

(¹) Telephone and fax contact details of the competent authority, including the country code. E-mail to be provided if available.
(²) Insertion of associated air operator certificate (AOC) number.
(³) Insertion of the operator's registered name and the operator's trading name, if different. Insert 'Dba' before the trading name (for 'Doing business as').
(⁴) Issue date of the operations specifications (dd-mm-yyyy) and signature of the competent authority representative.
(⁵) Insertion of ICAO designation of the aircraft make, model and series, or master series, if a series has been designated (e.g. Boeing-737-3K2 or Boeing-777-232).
(⁶) Either the registration marks are listed in the operations specifications or in the operations manual. In the latter case the related operations specifications must make a reference to the related page in the operation manual. In case not all specific approvals apply to the aircraft model, the registration marks of the aircraft could be entered in the remark column to the related specific approval.
(⁷) Listing of geographical area(s) of authorised operation (by geographical coordinates or specific routes, flight information region or national or regional boundaries).
(⁸) Listing of applicable special limitations (e.g. VFR only, Day only, etc.).
(⁹) List in this column the most permissive criteria for each approval or the approval type (with appropriate criteria).
(¹⁰) Insertion of applicable precision approach category: CAT I, II, IIIA, IIIB or IIIC. Insertion of minimum runway visual range (RVR) in meters and decision height (DH) in feet. One line is used per listed approach category.
(¹¹) Insertion of approved minimum take-off RVR in meters. One line per approval may be used if different approvals are granted.
(¹²) Not applicable (N/A) box may be checked only if the aircraft maximum ceiling is below FL290.
(¹³) Extended range operations (ETOPS) currently applies only to two-engined aircraft. Therefore the Not applicable (N/A) box may be checked if the aircraft model has more or less than two engines.
(¹⁴) The threshold distance may also be listed (in NM), as well as the engine type.
(¹⁵) Performance-based navigation (PBN): one line is used for each PBN approval (e.g. area navigation (RNAV) 10, RNAV 1, required navigation performance (RNP) 4,...), with appropriate limitations or conditions listed in the 'Specifications' and/or 'Remarks'columns.
(¹⁶) Limitations, conditions and regulatory basis for operational approval associated with the PBN approval (e.g. global navigation satellite system (GNSS), distance measuring equipment/DME/inertial reference unit (DME/DME/IRU), ...).
(¹⁷) Approval to conduct the training course and examination to be completed by applicants for a cabin crew attestation as specified in Annex V (Part-CC) to Commission Regulation (EU) No 290/2012.
(¹⁸) Approval to issue cabin crew attestations as specified in Annex V (Part-CC) to Commission Regulation (EU) No 290/2012.
(¹⁹) The name of the person/organisation responsible for ensuring that the continuing airworthiness of the aircraft is maintained and a reference to the regulation that requires the work, i.e. Annex I (Part-M), Subpart G to Commission Regulation (EC) No 2042/2003.
(²⁰) Other approvals or data can be entered here, using one line (or one multi-line block) per authorisation (e.g. short landing operations, steep approach operations, helicopter operations to/from a public interest site, helicopter operations over a hostile environment located outside a congested area, helicopter operations without a safe forced landing capability, operations with increased bank angles, maximum distance from an adequate aerodrome for two-engined aeroplanes without an ETOPS approval, aircraft used for non-commercial operations).

EASA FORM 139 Issue 1

ORO.AOC.100 Application for an air operator certificate

(a) Without prejudice to Regulation (EC) No 1008/2008 of the European Parliament and the Council (1), prior to commencing commercial air operations, the operator shall apply for and obtain an air operator certificate (AOC) issued by the competent authority.

(b) The operator shall provide the following information to the competent authority:

(1) the official name and business name, address, and mailing address of the applicant;

(2) a description of the proposed operation, including the type(s), and number of aircraft to be operated;

(3) a description of the management system, including organisational structure;

(4) the name of the accountable manager;

(5) the names of the nominated persons required by ORO.AOC.135(a) together with their qualifications and experience; and

(6) a copy of the operations manual required by ORO.MLR.100.

(7) a statement that all the documentation sent to the competent authority have been verified by the applicant and found in compliance with the applicable requirements.

(c) Applicants shall demonstrate to the competent authority that:

(1) they comply with all the applicable requirements of Annex IV to Regulation (EC) No 216/2008, this Annex and Annex IV (Part-CAT) and Annex V (Part-SPA) to this Regulation, as applicable;

(2) all aircraft operated have a certificate of airworthiness (CofA) in accordance with Regulation (EC) No 1702/2003; and

(3) its organisation and management are suitable and properly matched to the scale and scope of the operation.

ORO.AOC.105 Operations specifications and privileges of an AOC holder

The privileges of the operator, including those granted in accordance with Annex V (Part-SPA), shall be specified in the operations specifications of the certificate.

ORO.AOC.135 Personnel requirements

(a) In accordance with ORO.GEN.210(b), the operator shall nominate persons responsible for the management and supervision of the following areas:

(1) flight operations;

(2) crew training;

(3) ground operations; and

(4) continuing airworthiness in accordance with Regulation (EC) No 2042/2003.

(b) Adequacy and competency of personnel

(1) The operator shall employ sufficient personnel for the planned ground and flight operations.

(2) All personnel assigned to, or directly involved in, ground and flight operations shall:

(i) be properly trained;

(ii) demonstrate their capabilities in the performance of their assigned duties; and

(iii) be aware of their responsibilities and the relationship of their duties to the operation as a whole.

(c) Supervision of personnel

(1) The operator shall appoint a sufficient number of personnel supervisors, taking into account the structure of the operator's organisation and the number of personnel employed.

(2) The duties and responsibilities of these supervisors shall be defined, and any other necessary arrangements shall be made to ensure that they can discharge their supervisory responsibilities.

(3) The supervision of crew members and personnel involved in the operation shall be exercised by individuals with adequate experience and the skills to ensure the attainment of the standards specified in the operations manual.

ORO.AOC.140 Facility requirements

In accordance with ORO.GEN.215, the operator shall:

(a) make use of appropriate ground handling facilities to ensure the safe handling of its flights;

(b) arrange operational support facilities at the main operating base, appropriate for the area and type of operation; and

(c) ensure that the available working space at each operating base is sufficient for personnel whose actions may affect the safety of flight operations. Consideration shall be given to the needs of ground crew, personnel concerned with operational control, the storage and display of essential records and flight planning by crews.

ORO.AOC.150 Documentation requirements

(a) The operator shall make arrangements for the production of manuals and any other documentation required and associated amendments.

(b) The operator shall be capable of distributing operational instructions and other information without delay.

3.4 Operational Procedures Requirements

ORO.GEN.110 Operator responsibilities

(a) The operator is responsible for the operation of the aircraft in accordance with Annex IV to Regulation (EC) No 216/2008, the relevant requirements of this Annex and its certificate.

(b) Every flight shall be conducted in accordance with the provisions of the operations manual.

(c) The operator shall establish and maintain a system for exercising operational control over any flight operated under the terms of its certificate.

(d) The operator shall ensure that its aircraft are equipped and its crews are qualified as required for the area and type of operation.

(e) The operator shall ensure that all personnel assigned to, or directly involved in, ground and flight operations are properly instructed, have demonstrated their abilities in their particular duties and are aware of their responsibilities and the relationship of such duties to the operation as a whole.

(f) The operator shall establish procedures and instructions for the safe operation of each aircraft type, containing ground staff and crew member duties and responsibilities for all types of operation on the ground and in flight. These procedures shall not require crew members to perform any activities during critical phases of flight other than those required for the safe operation of the aircraft.

(g) The operator shall ensure that all personnel are made aware that they shall comply with the laws, regulations and procedures of those States in which operations are conducted and that are pertinent to the performance of their duties.

(h) The operator shall establish a checklist system for each aircraft type to be used by crew members in all phases of flight under normal, abnormal and emergency conditions to ensure that the operating procedures in the operations manual are followed. The design and utilisation of checklists shall observe human factors principles and take into account the latest relevant documentation from the aircraft manufacturer.

(i) The operator shall specify flight planning procedures to provide for the safe conduct of the flight based on considerations of aircraft performance, other operating limitations and relevant expected conditions on the route to be followed and at the aerodromes or operating sites concerned. These procedures shall be included in the operations manual.

(j) The operator shall establish and maintain dangerous goods training programmes for personnel as required by the technical instructions which shall be subject to review and approval by the competent authority. Training programmes shall be commensurate with the responsibilities of personnel.

ORO.MLR.100 Operations manual — general

(a) The operator shall establish an operations manual (OM) as specified under 8.b of Annex IV to Regulation (EC) No 216/2008.

(b) The content of the OM shall reflect the requirements set out in this Annex, Annex IV (Part-CAT) and Annex V (Part-SPA), as applicable, and shall not contravene the conditions contained in the operations specifications to the air operator certificate (AOC).

(c) The OM may be issued in separate parts.

(d) All operations personnel shall have easy access to the portions of the OM that are relevant to their duties.

(e) The OM shall be kept up to date. All personnel shall be made aware of the changes that are relevant to their duties.

(f) Each crew member shall be provided with a personal copy of the relevant sections of the OM pertaining to their duties. Each holder of an OM, or appropriate parts of it, shall be responsible for keeping their copy up to date with the amendments or revisions supplied by the operator.

(g) For AOC holders:

(1) for amendments required to be notified in accordance with ORO.GEN.115(b) and ORO.GEN.130(c), the operator shall supply the competent authority with intended amendments in advance of the effective date; and

(2) for amendments to procedures associated with prior approval items in accordance with ORO.GEN.130, approval shall be obtained before the amendment becomes effective.

(h) Notwithstanding (g), when immediate amendments or revisions are required in the interest of safety, they may be published and applied immediately, provided that any approval required has been applied for.

(i) The operator shall incorporate all amendments and revisions required by the competent authority.

(j) The operator shall ensure that information taken from approved documents, and any amendment thereof, is correctly reflected in the OM. This does not prevent the operator from publishing more conservative data and procedures in the OM.

(k) The operator shall ensure that all personnel are able to understand the language in which those parts of the OM which pertain to their duties and responsibilities are written. The content of the OM shall be presented in a form that can be used without difficulty and observes human factors principles.

ORO.MLR.101 Operations manual — structure

The main structure of the OM shall be as follows:

(a) Part A: General/Basic, comprising all non-type-related operational policies, instructions and procedures;

(b) Part B: Aircraft operating matters, comprising all type-related instructions and procedures, taking into account differences between types/classes, variants or individual aircraft used by the operator;

(c) Part C: Commercial air transport operations, comprising route/role/area and aerodrome/operating site instructions and information;

(d) Part D: Training, comprising all training instructions for personnel required for a safe operation.

ORO.GEN.210 Personnel requirements

(a) The operator shall appoint an accountable manager, who has the authority for ensuring that all activities can be financed and carried out in accordance with the applicable requirements. The accountable manager shall be responsible for establishing and maintaining an effective management system.

(b) A person or group of persons shall be nominated by the operator, with the responsibility of ensuring that the operator remains in compliance with the applicable requirements. Such person(s) shall be ultimately responsible to the accountable manager.

(c) The operator shall have sufficient qualified personnel for the planned tasks and activities to be performed in accordance with the applicable requirements.

(d) The operator shall maintain appropriate experience, qualification and training records to show compliance with point (c).

(e) The operator shall ensure that all personnel are aware of the rules and procedures relevant to the exercise of their duties.

ORO.AOC.135 Personnel requirements

(a) In accordance with ORO.GEN.210(b), the operator shall nominate persons responsible for the management and supervision of the following areas:

(1) flight operations;

(2) crew training;

(3) ground operations; and

(4) continuing airworthiness in accordance with Regulation (EC) No 2042/2003.

(b) Adequacy and competency of personnel

(1) The operator shall employ sufficient personnel for the planned ground and flight operations.

(2) All personnel assigned to, or directly involved in, ground and flight operations shall:

(i) be properly trained;

(ii) demonstrate their capabilities in the performance of their assigned duties; and

(iii) be aware of their responsibilities and the relationship of their duties to the operation as a whole.

(c) Supervision of personnel

(1) The operator shall appoint a sufficient number of personnel supervisors, taking into account the structure of the operator's organisation and the number of personnel employed.

(2) The duties and responsibilities of these supervisors shall be defined, and any other necessary arrangements shall be made to ensure that they can discharge their supervisory responsibilities.

(3) The supervision of crew members and personnel involved in the operation shall be exercised by individuals with adequate experience and the skills to ensure the attainment of the standards specified in the operations manual.

CAT.OP.MPA.100 Use of air traffic services

(a) The operator shall ensure that:

(1) air traffic services (ATS) appropriate to the airspace and the applicable rules of the air are used for all flights whenever available;

(2) in-flight operational instructions involving a change to the ATS flight plan, when practicable, are coordinated with the appropriate ATS unit before transmission to an aircraft.

(b) Notwithstanding (a), the use of ATS is not required unless mandated by air space requirements for:

(1) operations under VFR by day of other-than-complex motor-powered aeroplanes;

(2) helicopters with an MCTOM of 3175 kg or less operated by day and over routes navigated by reference to visual landmarks; or

(3) local helicopter operations,

provided that search and rescue service arrangements can be maintained.

CAT.OP.MPA.125 Instrument departure and approach procedures

(a) The operator shall ensure that instrument departure and approach procedures established by the State of the aerodrome are used.

(b) Notwithstanding (a), the commander may accept an ATC clearance to deviate from a published departure or arrival route, provided obstacle clearance criteria are observed and full account is taken of the operating conditions. In any case, the final approach shall be flown visually or in accordance with the established instrument approach procedures.

(c) Notwithstanding (a), the operator may use procedures other than those referred to in (a) provided they have been approved by the State in which the aerodrome is located and are specified in the operations manual.

CAT.OP.MPA.155 Carriage of special categories of passengers (SCPs)

(a) Persons requiring special conditions, assistance and/or devices when carried on a flight shall be considered as SCPs including at least:

(1) persons with reduced mobility (PRMs) who, without prejudice to Regulation (EC) No 1107/2006, are understood to be any person whose mobility is reduced due to any physical disability, sensory or locomotory, permanent or temporary, intellectual disability or impairment, any other cause of disability, or age;

(2) infants and unaccompanied children; and

(3) deportees, inadmissible passengers or prisoners in custody.

(b) SCPs shall be carried under conditions that ensure the safety of the aircraft and its occupants according to procedures established by the operator.

(c) SCPs shall not be allocated, nor occupy, seats that permit direct access to emergency exits or where their presence could:

(1) impede crew members in their duties;

(2) obstruct access to emergency equipment; or

(3) impede the emergency evacuation of the aircraft.

(d) The commander shall be notified in advance when SCPs are to be carried on board.

CAT.OP.MPA.160 Stowage of baggage and cargo

The operator shall establish procedures to ensure that:

(a) only hand baggage that can be adequately and securely stowed is taken into the passenger compartment; and

(b) all baggage and cargo on board that might cause injury or damage, or obstruct aisles and exits if displaced, is stowed so as to prevent movement.

CAT.OP.MPA.165 Passenger seating

The operator shall establish procedures to ensure that passengers are seated where, in the event that an emergency evacuation is required, they are able to assist and not hinder evacuation of the aircraft.

CAT.OP.MPA.230 Securing of passenger compartment and galley(s)

(a) The operator shall establish procedures to ensure that before taxiing, take-off and landing all exits and escape paths are unobstructed.

(b) The commander shall ensure that before take-off and landing, and whenever deemed necessary in the interest of safety, all equipment and baggage are properly secured.

3.5   All Weather Operations Requirements – Low Visibility Operations

CAT.OP.MPA.110 Aerodrome operating minima

(a) The operator shall establish aerodrome operating minima for each departure, destination or alternate aerodrome planned to be used. These minima shall not be lower than those established for such aerodromes by the State in which the aerodrome is located, except when specifically approved by that State. Any increment specified by the competent authority shall be added to the minima.

(b) The use of a head-up display (HUD), head-up guidance landing system (HUDLS) or enhanced vision system (EVS) may allow operations with lower visibilities than the established aerodrome operating minima if approved in accordance with SPA.LVO.

(c) When establishing aerodrome operating minima, the operator shall take the following into account:

(1) the type, performance and handling characteristics of the aircraft;

(2) the composition, competence and experience of the flight crew;

(3) the dimensions and characteristics of the runways/final approach and take-off areas (FATOs) that may be selected for use;

(4) the adequacy and performance of the available visual and non-visual ground aids;

(5) the equipment available on the aircraft for the purpose of navigation and/or control of the flight path during the take-off, the approach, the flare, the landing, rollout and the missed approach;

(6) for the determination of obstacle clearance, the obstacles in the approach, missed approach and the climb-out areas necessary for the execution of contingency procedures;

(7) the obstacle clearance altitude/height for the instrument approach procedures;

(8) the means to determine and report meteorological conditions; and

(9) the flight technique to be used during the final approach.

(d) The operator shall specify the method of determining aerodrome operating minima in the operations manual.

(e) The minima for a specific approach and landing procedure shall only be used if all the following conditions are met:

(1) the ground equipment shown on the chart required for the intended procedure is operative;

(2) the aircraft systems required for the type of approach are operative;

(3) the required aircraft performance criteria are met; and

(4) the crew is appropriately qualified.

CAT.OP.MPA.320 Aircraft categories

(a) Aircraft categories shall be based on the indicated airspeed at threshold (V_{AT}) which is equal to the stalling speed (V_{S0}) multiplied by 1.3 or one-g (gravity) stall speed (V_{S1g}) multiplied by 1.23 in the landing configuration at the maximum certified landing mass. If both V_{S0} and VS_{1g} are available, the higher resulting V_{AT} shall be used.

(b) The aircraft categories specified in the table below shall be used.

Aircraft category	V_{AT}
A	< 91 KT
B	91- 120 KT
C	121 – 140 KT
D	141 – 165 KT
E	166 – 210 KT

3.5.1 Terminology

Decision Altitude / Height – DA/H
A specified altitude or height in the Precision Approach to a Runway at which a missed approach must be initiated if the required visual reference to continue the approach has not been established.

Decision altitude is referenced to mean sea level (MSL) and decision height is referenced to the Runway Threshold (THR) elevation.

Note: The required visual reference means that section of the visual aids or of the approach area, which should have been in view for sufficient time for the pilot to have made an assessment of the aircraft position and rate of change of the position, in relation to the desired flight path. In Category III operations with a decision height the required visual reference is that specified for the particular procedure and operation.

Minimum Descent Altitude / Height – MDA/H

Minimum descent altitude (MDA) or minimum descent height (MDH) is a specified altitude or height in a Non-precision Approach or Circling Approach below which the descent must not be made without the required visual reference.

MDA is referenced to MSL. MDH is referenced to the aerodrome (AD) elevation or the THR elevation if that is more than 2 m (or 7 feet) below the aerodrome elevation. An MDH for a circling approach is referenced to the aerodrome elevation.

Note: Similar to the DA/DH, the required visual reference means that section of the visual aids or of the approach area which should have been in view for sufficient time for the pilot to have made an assessment of the aircraft position and the rate of change for position in relation to the desired flight plan. In the case of a circling approach, the required visual reference is the runway environment.

Obstacle Clearing Altitude / Height –OCA/H

Obstacle clearing altitude (OCA) or Obstacle Clearing Height (OCH) is the lowest altitude / height above the elevation of the relevant runway threshold or the aerodrome elevation as applicable, used in establishing compliance with the appropriate obstacle clearance criteria.

 Note: OCA is referenced to MSL and OCH to the THR elevation or in the case of non-precision approaches to the AD elevation or THR elevation if that is more than 2 m, or 7 feet below the AD elevation. An OCH for a circling approach is referenced to the AD elevation and is established by the state.

Circling

The visual phase of an instrument approach to bring an aircraft into position for landing on a runway which is not suitably located for a straight-in approach.

Low Visibility Procedures (LVP)

Procedures applied at an aerodrome for the purpose of ensuring safe operations during Category II and III approaches and Low Visibility Takeoffs.

Low Visibility Takeoff (LVTO)

A takeoff where the Runway Visual Range (RVR) is less than 400 m.

Flight control system

A system which includes an automatic landing system and/or a hybrid landing system.

Fail-Passive flight control system

A flight control system is fail passive if, in the event of a failure, there is no significant out of trim condition or deviation of flight path or attitude but the landing is not completed automatically. For a fail passive automatic flight control system the pilot assumes control of the aeroplane after a failure.

Fail-Operational flight control system

A flight control system is fail-operational if, in the event of a failure below alert height, the approach, flare and landing, can be completed automatically. In the event of a failure, the automatic landing system will operate as a fail-passive system.

Fail-operational hybrid landing system

A system which consists of a primary fail-passive automatic landing system and a secondary independent guidance system enabling the pilot to complete a landing manually after failure of the primary system.

CRANFIELD AVIATION TRAINING SCHOOL LTD. PART-FCL GBR.ATO-0136
CATS INNOVATION CENTRE, LUTON, Bedfordshire LU2 8DL U.K.   www.catsaviation.com
3-21

Operational Procedures

Visual approach

An approach when either part or all of an instrument approach procedure is not completed and the approach is executed with visual reference to the terrain.

AMC1 CAT.OP.MPA.110 Aerodrome operating minima

TAKE-OFF OPERATIONS — AEROPLANES

(a) General

(1) Take-off minima should be expressed as visibility or runway visual range (RVR) limits, taking into account all relevant factors for each aerodrome planned to be used and aircraft characteristics. Where there is a specific need to see and avoid obstacles on departure and/or for a forced landing, additional conditions, e.g. ceiling, should be specified.

(2) The commander should not commence take-off unless the weather conditions at the aerodrome of departure are equal to or better than applicable minima for landing at that aerodrome unless a weather-permissible take-off alternate aerodrome is available.

(3) When the reported meteorological visibility (VIS) is below that required for take-off and RVR is not reported, a take-off should only be commenced if the commander can determine that the visibility along the take-off runway is equal to or better than the required Minimum.

(4) When no reported meteorological visibility or RVR is available, a take-off should only be commenced if the commander can determine that the visibility along the take-off runway is equal to or better than the required minimum.

(b) Visual reference

(1) The take-off minima should be selected to ensure sufficient guidance to control the aircraft in the event of both a rejected take-off in adverse circumstances and a continued take-off after failure of the critical engine.

(2) For night operations, ground lights should be available to illuminate the runway and any Obstacles.

(c) Required RVR/VIS — aeroplanes

(1) For multi-engined aeroplanes, with performance such that in the event of a critical engine failure at any point during take-off the aeroplane can either stop or continue the take-off to a height of 1500' above the aerodrome while clearing obstacles by the required margins, the take-off minima specified by the operator should be expressed as RVR/CMV (converted meteorological visibility) values not lower than those specified in Table 1.A.

(2) For multi-engined aeroplanes without the performance to comply with the conditions in (c)(1) in the event of a critical engine failure, there may be a need to re-land immediately and to see and avoid obstacles in the take-off area. Such aeroplanes may be operated to the following take-off minima provided they are able to comply with the applicable obstacle clearance criteria, assuming engine failure at the height specified. The take-off minima specified by the operator should be based upon the height from which the one-engine inoperative (OEI) net take-off flight path can be constructed. The RVR minima used should not be lower than either of the values specified in Table 1.A or Table 2.A.

(3) When RVR or meteorological visibility is not available, the commander should not commence take-off unless he/she can determine that the actual conditions satisfy the applicable take-off minima.

Table 1.A   Take-off — aeroplanes (without an approval for low visibility take-off (LVTO)) RVR/VIS

Facilities	RVR/VIS (m) *
Day only: Nil**	500
Day: at least runway edge lights or runway centreline markings Night: at least runway edge lights and runway end lights or runway centreline lights and runway end lights	400

*: The reported RVR/VIS value representative of the initial part of the take-off run can be replaced by pilot assessment.
**: The pilot is able to continuously identify the take-off surface and maintain directional control.

Table 2.A   Take-off — aeroplanes

Assumed engine failure height above the runway versus RVR/VIS

Assumed engine failure height above the takeoff runway (ft)	RVR / VIS (m) **
<50	400 (200 with LVTO approval)
51 – 100	400 (300 with LVTO approval)
101 – 150	400
151 – 200	500
201 – 300	1000
>300*	1500

*: 1500 m is also applicable if no positive take-off flight path can be constructed.
**: The reported RVR/VIS value representative of the initial part of the take-off run can be replaced by pilot assessment.

AMC3 CAT.OP.MPA.110 Aerodrome operating minima NPA, APV, CAT I OPERATIONS

(83) 'non-precision approach (NPA) operation' means an instrument approach with a minimum descent height (MDH), or DH when flying a CDFA technique, not lower than 250' and an RVR/CMV of not less than 750 m for aeroplanes and 600 m for helicopters;

(11) 'approach procedure with vertical guidance (APV) operation' means an instrument approach which utilises lateral and vertical guidance, but does not meet the requirements established for precision approach and landing operations, with a decision height (DH) not lower than 250' and a runway visual range (RVR) of not less than 600 m;

(13) 'category I (CAT I) approach operation' means a precision instrument approach and landing using an instrument landing system (ILS), microwave landing system (MLS), GLS (ground-based augmented global navigation satellite system (GNSS/GBAS) landing system), precision approach radar (PAR) or GNSS using a satellite-based augmentation system (SBAS) with a decision height (DH) not lower than 200' and with a runway visual range (RVR) not less than 550 m for aeroplanes and 500 m for helicopters;

AMC3 CAT.OP.MPA.110 Aerodrome operating minima

NPA, APV, CAT I OPERATIONS

(a) The decision height (DH) to be used for a non-precision approach (NPA) flown with the continuous descent final approach (CDFA) technique, approach procedure with vertical guidance (APV) or category (CAT) I operation should not be lower than the highest of:

(1) the minimum height to which the approach aid can be used without the required visual reference;

(2) the obstacle clearance height (OCH) for the category of aircraft;

(3) the published approach procedure DH where applicable;

(4) the system minimum specified in Table 3; or

(5) the minimum DH specified in the aircraft flight manual (AFM) or equivalent document, if stated.

(b) The minimum descent height (MDH) for an NPA operation flown without the CDFA technique should not be lower than the highest of:

(1) the OCH for the category of aircraft;

(2) the system minimum specified in Table 3; or

(3) the minimum MDH specified in the AFM, if stated.

AMC1 CAT.OP.MPA.305(e) Commencement and continuation of approach

VISUAL REFERENCES FOR INSTRUMENT APPROACH OPERATIONS

(a) NPA, APV and CAT I operations

At DH or MDH, at least one of the visual references specified below should be distinctly visible and identifiable to the pilot:

(1) elements of the approach lighting system;
(2) the threshold;
(3) the threshold markings;
(4) the threshold lights;
(5) the threshold identification lights;
(6) the visual glide slope indicator;
(7) the touchdown zone or touchdown zone markings;
(8) the touchdown zone lights;
(9) FATO/runway edge lights; or
(10) other visual references specified in the operations manual.

Facility	Lowest DH/MDH (ft)
GNSS (LNAV)	250
GNSS/Baro-VNAV (LNAV/ VNAV)	250
LOC with or without DME	250
SRA (terminating at ½ NM)	250
SRA (terminating at 1 NM)	300
SRA (terminating at 2 NM or more)	350
VOR	300
VOR/DME	250
NDB	350
NDB/DME	300
VDF	350

Table 3 System minima

AMC4 CAT.OP.MPA.110 Aerodrome operating minima

CRITERIA FOR ESTABLISHING RVR/CMV

(a) Aeroplanes

The following criteria for establishing RVR/CMV should apply:

(1) In order to qualify for the lowest allowable values of RVR/CMV specified in Table 6.A, the instrument approach should meet at least the following facility specifications and associated conditions:

(i) Instrument approaches with designated vertical profile up to and including 4.5° for category A and B aeroplanes, or 3.77° for category C and D aeroplanes where the facilities are:

(A) ILS/microwave landing system (MLS)/GBAS landing system (GLS)/precision approach radar (PAR); or

(B) APV; and

where the final approach track is offset by not more than 15° for category A and B aeroplanes or by not more than 5° for category C and D aeroplanes.

(ii) Instrument approach operations flown using the CDFA technique with a nominal vertical profile, up to and including 4.5° for category A and B aeroplanes, or 3.77° for category C and D aeroplanes, where the facilities are NDB, NDB/DME, VOR, VOR/DME, LOC, LOC/DME, VDF, SRA or GNSS/LNAV, with a final approach segment of at least 3 NM, which also fulfil the following criteria:

(A) the final approach track is offset by not more than 15° for category A and B aeroplanes or by not more than 5° for category C and D aeroplanes;

(B) the final approach fix (FAF) or another appropriate fix where descent is initiated is available, or distance to threshold (THR) is available by flight management system/GNSS (FMS/GNSS) or DME; and

(C) if the missed approach point (MAPt) is determined by timing, the distance from FAF or another appropriate fix to THR is ≤ 8 NM.

(iii) Instrument approaches where the facilities are NDB, NDB/DME, VOR, VOR/DME, LOC, LOC/DME, VDF, SRA or GNSS/LNAV, not fulfilling the criteria in (a)(1)(ii), or with an MDH ≥ 1 200'.

(2) The missed approach operation, after an approach operation has been flown using the CDFA technique, should be executed when reaching the DA/H or the MAPt, whichever occurs first. The lateral part of the missed approach procedure should be flown via the MAPt unless otherwise stated on the approach chart.

AMC5 CAT.OP.MPA.110 Aerodrome operating minima

DETERMINATION OF RVR/CMV/VIS MINIMA FOR NPA, APV, CAT I — AEROPLANES

(a) Aeroplanes

The RVR/CMV/VIS minima for NPA, APV and CAT I operations should be determined as follows:

(1) The minimum RVR/CMV/VIS should be the highest of the values specified in Table 5 or Table 6.A, but not greater than the maximum values specified in Table 6.A, where applicable.

(2) The values in Table 5 should be derived from the formula below,

Required RVR/VIS (m) = [(DH/MDH (ft) x 0.3048) / tanα] — length of approach lights (m) where α is the calculation angle, being a default value of 3.00° increasing in steps of 0.10° for each line in Table 5 up to 3.77° and then remaining constant.

(3) If the approach is flown with a level flight segment at or above MDA/H, 200 m should be added for category A and B aeroplanes and 400 m for category C and D aeroplanes to the minimum RVR/CMV/VIS value resulting from the application of Tables 5 and 6.A.

(4) An RVR of less than 750 m as indicated in Table 5 may be used:

(i) for CAT I operations to runways with full approach lighting system (FALS), runway touchdown zone lights (RTZL) and runway centreline lights (RCLL);

(ii) for CAT I operations to runways without RTZL and RCLL when using an approved head-up guidance landing system (HUDLS), or equivalent approved system, or when conducting a coupled approach or flight-director-flown approach to a DH. The ILS should not be published as a restricted facility; and

(iii) for APV operations to runways with FALS, RTZL and RCLL when using an approved head-up display (HUD).

(5) Lower values than those specified in Table 5, for HUDLS and auto-land operations may be used if approved in accordance with Annex V (Part-SPA), Subpart E (SPA.LVO).

(6) The visual aids should comprise standard runway day markings and approach and runway lights as specified in Table 4. The competent authority may approve that RVR values relevant to a basic approach lighting system (BALS) are used on runways where the approach lights are restricted in length below 210 m due to terrain or water, but where at least one cross-bar is available.

(7) For night operations or for any operation where credit for runway and approach lights is required, the lights should be on and serviceable except as provided for in Table 9.

(8) For single-pilot operations, the minimum RVR/VIS should be calculated in accordance with the following additional criteria:

(i) an RVR of less than 800 m as indicated in Table 5 may be used for CAT I approaches provided any of the following is used at least down to the applicable DH:

(A) a suitable autopilot, coupled to an ILS, MLS or GLS that is not published as restricted; or
(B) an approved HUDLS, including, where appropriate, enhanced vision system (EVS), or equivalent approved system;

(ii) where RTZL and/or RCLL are not available, the minimum RVR/CMV should not be less than 600 m; and

(iii) an RVR of less than 800 m as indicated in Table 5 may be used for APV operations to runways with FALS, RTZL and RCLL when using an approved HUDLS, or equivalent approved system, or when conducting a coupled approach to a DH equal to or greater than 250'.

Class of lighting facility	Length, configuration and intensity of approach lights
FALS (full approach light system)	CAT I Lighting System (HIALS 720 m ≥) distance coded centreline, Barrette centreline
IALS (intermediate approach light system)	Simple approach lighting system (HIALS 420-719 m) single source, Barrette
BALS (basic approach light system)	Any other approach lighting System (HIALS, MIALS or ALS 210-419 m
NALS (no approach light system)	Any other approach lighting system (HIALS, MIALS or ALS < 210 m) or no approach lights

Table 4 Approach light systems

DH or MDH			Class of Lighting Facility			
			FALS	IALS	BALS	NALS
			See (a)(4),(5),(8) above for RVR <750/800 m			
Feet			RVR/CMV (m)			
200	-	210	550	750	1000	1200
211	-	220	550	800	1000	1200
221	-	230	550	800	1000	1200
231	-	240	550	800	1000	1200
241	-	250	550	800	1000	1300
251	-	260	600	800	1100	1300
261	-	280	600	900	1100	1300
281	-	300	650	900	1200	1400
301	-	320	700	1000	1200	1400
321	-	340	800	1100	1300	1500
341	-	360	900	1200	1400	1600
361	-	380	1000	1300	1500	1700
381	-	400	1100	1400	1600	1800
401	-	420	1200	1500	1700	1900
421	-	440	1300	1600	1800	2000
441	-	460	1400	1700	1900	2100
461	-	480	1500	1800	2000	2200
481	-	500	1500	1800	2100	2300
501	-	520	1600	1900	2100	2400
521	-	540	1700	2000	2200	2400
541	-	560	1800	2100	2300	2500
561	-	580	1900	2200	2400	2600
581	-	600	2000	2300	2500	2700
601	-	620	2100	2400	2600	2800
621	-	640	2200	2500	2700	2900
641	-	660	2300	2600	2800	3000
661	-	680	2400	2700	2900	3100
681	-	700	2500	2800	3000	3200
701	-	720	2600	2900	3100	3300
721	-	740	2700	3000	3200	3400
741	-	760	2900	3000	3300	3500
761	-	800	3100	3200	3400	3600
801	-	850	3300	3400	3600	3800
851	-	900	3600	3600	3800	4000
901	-	950	3800	3900	4100	4300
951	-	1000	4100	4100	4300	4500
1001	-	1100	4600	4400	4600	4900
1101	-	1200	5000	4900	5000	5000
1201 and above			5000	5000	5000	5000

Table 5 RVR / CMV (See Table 11) versus DH / MDH

Facility / conditions	RVR / CMV (m)	Aeroplane category			
		A	B	C	D
ILS, MLS, GLS, PAR, GNSS/SBAS, GNSS/VNAV	Min	According to Table 5			
	Max	1500	1500	2400	2400
NDB, NDB/DME, VOR, VOR/DME, LOC, LOC/DME, VDF, SRA, GNSS/LNAV with a procedure that fulfils the criteria in AMC4 CAT.OP.MPA.110, (a)(1)(ii)	Min	750	750	750	750
	Max	1500	1500	2400	2400
For NDB, NDB/DME, VOR, VOR/DME, LOC, LOC/DME, VDF, SRA, GNSS/LNAV: not fulfilling the criteria in in AMC4 CAT.OP.MPA.110, (a)(1)(ii), or with a DH or MDH ≥1200'	Min	1000	1000	1200	1200
	Max	According to Table 5, if flown using the CDFA technique, otherwise an add-on of 200 m for Category A and B aeroplanes and 400 m for Category C and D aeroplanes applies to the values in Table 5 but not to result in a value exceeding 5000 m.			

Table 6.A CAT I, APV, NPA — aeroplanes
Minimum and maximum applicable RVR/CMV (lower and upper cut-off limits)

AMC3 SPA.LVO.100 Low visibility operations

LTS CAT I OPERATIONS

Lower than standard category I (LTS CAT I) operation' means a category I instrument approach and landing operation using category I DH, with an RVR lower than would normally be associated with the applicable DH but not lower than 400 m

(a) For lower than Standard Category I (LTS CAT I) operations the following provisions should apply:

(1) The decision height (DH) of an LTS CAT I operation should not be lower than the highest of:

(i) the minimum DH specified in the AFM, if stated;

(ii) the minimum height to which the precision approach aid can be used without the specified visual reference;

(iii) the applicable obstacle clearance height (OCH) for the category of aeroplane;

(iv) the DH to which the flight crew is qualified to operate; or

(v) 200'.

(2) An instrument landing system / microwave landing system (ILS/MLS) that supports an LTS CAT I operation should be an unrestricted facility with a straight-in course, ≤ 3° offset, and the ILS should be certified to:

(i) class I/T/1 for operations to a minimum of 450 m RVR; or

(ii) class II/D/2 for operations to less than 450 m RVR.

Single ILS facilities are only acceptable if level 2 performance is provided.

(3) The following visual aids should be available:

(i) standard runway day markings, approach lights, runway edge lights, threshold lights and runway end lights;

(ii) for operations with an RVR below 450 m, additionally touch-down zone and/or runway centre line lights.

(4) The lowest RVR / converted meteorological visibility (CMV) minima to be used are specified in Table 2.

Lower than Standard Category I minima						
DH (feet)			Class of lighting facility			
			FALS	IALS	BALS	NALS
			RVR / CMV (m)			
200	-	210	400	500	600	750
211	-	220	450	550	650	800
221	-	230	500	600	700	900
231	-	240	500	650	750	1000
241	-	249	550	700	800	1100

Table 6b Lower than Standard Category I Minimum RVR / CMV versus approach light system

AMC1 CAT.OP.MPA.305(e) Commencement and continuation of approach

VISUAL REFERENCES FOR INSTRUMENT APPROACH OPERATIONS

(b) LTS CAT I operations

At DH, the visual references specified below should be distinctly visible and identifiable to the Pilot:

(1) a segment of at least three consecutive lights, being the centreline of the approach lights, or touchdown zone lights, or runway centreline lights, or runway edge lights, or a combination of them;

(2) this visual reference should include a lateral element of the ground pattern, such as an approach light crossbar or the landing threshold or a barrette of the touchdown zone light unless the operation is conducted utilising an approved HUDLS usable to at least 150'.

SPA.LVO.110 General operating requirements

(a) The operator shall only conduct LTS CAT I operations if:

(1) each aircraft concerned is certified for operations to conduct CAT II operations; and

(2) the approach is flown:

(i) auto-coupled to an auto-land that needs to be approved for CAT IIIA operations; or

(ii) using an approved head-up display landing system (HUDLS) to at least 150' above the threshold.

3.5.1.1 Precision approach — Category II and other than Standard Category II operations

Category II (CAT II) operation' means a precision instrument approach and landing operation using ILS or MLS with: (a) DH below 200' but not lower than 100'; and (b) RVR of not less than 300 m

Other than standard category II (OTS CAT II) operation' means a precision instrument approach and landing operation using ILS or MLS where some or all of the elements of the precision approach category II light system are not available, and with: (a) DH below 200' but not lower than 100'; and (b) RVR of not less than 350 m

AMC1 CAT.OP.MPA.305(e) Commencement and continuation of approach

VISUAL REFERENCES FOR INSTRUMENT APPROACH OPERATIONS

(c) CAT II or OTS CAT II operations

At DH, the visual references specified below should be distinctly visible and identifiable to the pilot:

(1) a segment of at least three consecutive lights being the centreline of the approach lights, or touchdown zone lights, or runway centreline lights, or runway edge lights, or a combination of them;

(2) this visual reference should include a lateral element of the ground pattern, such as an approach light crossbar or the landing threshold or a barrette of the touchdown zone light unless the operation is conducted utilising an approved HUDLS to touchdown.

AMC4 SPA.LVO.100 Low visibility operations

CAT II AND OTS CAT II OPERATIONS

(a) For CAT II and other than Standard Category II (OTS CAT II) operations the following provisions should apply:

(1) The ILS / MLS that supports OTS CAT II operation should be an unrestricted facility with a straight in course (≤ 3° offset) and the ILS should be certified to class II/D/2. Single ILS facilities are only acceptable if level 2 performance is provided.

(2) The DH for CAT II and OTS CAT II operation should not be lower than the highest of:

(i) the minimum DH specified in the AFM, if stated;

(ii) the minimum height to which the precision approach aid can be used without the specified visual reference;

(iii) the applicable OCH for the category of aeroplane;

(iv) the DH to which the flight crew is qualified to operate; or

(v) 100'.

(3) The following visual aids should be available:

(i) standard runway day markings and approach and the following runway lights: runway edge lights, threshold lights and runway end lights;

(ii) for operations in RVR below 450 m, additionally touch-down zone and/or runway centre line lights;

(iii) for operations with an RVR of 400 m or less, additionally centre line lights.

(4) The lowest RVR minima to be used are specified:

(i) for CAT II operations in Table 3; and

(ii) for OTS CAT II operations in Table 4.

(b) For OTS CAT II operations, the terrain ahead of the runway threshold should have been surveyed.

DH(feet)	Category II minima	
	Auto-coupled/Approved HUDLS to below DH*	
	Aeroplane Category A, B and C RVR (m)	Aeroplane Category D RVR (m)
100 – 120	300	300 / 350**
121 – 140	400	400
141 – 199	450	450

*: This means continued use of the automatic flight control system or the HUDLS down to a height of 80 % of the DH.
**: An RVR of 300 m may be used for a category D aircraft conducting an auto-land.

Table 3: CAT II operation minima
RVR vs. DH

DH (feet)	Other than Standard Category II minima				
	Auto-land or approved HUDLS utilised to touchdown				
	Class of lighting facility				
	FALS		IALS	BALS	NALS
	CAT A-C	CAT D	CAT A-D	CAT A-D	CAT A-D
	RVR (m)				
100-120	350	400	450	600	700
121-140	400	450	500	600	700
141-160	400	500	500	600	750
161-199	400	500	550	650	750

Table 4: OTS CAT II operation minima
RVR vs. approach lighting system

AMC5 SPA.LVO.100 Low visibility operations

CAT III OPERATIONS

(15) 'category IIIA (CAT IIIA) operation' means a precision instrument approach and landing operation using ILS or MLS with:

(a) DH lower than 100'; and

(b) RVR not less than 200 m;

(16) 'category IIIB (CAT IIIB) operation' means a precision instrument approach and landing operation using ILS or MLS with:

(a) DH lower than 100', or no DH; and

(b) RVR lower than 200 m but not less than 75 m;

AMC1 CAT.OP.MPA.305(e) Commencement and continuation of approach

VISUAL REFERENCES FOR INSTRUMENT APPROACH OPERATIONS

(d) CAT III operations

(1) For CAT IIIA operations and for CAT IIIB operations conducted either with fail-passive flight control systems or with the use of an approved HUDLS: at DH, a segment of at least three consecutive lights being the centreline of the approach lights, or touchdown zone lights, or runway centreline lights, or runway edge lights, or a combination of these is attained and can be maintained by the pilot.

(2) For CAT IIIB operations conducted either with fail-operational flight control systems or with a fail-operational hybrid landing system using a DH: at DH, at least one centreline light is attained and can be maintained by the pilot.

(3) For CAT IIIB operations with no DH, there is no specification for visual reference with the runway prior to touchdown.

The following provisions should apply to CAT III operations:

(a) Where the DH and RVR do not fall within the same category, the RVR should determine in which category the operation is to be considered.

(b) For operations in which a DH is used, the DH should not be lower than:

(1) the minimum DH specified in the AFM, if stated;

(2) the minimum height to which the precision approach aid can be used without the specified visual reference; or

(3) the DH to which the flight crew is qualified to operate.

(c) Operations with no DH should only be conducted if:

(1) the operation with no DH is specified in the AFM;

(2) the approach aid and the aerodrome facilities can support operations with no DH; and

(3) the flight crew is qualified to operate with no DH.

(d) The lowest RVR minima to be used are specified in Table 5.

Category III minima			
Category	Decision height (ft)*	Roll-out control / Guidance System	RVR (m)
IIIA	Less than 100	Not required	200
IIIB	Less than 100	Fail-passive	150**
IIIB	Less than 50	Fail-passive	125
IIIB	Less than 50 or No decision Height	Fail-operational***	75
*: Flight control system redundancy is determined under CS-AWO by the minimum certificated decision height. **: For aeroplanes certificated in accordance with CS-AWO 321(b)3. or equivalent. ***: The fail-operational system referred to may consist of a fail-operational hybrid system.			

Table 5: CAT III operations minima
RVR vs. DH and rollout control/guidance system

AMC6 SPA.LVO.100 Low visibility operations

OPERATIONS UTILISING EVS

The pilot using a certified enhanced vision system (EVS) in accordance with the procedures and limitations of the AFM:

(a) may reduce the RVR/CMV value in column 1 to the value in column 2 of Table 6 for CAT I operations, APV operations and NPA operations flown with the CDFA technique;

(b) for CAT I operations:

(1) may continue an approach below DH to 100' above the runway threshold elevation provided that a visual reference is displayed and identifiable on the EVS image; and

(2) should only continue an approach below 100' above the runway threshold elevation provided that a visual reference is distinctly visible and identifiable to the pilot without reliance on the EVS;

(c) for APV operations and NPA operations flown with the CDFA technique:

(1) may continue an approach below DH/MDH to 200' above the runway threshold elevation provided that a visual reference is displayed and identifiable on the EVS image; and

(2) should only continue an approach below 200' above the runway threshold elevation provided that a visual reference is distinctly visible and identifiable to the pilot without reliance on the EVS.

RVR / CMV (m) normally required	RVR / CMV (m) for approach utilising EVS	RVR / CMV (m) normally required	RVR / CMV (m) for approach utilising EVS	RVR / CMV (m) normally required	RVR / CMV (m) for approach utilising EVS
550	350	1900	1300	3500	2300
600	400	2000	1300	3600	2400
650	450	2100	1400	3700	2400
700	450	2200	1500	3800	2500
750	500	2300	1500	3900	2600
800	550	2400	1600	4000	2600
900	600	2500	1700	4100	2700
1000	650	2600	1700	4200	2800
1100	750	2700	1800	4300	2800
1200	800	2800	1900	4400	2900
1300	900	2900	1900	4500	3000
1400	900	3000	2000	4600	3000
1500	1000	3100	2000	4700	3100
1600	1100	3200	2100	4800	3200
1700	1100	3300	2200	4900	3200
1800	1200	3400	2200	5000	3300

Table 6: Operations utilising EVS
RVR/CMV reduction vs. normal RVR/CMV

AMC7 CAT.OP.MPA.110 Aerodrome operating minima

CIRCLING OPERATIONS — AEROPLANES

(a) Circling minima

The following standards should apply for establishing circling minima for operations with aeroplanes:

(1) the MDH for circling operation should not be lower than the highest of:

(i) the published circling OCH for the aeroplane category;

(ii) the minimum circling height derived from Table 7; or

(iii) the DH/MDH of the preceding instrument approach procedure;

(2) the MDA for circling should be calculated by adding the published aerodrome elevation to the MDH, as determined by (a)(1); and

(3) the minimum visibility for circling should be the highest of:

(i) the circling visibility for the aeroplane category, if published;

(ii) the minimum visibility derived from Table 7; or

(iii) the RVR/CMV derived from Tables 5 and 6.A for the preceding instrument approach Procedure.

The lowest minima to be used by an operator for circling are:

	Aeroplane Category			
	A	B	C	D
MDH	400'	500'	600'	700'
Minimum meteorological visibility	1500 m	1600 m	2400 m	3600 m

Table 7   Circling — aeroplanes
MDH and minimum visibility vs aeroplane category

(b) Conduct of flight — general:

(1) the MDH and OCH included in the procedure are referenced to aerodrome elevation;

(2) the MDA is referenced to mean sea level;

(3) for these procedures, the applicable visibility is the meteorological visibility; and

(4) operators should provide tabular guidance of the relationship between height above threshold and the in-flight visibility required to obtain and sustain visual contact during the circling manoeuvre.

(c) Instrument approach followed by visual manoeuvring (circling) without prescribed tracks

(1) When the aeroplane is on the initial instrument approach, before visual reference is stabilised, but not below MDA/H, the aeroplane should follow the corresponding instrument approach procedure until the appropriate instrument MAPt is reached.

(2) At the beginning of the level flight phase at or above the MDA/H, the instrument approach track determined by radio navigation aids, RNAV, RNP, ILS, MLS or GLS should be maintained until the pilot:

(i) estimates that, in all probability, visual contact with the runway of intended landing or the runway environment will be maintained during the entire circling procedure;

(ii) estimates that the aeroplane is within the circling area before commencing circling; and

(iii) is able to determine the aeroplane's position in relation to the runway of intended landing with the aid of the appropriate external references.

(3) When reaching the published instrument MAPt and the conditions stipulated in (c)(2) are unable to be established by the pilot, a missed approach should be carried out in accordance with that instrument approach procedure.

(4) After the aeroplane has left the track of the initial instrument approach, the flight phase outbound from the runway should be limited to an appropriate distance, which is required to align the aeroplane onto the final approach. Such manoeuvres should be conducted to enable the aeroplane:

(i) to attain a controlled and stable descent path to the intended landing runway; and

(ii) to remain within the circling area and in such way that visual contact with the runway of intended landing or runway environment is maintained at all times.

(5) Flight manoeuvres should be carried out at an altitude/height that is not less than the circling MDA/H.

(6) Descent below MDA/H should not be initiated until the threshold of the runway to be used has been appropriately identified. The aeroplane should be in a position to continue with a normal rate of descent and land within the touchdown zone.

(d) Instrument approach followed by a visual manoeuvring (circling) with prescribed track

(1) The aeroplane should remain on the initial instrument approach procedure until one of the following is reached:

(i) the prescribed divergence point to commence circling on the prescribed track; or

(ii) the MAPt.

(2) The aeroplane should be established on the instrument approach track determined by the radio navigation aids, RNAV, RNP, ILS, MLS or GLS in level flight at or above the MDA/H at or by the circling manoeuvre divergence point.

(3) If the divergence point is reached before the required visual reference is acquired, a missed approach should be initiated not later than the MAPt and completed in accordance with the instrument approach procedure.

(4) When commencing the prescribed circling manoeuvre at the published divergence point, the subsequent manoeuvres should be conducted to comply with the published routing and published heights/altitudes.

(5) Unless otherwise specified, once the aeroplane is established on the prescribed track(s), the published visual reference does not need to be maintained unless:

(i) required by the State of the aerodrome; or

(ii) the circling MAPt (if published) is reached.

(6) If the prescribed circling manoeuvre has a published MAPt and the required visual reference has not been obtained by that point, a missed approach should be executed in accordance with (e)(2) and (e)(3).

(7) Subsequent further descent below MDA/H should only commence when the required visual reference has been obtained.

(8) Unless otherwise specified in the procedure, final descent should not be commenced from MDA/H until the threshold of the intended landing runway has been identified and the aeroplane is in a position to continue with a normal rate of descent to land within the touchdown zone.

(e) Missed approach

(1) Missed approach during the instrument procedure prior to circling:

(i) if the missed approach procedure is required to be flown when the aeroplane is positioned on the instrument approach track defined by radio-navigation aids RNAV, RNP, or ILS, MLS, and before commencing the circling manoeuvre, the published missed approach for the instrument approach should be followed; or

(ii) if the instrument approach procedure is carried out with the aid of an ILS, MLS or an stabilised approach (SAp), the MAPt associated with an ILS, MLS procedure without glide path (GP-out procedure) or the SAp, where applicable, should be used.

(2) If a prescribed missed approach is published for the circling manoeuvre, this overrides the manoeuvres prescribed below.

(3) If visual reference is lost while circling to land after the aeroplane has departed from the initial instrument approach track, the missed approach specified for that particular instrument approach should be followed. It is expected that the pilot will make an initial climbing turn toward the intended landing runway to a position

overhead the aerodrome where the pilot will establish the aeroplane in a climb on the instrument missed approach segment.

(4) The aeroplane should not leave the visual manoeuvring (circling) area, which is obstacle-protected, unless:

(i) established on the appropriate missed approach procedure; or

(ii) at minimum sector altitude (MSA).

(5) All turns should be made in the same direction and the aeroplane should remain within the circling protected area while climbing either:

(i) to the altitude assigned to any published circling missed approach manoeuvre if applicable;

(ii) to the altitude assigned to the missed approach of the initial instrument approach;

(iii) to the MSA; or

(iv) to the minimum holding altitude (MHA) applicable to transition to a holding facility or fix, or continue to climb to an MSA;

or as directed by ATS.

When the missed approach procedure is commenced on the 'downwind' leg of the circling manoeuvre, an 'S' turn may be undertaken to align the aeroplane on the initial instrument approach missed approach path, provided the aeroplane remains within the protected circling area.

The commander should be responsible for ensuring adequate terrain clearance during the above-stipulated manoeuvres, particularly during the execution of a missed approach initiated by ATS.

(6) Because the circling manoeuvre may be accomplished in more than one direction, different patterns will be required to establish the aeroplane on the prescribed missed approach course depending on its position at the time visual reference is lost. In particular, all turns are to be in the prescribed direction if this is restricted, e.g. to the west/east (left or right hand) to remain within the protected circling area.

(7) If a missed approach procedure is published for a particular runway onto which the aeroplane is conducting a circling approach and the aeroplane has commenced a manoeuvre to align with the runway, the missed approach for this direction may be accomplished. The ATS unit should be informed of the intention to fly the published missed approach procedure for that particular runway.

(8) The commander should advise ATS when any missed approach procedure has been commenced, the height/altitude the aeroplane is climbing to and the position the aeroplane is proceeding towards and/or heading the aeroplane is established on.

AMC8 CAT.OP.MPA.110 Aerodrome operating minima

ONSHORE CIRCLING OPERATIONS — HELICOPTERS

For circling, the specified MDH should not be less than 250', and the meteorological visibility not less than 800 m.

AMC9 CAT.OP.MPA.110 Aerodrome operating minima

VISUAL APPROACH OPERATIONS

The operator should not use an RVR of less than 800 m for a visual approach operation.

AMC10 CAT.OP.MPA.110 Aerodrome operating minima

CONVERSION OF REPORTED METEOROLOGICAL VISIBILITY TO RVR

(a) A conversion from meteorological visibility to RVR/CMV should not be used:

(1) when reported RVR is available;

(2) for calculating take-off minima; and

(3) for any RVR minima less than 800 m.

(b) If the RVR is reported as being above the maximum value assessed by the aerodrome operator, e.g. 'RVR more than 1500 m', it should not be considered as a reported value for (a)(1).

(c) When converting meteorological visibility to RVR in circumstances other than those in (a), the conversion factors specified in Table 8 should be used.

Lighting elements in operation	RVR / CMV = Reported Meteorological Visibility x	
	Day	Night
High intensity approach and runway lighting	1.5	2.0
Any type of lighting installation other than above	1.0	1.5
No lighting	1.0	Not applicable

Table 8   Conversion of reported meteorological visibility to RVR/CMV

ANNEX V Specific Approvals [Part-SPA] SUBPART E: LOW VISIBILITY OPERATIONS (LVO)

SPA.LVO.100 Low visibility operations

The operator shall only conduct the following low visibility operations (LVO) when approved by the competent authority:

(a) low visibility take-off (LVTO) operation;

(b) lower than standard category I (LTS CAT I) operation;

(c) standard category II (CAT II) operation;

(d) other than standard category II (OTS CAT II) operation;

(e) standard category III (CAT III) operation;

(f) approach operation utilising enhanced vision systems (EVS) for which an operational credit is applied to reduce the runway visual range (RVR) minima by no more than one third of the published RVR.

SPA.LVO.105 LVO approval

To obtain an LVO approval from the competent authority, the operator shall demonstrate compliance with the requirements of this Subpart.

SPA.LVO.110 General operating requirements

(a) The operator shall only conduct LTS CAT I operations if:

(1) each aircraft concerned is certified for operations to conduct CAT II operations; and

(2) the approach is flown:

(i) auto-coupled to an auto-land that needs to be approved for CAT IIIA operations; or
(ii) using an approved head-up display landing system (HUDLS) to at least 150' above the threshold.

(b) The operator shall only conduct CAT II, OTS CAT II or CAT III operations if:

(1) each aircraft concerned is certified for operations with a decision height (DH) below 200', or no DH, and equipped in accordance with the applicable airworthiness requirements;
(2) a system for recording approach and/or automatic landing success and failure is established and maintained to monitor the overall safety of the operation;
(3) the DH is determined by means of a radio altimeter;
(4) the flight crew consists of at least two pilots;
(5) all height call-outs below 200' above the aerodrome threshold elevation are determined by a radio altimeter.

(c) The operator shall only conduct approach operations utilising an EVS if:

(1) the EVS is certified for the purpose of this Subpart and combines infra-red sensor image and flight information on the HUD;
(2) for operations with an RVR below 550 m, the flight crew consists of at least two pilots;
(3) for CAT I operations, natural visual reference to runway cues is attained at least at 100' above the aerodrome threshold elevation;

(4) for approach procedure with vertical guidance (APV) and non-precision approach (NPA) operations flown with CDFA technique, natural visual reference to runway cues is attained at least at 200' above the aerodrome threshold elevation and the following requirements are complied with:

(i) the approach is flown using an approved vertical flight path guidance mode;
(ii) the approach segment from final approach fix (FAF) to runway threshold is straight and the difference between the final approach course and the runway centreline is not greater than 2°;
(iii) the final approach path is published and not greater than 3.7°;
(iv) the maximum cross-wind components established during certification of the EVS are not exceeded.

SPA.LVO.115 Aerodrome related requirements

(a) The operator shall not use an aerodrome for LVOs below a visibility of 800 m unless:

(1) the aerodrome has been approved for such operations by the State of the aerodrome; and
(2) low visibility procedures (LVP) have been established.

(b) If the operator selects an aerodrome where the term LVP is not used, the operator shall ensure that there are equivalent procedures that adhere to the requirements of LVP at the aerodrome. This situation shall be clearly noted in the operations manual or procedures manual including guidance to the flight crew on how to determine that the equivalent LVP are in effect.

SPA.LVO.120 Flight crew training and qualifications

The operator shall ensure that, prior to conducting an LVO:

(a) each flight crew member:

(1) complies with the training and checking requirements prescribed in the operations manual, including flight simulation training device (FSTD) training, in operating to the limiting values of RVR/VIS (visibility) and DH specific to the operation and the aircraft type;
(2) is qualified in accordance with the standards prescribed in the operations manual;

(b) the training and checking is conducted in accordance with a detailed syllabus.

SPA.LVO.125 Operating procedures

(a) The operator shall establish procedures and instructions to be used for LVOs. These procedures and instructions shall be included in the operations manual or procedures manual and contain the duties of flight crew members during taxiing, take-off, approach, flare, landing, rollout and missed approach operations, as appropriate.

(b) Prior to commencing an LVO, the pilot-in-command/commander shall be satisfied that:

(1) the status of the visual and non-visual facilities is sufficient;
(2) appropriate LVPs are in force according to information received from air traffic services (ATS);
(3) flight crew members are properly qualified.

SPA.LVO.130 Minimum equipment

(a) The operator shall include the minimum equipment that has to be serviceable at the commencement of an LVO in accordance with the aircraft flight manual (AFM) or other approved document in the operations manual or procedures manual, as applicable.

(b) The pilot-in-command/commander shall be satisfied that the status of the aircraft and of the relevant airborne systems is appropriate for the specific operation to be conducted.

Minimum Visibilities for VFR Operations

An operator shall ensure that VFR flights are conducted in accordance with the Visual Flight Rules and in accordance with the table in below:

Airspace class	B C D E	F G	
		Above 900 m (3000') AMSL or above 300 m (1000') above terrain, whichever is the higher	At and below 900 m (3000') AMSL or 300 m (1000') above terrain, whichever is the higher
Distance from cloud	1500 m horizontally 300m (1000') vertically		Clear of cloud and in sight of the surface
Flight visibility	8 km at and above 3050 m (10000') AMSL (Note 1) 5 km below 3050 m (10000') AMSL		5 km (Note 2)

Note 1: When the height of the transition altitude is lower than 3050 m (10000') AMSL, FL 100 should be used in lieu of 10000'.

Note 2: Cat A and B aeroplanes may be operated in flight visibilities down to 3000 m, provided the appropriate ATS authority permits use of a flight visibility less than 5 km, and the circumstances are such, that the probability of encounters with other traffic is low, and the IAS is 140 KT or less.

(a) Special VFR flights are not commenced when the visibility is less than 3 km and not otherwise conducted when the visibility is less than 1.5 km.

3.6   *Instrument and Equipment Requirements*

CAT.IDE.A.110 Spare electrical fuses

(a) Aeroplanes shall be equipped with spare electrical fuses, of the ratings required for complete circuit protection, for replacement of those fuses that are allowed to be replaced in flight.

(b) The number of spare fuses that are required to be carried shall be the higher of:

(1) 10 % of the number of fuses of each rating; or

(2) three fuses for each rating.

CAT.IDE.A.115 Operating lights

(a) Aeroplanes operated by day shall be equipped with:

(1) an anti-collision light system;

(2) lighting supplied from the aeroplane's electrical system to provide adequate illumination for all instruments and equipment essential to the safe operation of the aeroplane;

(3) lighting supplied from the aeroplane's electrical system to provide illumination in all passenger compartments; and

(4) an independent portable light for each required crew member readily accessible to crew members when seated at their designated stations.

(b) Aeroplanes operated at night shall in addition be equipped with:

(1) navigation/position lights;

(2) two landing lights or a single light having two separately energised filaments; and

(3) lights to conform with the International Regulations for Preventing Collisions at Sea if the aeroplane is operated as a seaplane.

CAT.IDE.A.120 Equipment to clear windshield

Aeroplanes with an MCTOM of more than 5700 kg shall be equipped at each pilot station with a means to maintain a clear portion of the windshield during precipitation.

CAT.IDE.A.155 Airborne collision avoidance system (ACAS)

Unless otherwise provided for by Regulation (EU) No 1332/2011, turbine-powered aeroplanes with an MCTOM of more than 5700 kg or an MOPSC of more than 19 shall be equipped with ACAS II.

CAT.IDE.A.160 Airborne weather detecting equipment

The following shall be equipped with airborne weather detecting equipment when operated at night or in IMC in areas where thunderstorms or other potentially hazardous weather conditions, regarded as detectable with airborne weather detecting equipment, may be expected to exist along the route:

(a) pressurised aeroplanes;
(b) non-pressurised aeroplanes with an MCTOM of more than 5700 kg; and
(c) non-pressurised aeroplanes with an MOPSC of more than nine.

CAT.IDE.A.165 Additional equipment for operations in icing conditions at night

(a) Aeroplanes operated in expected or actual icing conditions at night shall be equipped with a means to illuminate or detect the formation of ice.

(b) The means to illuminate the formation of ice shall not cause glare or reflection that would handicap crew members in the performance of their duties.

CAT.IDE.A.170 Flight crew interphone system

Aeroplanes operated by more than one flight crew member shall be equipped with a flight crew interphone system, including headsets and microphones for use by all flight crew members.

CAT.IDE.A.175 Crew member interphone system

Aeroplanes with an MCTOM of more than 15 000 kg, or with an MOPSC of more than 19 shall be equipped with a crew member interphone system, except for aeroplanes first issued with an individual CofA before 1 April 1965 and already registered in a Member State on 1 April 1995.

CAT.IDE.A.180 Public address system

Aeroplanes with an MOPSC of more than 19 shall be equipped with a public address system.

CAT.IDE.A.185 Cockpit voice recorder

(a) The following aeroplanes shall be equipped with a cockpit voice recorder (CVR):

(1) aeroplanes with an MCTOM of more than 5 700 kg; and

(2) multi-engined turbine-powered aeroplanes with an MCTOM of 5 700 kg or less, with an MOPSC of more than nine and first issued with an individual CofA on or after 1 January 1990.

(b) The CVR shall be capable of retaining the data recorded during at least:

(1) the preceding two hours in the case of aeroplanes referred to in (a)(1) when the individual CofA has been issued on or after 1 April 1998;

(2) the preceding 30 minutes for aeroplanes referred to in (a)(1) when the individual CofA has been issued before 1 April 1998; or

(3) the preceding 30 minutes, in the case of aeroplanes referred to in (a)(2).

(c) The CVR shall record with reference to a timescale:

(1) voice communications transmitted from or received in the flight crew compartment by radio;

(2) flight crew members' voice communications using the interphone system and the public address system, if installed;

(3) the aural environment of the flight crew compartment, including without interruption:
(i) for aeroplanes first issued with an individual CofA on or after 1 April 1998, the audio signals received from each boom and mask microphone in use;

(ii) for aeroplanes referred to in (a)(2) and first issued with an individual CofA before 1 April 1998, the audio signals received from each boom and mask microphone, where practicable;

and

(4) voice or audio signals identifying navigation or approach aids introduced into a headset or speaker.

(d) The CVR shall start to record prior to the aeroplane moving under its own power and shall continue to record until the termination of the flight when the aeroplane is no longer capable of moving under its own power. In addition, in the case of aeroplanes issued with an individual CofA on or after 1 April 1998, the CVR shall start automatically to record prior to the aeroplane moving under its own power and continue to record until the termination of the flight when the aeroplane is no longer capable of moving under its own power.

(e) In addition to (d), depending on the availability of electrical power, the CVR shall start to record as early as possible during the cockpit checks prior to engine start at the beginning of the flight until the cockpit checks immediately following engine shutdown at the end of the flight, in the case of:

(1) aeroplanes referred to in (a)(1) and issued with an individual CofA after 1 April 1998; or

(2) aeroplanes referred to in (a)(2).

(f) The CVR shall have a device to assist in locating it in water.

CAT.IDE.A.190 Flight data recorder

(a) The following aeroplanes shall be equipped with a flight data recorder (FDR) that uses a digital method of recording and storing data and for which a method of readily retrieving that data from the storage medium is available:

(1) aeroplanes with an MCTOM of more than 5 700 kg and first issued with an individual CofA on or after 1 June 1990;

(2) turbine-engined aeroplanes with an MCTOM of more than 5 700 kg and first issued with an individual CofA before 1 June 1990; and

(3) multi-engined turbine-powered aeroplanes with an MCTOM of 5 700 kg or less, with an MOPSC of more than nine and first issued with an individual CofA on or after 1 April 1998.

(b) The FDR shall record:

(1) time, altitude, airspeed, normal acceleration and heading and be capable of retaining the data recorded during at least the preceding 25 hours for aeroplanes referred to in (a)(2) with an MCTOM of less than 27000 kg;

(2) the parameters required to determine accurately the aeroplane flight path, speed, attitude, engine power and configuration of lift and drag devices and be capable of retaining the data recorded during at least the preceding 25 hours, for aeroplanes referred to in (a)(1) with an MCTOM of less than 27 000 kg and first issued with an individual CofA before 1 January 2016;

(3) the parameters required to determine accurately the aeroplane flight path, speed, attitude, engine power, configuration and operation and be capable of retaining the data recorded during at least the preceding 25 hours, for aeroplanes referred to in (a)(1) and (a)(2) with an MCTOM of over 27 000 kg and first issued with an individual CofA before 1 January 2016;

(4) the parameters required to determine accurately the aeroplane flight path, speed, attitude, engine power and configuration of lift and drag devices and be capable of retaining the data recorded during at least the preceding 10 hours, in the case of aeroplanes referred to in (a)(3) and first issued with an individual CofA before 1 January 2016; or

(5) the parameters required to determine accurately the aeroplane flight path, speed, attitude, engine power, configuration and operation and be capable of retaining the data recorded during at least the preceding 25 hours, for aeroplanes referred to in (a)(1) and (a)(3) and first issued with an individual CofA on or after 1 January 2016.

(c) Data shall be obtained from aeroplane sources that enable accurate correlation with information displayed to the flight crew.

(d) The FDR shall start to record the data prior to the aeroplane being capable of moving under its own power and shall stop after the aeroplane is incapable of moving under its own power. In addition, in the case of aeroplanes issued with an individual CofA on or after 1 April 1998, the FDR shall start automatically to record the data prior to the aeroplane being capable of moving under its own power and shall stop automatically after the aeroplane is incapable of moving under its own power.

(e) The FDR shall have a device to assist in locating it in water.

CAT.IDE.A.200 Combination recorder

Compliance with CVR and FDR requirements may be achieved by:

(a) one flight data and cockpit voice combination recorder in the case of aeroplanes required to be equipped with a CVR or an FDR;

(b) one flight data and cockpit voice combination recorder in the case of aeroplanes with an MCTOM of 5 700 kg or less and required to be equipped with a CVR and an FDR; or

(c) two flight data and cockpit voice combination recorders in the case of aeroplanes with an MCTOM of more than 5 700 kg and required to be equipped with a CVR and an FDR.

CAT.IDE.A.205 Seats, seat safety belts, restraint systems and child restraint devices

(a) Aeroplanes shall be equipped with:

(1) a seat or berth for each person on board who is aged 24 months or more;

(2) a seat belt on each passenger seat and restraining belts for each berth except as specified in (3);

(3) a seat belt with upper torso restraint system on each passenger seat and restraining belts on each berth in the case of aeroplanes with an MCTOM of less than 5 700 kg and with an MOPSC of less than nine, after 8 April 2015;

(4) a child restraint device (CRD) for each person on board younger than 24 months;

(5) a seat belt with upper torso restraint system incorporating a device that will automatically restrain the occupant's torso in the event of rapid deceleration:

(i) on each flight crew seat and on any seat alongside a pilot's seat;

(ii) on each observer seat located in the flight crew compartment;

(6) a seat belt with upper torso restraint system on each seat for the minimum required cabin crew.

(b) A seat belt with upper torso restraint system shall:

(1) have a single point release;

(2) on flight crew seats, on any seat alongside a pilot's seat and on the seats for the minimum required cabin crew, include two shoulder straps and a seat belt that may be used independently.

CAT.IDE.A.215 Internal doors and curtains

Aeroplanes shall be equipped with:

(a) in the case of aeroplanes with an MOPSC of more than 19, a door between the passenger compartment and the flight crew compartment, with a placard indicating 'crew only' and a locking means to prevent passengers from opening it without the permission of a member of the flight crew;

(b) a readily accessible means for opening each door that separates a passenger compartment from another compartment that has emergency exits;

(c) a means for securing in the open position any doorway or curtain separating the passenger compartment from other areas that need to be accessed to reach any required emergency exit from any passenger seat;

d) a placard on each internal door or adjacent to a curtain that is the means of access to a passenger emergency exit, to indicate that it must be secured open during take-off and landing; and

(e) a means for any member of the crew to unlock any door that is normally accessible to passengers and that can be locked by passengers.

CAT.IDE.A.220 First-aid kit

(a) Aeroplanes shall be equipped with first-aid kits, in accordance with Table 1.

(b) First-aid kits shall be:

(1) readily accessible for use; and
(2) kept up to date.

Number of passenger seats installed	Number of first-aid kits required
0-100	1
101-200	2
201-300	3
301-400	4
401-500	5
501 or more	6

Table 1   Number of first-aid kits required

3.7 *Communication and Navigation Equipment Requirements*

CAT.IDE.A.335 Audio selector panel

Aeroplanes operated under IFR shall be equipped with an audio selector panel operable from each required flight crew member station.

CAT.IDE.A.340 Radio equipment for operations under VFR over routes navigated by reference to visual landmarks

Aeroplanes operated under VFR over routes navigated by reference to visual landmarks shall be equipped with radio communication equipment necessary under normal radio propagation conditions to fulfil the following:

(a) communicate with appropriate ground stations;
(b) communicate with appropriate ATC stations from any point in controlled airspace within which flights are intended; and

(c) receive meteorological information.

CAT.IDE.A.345 Communication and navigation equipment for operations under IFR or under VFR over routes not navigated by reference to visual landmarks

(a) Aeroplanes operated under IFR or under VFR over routes that cannot be navigated by reference to visual landmarks shall be equipped with radio communication and navigation equipment in accordance with the applicable airspace requirements.

(b) Radio communication equipment shall include at least two independent radio communication systems necessary under normal operating conditions to communicate with an appropriate ground station from any point on the route, including diversions.

(c) Notwithstanding (b), aeroplanes operated for short haul operations in the North Atlantic minimum navigation performance specifications (NAT MNPS) airspace and not crossing the North Atlantic shall be equipped with at least one long range communication system, in case alternative communication procedures are published for the airspace concerned.

(d) Aeroplanes shall have sufficient navigation equipment to ensure that, in the event of the failure of one item of equipment at any stage of the flight, the remaining equipment shall allow safe navigation in accordance with the flight plan.

(e) Aeroplanes operated on flights in which it is intended to land in IMC shall be equipped with suitable equipment capable of providing guidance to a point from which a visual landing can be performed for each aerodrome at which it is intended to land in IMC and for any designated alternate aerodrome.

3.8 Flight and duty-time limitations and rest requirements

Subpart FTL establishes the requirements to be met by an operator and its crew members with regard to flight and duty time limitations and rest requirements for crew members.

3.8.1 Fatigue and acclimatisation to time zones

ICAO defines fatigue as 'A physiological state of reduced mental or physical performance capability resulting from sleep loss, extended wakefulness, circadian phase, and/or workload (mental and/or physical activity) that can impair a person's alertness and ability to perform safety related operational duties.'

The body's biological clock entrains to, i.e. gradually synchronises with, the natural light-dark cycle. A crew member is 'acclimatised' when their biological clock is synchronised to the time zone where the crew member is. Disruption of the body clock in those exposed to light at unusual and continually changing times is called circadian dysrhythmia. It is often called jet lag when it is caused by travel across time zones.

A crew member is considered to be acclimatised to a 2-hour wide time zone surrounding the local time at the point of departure ('reference time' in Table 1). When the local time at the place where a duty commences differs by more than 2 hours from the local time at the place where the next duty starts, the crew member, for the calculation of the maximum daily flight duty period (FDP), is considered to be acclimatised in accordance with the values in the Table 1.

Table 1

Time difference (h) between reference time and local time where the crew member starts the next duty	Time elapsed since reporting at reference time				
	<48	48–71:59	72–95:59	96–119:59	≥120
< 4	B	D	D	D	D
≤6	B	X	D	D	D
≤9	B	X	X	D	D
≤12	B	X	X	X	D

'B' means acclimatised to the local time of the departure time zone,

'D' means acclimatised to the local time where the crew member starts his/her next duty, and

'X' means that a crew member is in an unknown state of acclimatisation.

Thus from Table 1, for example, as a crew member departing from London and arriving in New York (-5 hours difference between reference time (London) and local time (New York)) you are acclimatised to the local time of the departure time zone (London). When you next report for duty to depart you must calculate if you are acclimatised to New York. Enter Table 1 with a difference in time of 5 hours. Then follow the table to the right. If the time elapsed since reporting in London is:

a) Less than 48 hours then you are still acclimatised to London (B)

b) 48-71:59 then you are in an unknown state of acclimatisation (X)

c) 72 hours or more then you are acclimatised to New York and the local time there is now your reference time (D)

A 'disruptive schedule' means a crew member's roster which disrupts the sleep opportunity during the optimal sleep time window by comprising an FDP or a combination of FDPs which encroach, start or finish during any portion of the day or of the night where a crew member is acclimatised. A schedule may be disruptive due to early starts, late finishes or night duties.

The so-called window of circadian low (WOCL) referred to in Subpart FTL means the period between 02:00 and 05:59 hours in the time zone to which a crew member is acclimatised, i.e. the time of the daily low point in core body temperature.

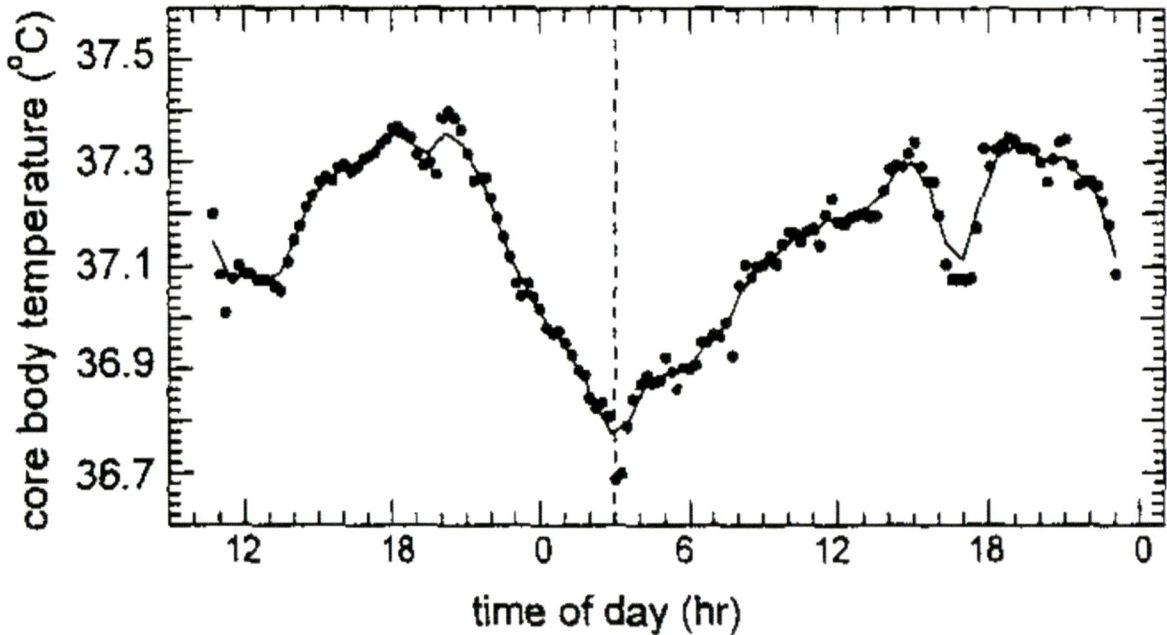

Circadian variation in core body temperature in five subjects measured by rectal probe. From Kryger MH, Roth T and Dement WC. Principles and practice of sleep medicine 3rd edition. WB Saunders Company: Philadelphia 2000.

3.8.2 ORO.FTL.205 Flight duty period (FDP)

ORO.FTL.205 states at (b) that:

(1) The maximum daily FDP without the use of extensions for acclimatised crew members shall be in accordance with the following table:

Table 2

Maximum daily FDP — Acclimatised crew members

Start of FDP at reference time	1–2 Sectors	3 Sectors	4 Sectors	5 Sectors	6 Sectors	7 Sectors	8 Sectors	9 Sectors	10 Sectors
0600–1329	13:00	12:30	12:00	11:30	11:00	10:30	10:00	09:30	09:00
1330–1359	12:45	12:15	11:45	11:15	10:45	10:15	09:45	09:15	09:00
1400–1429	12:30	12:00	11:30	11:00	10:30	10:00	09:30	09:00	09:00
1430–1459	12:15	11:45	11:15	10:45	10:15	09:45	09:15	09:00	09:00
1500–1529	12:00	11:30	11:00	10:30	10:00	09:30	09:00	09:00	09:00
1530–1559	11:45	11:15	10:45	10:15	09:45	09:15	09:00	09:00	09:00
1600–1629	11:30	11:00	10:30	10:00	09:30	09:00	09:00	09:00	09:00
1630–1659	11:15	10:45	10:15	09:45	09:15	09:00	09:00	09:00	09:00
1700–0459	11:00	10:30	10:00	09:30	09:00	09:00	09:00	09:00	09:00
0500–0514	12:00	11:30	11:00	10:30	10:00	09:30	09:00	09:00	09:00
0515–0529	12:15	11:45	11:15	10:45	10:15	09:45	09:15	09:00	09:00
0530–0544	12:30	12:00	11:30	11:00	10:30	10:00	09:30	09:00	09:00
0545–0559	12:45	12:15	11:45	11:15	10:45	10:15	09:45	09:15	09:00

(2) The maximum daily FDP when crew members are in an unknown state of acclimatisation shall be in accordance with the following table:

Table 3

Crew members in an unknown state of acclimatisation

Maximum daily FDP according to sectors						
1-2	3	4	5	6	7	8
11:00	10:30	10:00	09:30	09:00	09:00	09:00

(3) The maximum daily FDP when crew members are in an unknown state of acclimatisation and the operator has implemented a FRM, shall be in accordance with the following table:

Table 4

Crew members in an unknown state of acclimatisation under FRM

The values in the following table may apply provided the operator's FRM continuously monitors that the required safety performance is maintained.

Maximum daily FDP according to sectors						
1-2	3	4	5	6	7	8
12:00	11:30	11:00	10:30	10:00	09:30	09:00

ORO.FTL.205 states at (d) and (e) the maximum daily FDP for acclimatised crew members with the use of extensions with and without in-flight rest:

(d) Maximum daily FDP for acclimatised crew members with the use of extensions without in-flight rest.

(1) The maximum daily FDP may be extended by up to 1 hour not more than twice in any 7 consecutive days. In that case:

(i) the minimum pre-flight and post-flight rest periods shall be increased by 2 hours; or

(ii) the post-flight rest period shall be increased by 4 hours.

(2) When extensions are used for consecutive FDPs, the additional pre- and post-flight rest between the two extended FDPs required under subparagraph 1 shall be provided consecutively.

(3) The use of the extension shall be planned in advance, and shall be limited to a maximum of:

(i) 5 sectors when the WOCL is not encroached; or

(ii) 4 sectors, when the WOCL is encroached by 2 hours or less; or

(iii) 2 sectors, when the WOCL is encroached by more than 2 hours.

(4) Extension of the maximum basic daily FDP without in-flight rest shall not be combined with extensions due to in-flight rest or split duty in the same duty period.

(5) Flight time specification schemes shall specify the limits for extensions of the maximum basic daily FDP in accordance with the certification specifications applicable to the type of operation, taking into account:

(i) the number of sectors flown; and

(ii) WOCL encroachment.

(e) Maximum daily FDP with the use of extensions due to in-flight rest

Flight time specification schemes shall specify the conditions for extensions of the maximum basic daily FDP with in-flight rest in accordance with the certification specifications applicable to the type of operation, taking into account:

(i) the number of sectors flown;

(ii) the minimum in-flight rest allocated to each crew member;

(iii) the type of in-flight rest facilities; and

(iv) the augmentation of the basic flight crew.

The commander may increase the maximum daily FDP due to unforeseen circumstances in flight operations at their discretion. AMC1 ORO.FTL.205(f) states that the exercise of commander's discretion should be considered exceptional and should be avoided at home base and/or company hubs where standby or reserve crew members should be available. An 'augmented flight crew' means a flight crew which comprises more than the minimum number required to operate the aircraft, allowing each flight crew member to leave the assigned post, for the purpose of in-flight rest, and to be replaced by another appropriately qualified flight crew member.

ORO.FTL.205 states at (f) that:

(1) The conditions to modify the limits on flight duty, duty and rest periods by the commander in the case of unforeseen circumstances in flight operations, which start at or after the reporting time, shall comply with the following:

(i) the maximum daily FDP which results after applying points (b) and (e) of point ORO.FTL.205 or point ORO.FTL.220 may not be increased by more than 2 hours unless the flight crew has been augmented, in which case the maximum flight duty period may be increased by not more than 3 hours;

(ii) if on the final sector within an FDP the allowed increase is exceeded because of unforeseen circumstances after take-off, the flight may continue to the planned destination or alternate aerodrome; and

(iii) the rest period following the FDP may be reduced but can never be less than 10 hours.

(2) In case of unforeseen circumstances which could lead to severe fatigue, the commander shall reduce the actual flight duty period and/or increase the rest period in order to eliminate any detrimental effect on flight safety.

(3) The commander shall consult all crew members on their alertness levels before deciding the modifications under subparagraphs 1 and 2.

(4) The commander shall submit a report to the operator when an FDP is increased or a rest period is reduced at his or her discretion.

(5) Where the increase of an FDP or reduction of a rest period exceeds 1 hour, a copy of the report, to which the operator shall add its comments, shall be sent by the operator to the competent authority not later than 28 days after the event.

(6) The operator shall implement a non-punitive process for the use of the discretion described under this provision and shall describe it in the operations manual.

3.8.3 ORO.FTL.210 Flight times and duty periods

ORO.FTL.210 states at (a), (b) and (c) that:

(a) The total duty periods to which a crew member may be assigned shall not exceed:

(1) 60 duty hours in any 7 consecutive days;

(2) 110 duty hours in any 14 consecutive days; and

(3) 190 duty hours in any 28 consecutive days, spread as evenly as practicable throughout that period.

(b) The total flight time of the sectors on which an individual crew member is assigned as an operating crew member shall not exceed:

(1) 100 hours of flight time in any 28 consecutive days;

(2) 900 hours of flight time in any calendar year; and

(3) 1 000 hours of flight time in any 12 consecutive calendar months.

(c) Post-flight duty shall count as duty period. The operator shall specify in its operations manual the minimum time period for post-flight duties.

3.8.4 ORO.FTL.225 Standby and duties at the airport

If an operator assigns crew members to standby or to any duty at the airport, the following shall apply in accordance with the certification specifications applicable to the type of operation:

(a) standby and any duty at the airport shall be in the roster and the start and end time of standby shall be defined and notified in advance to the crew members concerned to provide them with the opportunity to plan adequate rest;

(b) a crew member is considered on airport standby from reporting at the reporting point until the end of the notified airport standby period;

(c) airport standby shall count in full as duty period for the purpose of points ORO.FTL.210 and ORO.FTL.235;

(d) any duty at the airport shall count in full as duty period and the FDP shall count in full from the airport duty reporting time;

(e) the operator shall provide accommodation to the crew member on airport standby;

(f) flight time specification schemes shall specify the following elements:

(1) the maximum duration of any standby;

(2) the impact of the time spent on standby on the maximum FDP that may be assigned, taking into account facilities provided to the crew member to rest, and other relevant factors such as:

– the need for immediate readiness of the crew member,

– the interference of standby with sleep, and

– sufficient notification to protect a sleep opportunity between the call for duty and the assigned FDP;

(3) the minimum rest period following standby which does not lead to assignment of an FDP;

(4) how time spent on standby other than airport standby shall be counted for the purpose of cumulative duty periods.

3.8.5 ORO.FTL.235 Rest periods

ORO.FTL.235 states the minimum rest periods at home base and away from home base, by how much the minimum rest periods may be reduced, and the need for recurrent extended recovery rest periods and additional rest periods:

(a) Minimum rest period at home base.

(1) The minimum rest period provided before undertaking an FDP starting at home base shall be at least as long as the preceding duty period, or 12 hours, whichever is greater.

(2) By way of derogation from point (1), the minimum rest provided under point (b) applies if the operator provides suitable accommodation to the crew member at home base.

(b) Minimum rest period away from home base.

The minimum rest period provided before undertaking an FDP starting away from home base shall be at least as long as the preceding duty period, or 10 hours, whichever is greater. This period shall include an 8-hour sleep opportunity in addition to the time for travelling and physiological needs.

(c) Reduced rest

By derogation from points (a) and (b), flight time specification schemes may reduce the minimum rest periods in accordance with the certification specifications applicable to the type of operation and taking into account the following elements:

(1) the minimum reduced rest period;

(2) the increase of the subsequent rest period; and

(3) the reduction of the FDP following the reduced rest.

(d) Recurrent extended recovery rest periods

Flight time specification schemes shall specify recurrent extended recovery rest periods to compensate for cumulative fatigue. The minimum recurrent extended recovery rest period shall be 36 hours, including 2 local nights, and in any case the time between the end of one recurrent extended recovery rest period and the start of the next extended recovery rest period shall not be more than 168 hours. The recurrent extended recovery rest period shall be increased to 2 local days twice every month.

(e) Flight time specification schemes shall specify additional rest periods in accordance with the applicable certification specifications to compensate for:

(1) the effects of time zone differences and extensions of the FDP;

(2) additional cumulative fatigue due to disruptive schedules; and

(3) a change of home base.

3.8.6 ORO.FTL.245 Records of home base, flight times, duty and rest periods

ORO.FTL.245 states at (a) that:

(a) An operator shall maintain, for a period of 24 months:

(1) individual records for each crew member including:

(i) flight times;

(ii) start, duration and end of each duty period and FDP;

(iii) rest periods and days free of all duties; and

(iv) assigned home base;

(2) reports on extended flight duty periods and reduced rest periods.

Self Assessment Test 02

1. Who is responsible for the correct loading of the aircraft and for the load and trim sheet:
A) The operator
B) The loadmaster
C) The flight dispatcher
D) The captain

2. What is the period of validity for a C of A:
A) indefinite
B) 6 months
C) 24 months
D) 13 months

3. Who is responsible for the approval of the minimum equipment list:
A) State of aircraft manufacture
B) Aircraft manufacture
C) State of the operator
D) The operator

4. A flight data recorder must be carried on all commercial aircraft whose certified takeoff weight is greater than:
A) 20000 kg
B) 5700 kg
C) 10000 kg
D) 7500 kg

5. Flight Data Recorders (FDA's) shall be capable of retaining information from the last .... of their operations except for type II & FDR's that retain information from the last ....of their operation:
A) 12 h   1 h
B) 24 h   30 min
C) 25 h   30 min
D) 25 h   1 h

6. For aircraft certified from 1st January 1999 a ground proximity warning system (GPWS) shall be fitted, if the certified takeoff mass is in excess of:
A) 2500 kg
B) 10000 kg
C) 19000 kg
D) 5700 kg

7. According to chapter 11 of Annex 6 the completed journey log book should be retained for a period of:
A) 6 months
B) 9 months
C) 12 months
D) 1 month

8. (VFR Operating minima) states that the operator shall ensure for VFR flights that:
A) For VFR flights in class E airspace flight visibility at and above 3050 m (1000' is 5 km)
B) For VFR flights in class F airspace vertical distance from cloud is 250 m
C) For VFR flights in class B airspace at and above 3050 m (10000') the flight visibility is 8 km
D) For VFR flights in class D airspace the aircraft maintains clear of cloud

9. An aircraft commander cannot initiate an IFR flight unless the available information regarding the destination aerodrome or destination alternate are at the time of:
A) Takeoff are equal or better than the minimum conditions for aerodrome use
B) Arrival and for a reasonable period beforehand are better than the minimum conditions requested for aerodrome use
C) Arrival and for a predicted time thereafter equal to the minimum conditions required for aerodrome use
D) Arrival and equal or better than the minimum conditions for aerodrome use

10. The operator or commander of an aeroplane shall submit a flight occurrence report of any incident that has or may have endangered the safe operation of a flight within:
A) 24 h
B) 48 h
C) 36 h
D) 72 h

11. A category 1 precision approach may be carried out with a Runway Visual Range (RVR) of at least:
A) 350 m
B) 550 m
C) 650 m
D) 900 m

12. A category 1 precision approach is an approach with:
A) No decision height
B) A minimum decision height of 100'
C) A minimum decision height of 200'
D) A minimum decision height of 300'

13. A category C aircraft can carry out a circling approach only if the horizontal visibility is equal or greater than:
A) 1500 m
B) 2400 m
C) 1600 m
D) 3600 m

14. A category 2 precision approach is an approach with:
A) A minimum decision height of 100'
B) A minimum decision height of less than 100' but greater than 50'
C) A minimum decision height of 50'
D) No decision height

15. A category 2 precision approach may be carried out with a Runway Visual Range (RVR) of at least:
A) 500 m
B) 450 m
C) 400 m
D) 300 m

16. Aircraft categories according to their threshold speed (Vat) are calculated for approach procedure purposes. This speed is the stalling speed in the landing configuration multiplied by a factor of:
A) 1.23
B) 1.3
C) 1.45
D) 1.5

17. Which of the following documents must be carried on board the aircraft:
    1. Certificate of Registration
    2. Certificate of Airworthiness
    3. Noise certificate (if applicable)
    4. Air operators certificate
    5. Aircraft radio licence
    6. 3rd party liability insurance certificate
A) 1,2,4
B) 2,4,6
C) 1,2,3,5
D) 1,2,3,4,5,6

18. Aircraft in category C have threshold speed of:
A) 91 – 120 KT
B) 121 – 140 KT
C) 141 – 165 KT
D) Less than 91 KT

19. Which of the following documents are to be retained on the ground by the operator:
    1. Operational flight plan
    2. Aircraft technical log
    3. NOTAM's
    4. Mass & Balance "load & trim" sheets
    5. Special loads notification
A) 1,2
B) 1,3,5
C) 1,2,3,4,5
D) 1,2,4,5

20. A low visibility takeoff (LVTO) is defined as a takeoff where the RVR is less than:
A) 1500 m
B) 1000 m
C) 500 m
D) 400 m

Self Assessment Test 02 Answers

1	D
2	A
3	C
4	B
5	C
6	D
7	A
8	C
9	A
10	D
11	B
12	C
13	B
14	A
15	D
16	B
17	D
18	B
19	C
20	D

CHAPTER 4

Navigation Requirements for Long Range Flights

4.1 Introduction

The planning and operating of a long-range flight requires some additional and different procedures from a short medium-range flight. The main differences are:

- The comparative scarcity or non-existence of ground based navigational aids and radar surveillance
- The limitations of the on board navigation system
- The limitations of the ATC system and associated communications

The lack of these is more than made up by the availability of inertial guidance systems or more recently, global navigation satellite systems (GNSS).

4.2 Flight Management

4.2.1 Routes and areas of operation

CAT.OP.MPA.135 Routes and areas of operation — general

(a) The operator shall ensure that operations are only conducted along routes, or within areas, for which:

(1) ground facilities and services, including meteorological services, adequate for the planned operation are provided;

(2) the performance of the aircraft is adequate to comply with minimum flight altitude requirements;

(3) the equipment of the aircraft meets the minimum requirements for the planned operation; and

(4) appropriate maps and charts are available.

(b) The operator shall ensure that operations are conducted in accordance with any restriction on the routes or the areas of operation specified by the competent authority.

(c) (a)(1) shall not apply to operations under VFR by day of other-than-complex motor-powered aircraft on flights that depart from and arrive at the same aerodrome or operating site.

CAT.OP.MPA.136 Routes and areas of operation — single-engined aeroplanes

The operator shall ensure that operations of single-engined aeroplanes are only conducted along routes, or within areas, where surfaces are available that permit a safe forced landing to be executed.

CAT.OP.MPA.137 Routes and areas of operation — helicopters

The operator shall ensure that:
(a) for helicopters operated in performance class 3, surfaces are available that permit a safe forced landing to be executed, except when the helicopter has an approval to operate in accordance with CAT.POL.H.420;

(b) for helicopters operated in performance class 3 and conducting 'coastal transit' operations, the operations manual contains procedures to ensure that the width of the coastal corridor, and the equipment carried, is consistent with the conditions prevailing at the time.

4.2.2   *Factors to be considered by the Commander*

CAT.OP.MPA.175 Flight preparation

(a) An operational flight plan shall be completed for each intended flight based on considerations of aircraft performance, other operating limitations and relevant expected conditions on the route to be followed and at the aerodromes/ operating sites concerned.

(b) The flight shall not be commenced unless the commander is satisfied that:

(1) all items stipulated in 2.a.3 of Annex IV to Regulation (EC) No 216/2008 concerning the airworthiness and registration of the aircraft, instrument and equipment, mass and centre of gravity (CG) location, baggage and cargo and aircraft operating limitations can be complied with;

(2) the aircraft is not operated contrary to the provisions of the configuration deviation list (CDL);

(3) the parts of the operations manual that are required for the conduct of the flight are available;

(4) the documents, additional information and forms required to be available by CAT.GEN.MPA.180 are on board;

(5) current maps, charts and associated documentation or equivalent data are available to cover the intended operation of the aircraft including any diversion that may reasonably be expected;

(6) ground facilities and services required for the planned flight are available and adequate;

(7) the provisions specified in the operations manual in respect of fuel, oil, oxygen, minimum safe altitudes, aerodrome operating minima and availability of alternate aerodromes, where required, can be complied with for the planned flight; and

(8) any additional operational limitation can be complied with.

(c) Notwithstanding (a), an operational flight plan is not required for operations under VFR of:

(1) other-than-complex motor-powered aeroplane taking off and landing at the same aerodrome or operating site; or
(2) helicopters with an MCTOM of 3175 kg or less, by day and over routes navigated by reference to visual landmarks in a local area as specified in the operations manual.

4.2.3 Completion of Flight Plans

The requirements for the completion of operational flight plans are identical to the ICAO requirements. A flight must not be commenced unless an ATS flight plan has been submitted, or adequate information has been given which will allow the alerting services to be activated if required. The ATS flight plan should normally be filed at least 60 min before departure.

CAT.OP.MPA.190 Submission of the ATS flight plan

(a) If an ATS flight plan is not submitted because it is not required by the rules of the air, adequate information shall be deposited in order to permit alerting services to be activated if required.

(b) When operating from a site where it is impossible to submit an ATS flight plan, the ATS flight plan shall be transmitted as soon as possible after take-off by the commander or the operator.

4.3 *Choice of Route, Speed and Altitude*

4.3.1 *Selection of a Route*

Routes must be selected with due care towards the following:

- ATC requirements – Routes selected must be in accordance with any ATC restrictions or route structures that apply. This data can be found detailed in the Regional Navigation Procedures document.
- Availability of airfields – there must be adequate aerodromes available
- Aircraft limitations – the performance capabilities of the aeroplane will affect the route choice, limiting the choice for aeroplanes with lesser performance capabilities.

An operator shall only authorise use of aerodromes that are adequate for the type(s) of aeroplane and operation(s) concerned. An adequate aerodrome is an aerodrome, which the operator considers to be satisfactory, taking account of the applicable performance requirements and runway characteristics. In addition, it should be anticipated that, at the expected time of use, the aerodrome will be available and equipped with necessary ancillary services, such as ATS, sufficient lighting, communications, weather reporting, navigation aids and emergency services.

For an ETOPS en-route alternate aerodrome, the following additional points should be considered:

- The availability of an ATC facility; and
- The availability of at least one letdown aid (ground radar would so qualify) for an instrument approach.

4.3.2 *Twin-engine Operations*

CAT.OP.MPA.140 Maximum distance from an adequate aerodrome for two-engined aeroplanes without an ETOPS approval

(a) Unless approved by the competent authority in accordance with Annex V (Part-SPA), Subpart F, the operator shall not operate a two-engined aeroplane over a route that contains a point further from an adequate aerodrome, under standard conditions in still air, than:

(1) for performance class A aeroplanes with either:

(i) a maximum operational passenger seating configuration (MOPSC) of 20 or more; or

(ii) a maximum take-off mass of 45360 kg or more,

the distance flown in 60 minutes at the one-engine-inoperative (OEI) cruising speed determined in accordance with (b);

(2) for performance class A aeroplanes with:

(i) an MOPSC of 19 or less; and

(ii) a maximum take-off mass less than 45 360 kg,

the distance flown in 120 minutes or, subject to approval by the competent authority, up to 180 minutes for turbo-jet aeroplanes, at the OEI cruise speed determined in accordance with (b);

(3) for performance class B or C aeroplanes:

(i) the distance flown in 120 minutes at the OEI cruise speed determined in accordance with (b); or

(ii) 300 NM, whichever is less.

(b) The operator shall determine a speed for the calculation of the maximum distance to an adequate aerodrome for each two-engined aeroplane type or variant operated, not exceeding V MO (maximum operating speed) based upon the true airspeed that the aeroplane can maintain with one engine inoperative.

(c) The operator shall include the following data, specific to each type or variant, in the operations manual:

(1) the determined OEI cruising speed; and

(2) the determined maximum distance from an adequate aerodrome.

(d) To obtain the approval referred to in (a)(2), the operator shall provide evidence that:

(1) the aeroplane/engine combination holds an extended range operations with two-engined aeroplanes (ETOPS) type design and reliability approval for the intended operation;

(2) a set of conditions has been implemented to ensure that the aeroplane and its engines are maintained to meet the necessary reliability criteria; and

(3) the flight crew and all other operations personnel involved are trained and suitably qualified to conduct the intended operation.

4.3.2.1 Extended Range Operations with Two-Engined Aeroplanes (ETOPS)

An operator shall not conduct operations beyond the threshold distance determined in accordance with OPS 1 above unless approved to do so by the Authority (ETOPS approval).
Prior to conducting an ETOPS flight, an operator shall ensure that a suitable ETOPS en-route alternate is available, within either the approved diversion time or a diversion time based on the MEL generated serviceability status of the aeroplane, whichever is shorter.

4.3.2.2 Ditching

CAT.GEN.MPA.150 Ditching — aeroplanes

The operator shall only operate an aeroplane with a passenger seating configuration of more than 30 on overwater flights at a distance from land suitable for making an emergency landing, greater than 120 minutes at cruising speed, or 400 NM, whichever is less, if the aeroplane complies with the ditching provisions prescribed in the applicable airworthiness code

4.3.3 Performance Class A Aeroplanes Limitations

4.3.3.1 En-route – one engine inoperative

CAT.POL.A.215 En-route — one-engine-inoperative (OEI)

(a) The OEI en-route net flight path data shown in the AFM, appropriate to the meteorological conditions expected for the flight, shall allow demonstration of compliance with (b) or (c) at all points along the route. The net flight path shall have a positive gradient at 1500' above the aerodrome where the landing is assumed to be made after engine failure. In meteorological conditions requiring the operation of ice protection systems, the effect of their use on the net flight path shall be taken into account.

(b) The gradient of the net flight path shall be positive at least 1000' above all terrain and obstructions along the route within 9,3 km (5 NM) on either side of the intended track.

(c) The net flight path shall permit the aeroplane to continue flight from the cruising altitude to an aerodrome where a landing can be made in accordance with CAT.POL.A.225 or CAT.POL.A.230, as appropriate. The net flight path shall clear vertically, by at least 2000', all terrain and obstructions along the route within 9,3 km (5 NM) on either side of the intended track in accordance with the following:

(1) the engine is assumed to fail at the most critical point along the route;

(2) account is taken of the effects of winds on the flight path;

(3) fuel jettisoning is permitted to an extent consistent with reaching the aerodrome with the required fuel reserves, if a safe procedure is used; and

(4) the aerodrome where the aeroplane is assumed to land after engine failure shall meet the following criteria:

(i) the performance requirements at the expected landing mass are met; and

(ii) weather reports and/or forecasts and field condition reports indicate that a safe landing can be accomplished at the estimated time of landing.

(d) The operator shall increase the width margins of (b) and (c) to 18.5 km (10 NM) if the navigational accuracy does not meet at least required navigation performance 5 (RNP5).

4.3.3.2 En-route – aeroplanes with 3 or more engines, 2 engines inoperative

CAT.POL.A.220 En-route — aeroplanes with three or more engines, two engines inoperative

(a) At no point along the intended track shall an aeroplane having three or more engines be more than 90 minutes, at the all-engines long range cruising speed at standard temperature in still air, away from an aerodrome at which the performance requirements applicable at the expected landing mass are met, unless it complies with (b) to (f).

(b) The two-engines-inoperative en-route net flight path data shall allow the aeroplane to continue the flight, in the expected meteorological conditions, from the point where two engines are assumed to fail simultaneously to an aerodrome at which it is possible to land and come to a complete stop when using the prescribed procedure for a landing with two engines inoperative. The net flight path shall clear vertically, by at least 2000', all terrain and obstructions along the route within 9.3 km (5 NM) on either side of the intended track. At altitudes and in meteorological conditions requiring ice protection systems to be operable, the effect of their use on the net flight path data shall be taken into account. If the navigational accuracy does not meet at least RNP5, the operator shall increase the width margin given above to 18.5 km (10 NM).

(c) The two engines shall be assumed to fail at the most critical point of that portion of the route where the aeroplane is more than 90 minutes, at the all-engines long range cruising speed at standard temperature in still air, away from an aerodrome at which the performance requirements applicable at the expected landing mass are met.

(d) The net flight path shall have a positive gradient at 1 500' above the aerodrome where the landing is assumed to be made after the failure of two engines.

(e) Fuel jettisoning shall be permitted to an extent consistent with reaching the aerodrome with the required fuel reserves, if a safe procedure is used.

(f) The expected mass of the aeroplane at the point where the two engines are assumed to fail shall not be less than that which would include sufficient fuel to proceed to an aerodrome where the landing is assumed to be made, and to arrive there at least 1 500' directly over the landing area and thereafter to fly level for 15 minutes.

4.3.4 *Performance Class B Aeroplanes Limitations*

4.3.4.1 *En-Route - Multi-engined aeroplanes*

CAT.POL.A.315 En-route — multi-engined aeroplanes

(a) The aeroplane, in the meteorological conditions expected for the flight and in the event of the failure of one engine, with the remaining engines operating within the maximum continuous power conditions specified, shall be capable of continuing flight at or above the relevant minimum altitudes for safe flight stated in the operations manual to a point of 1 000' above an aerodrome at which the performance requirements can be met.

(b) It shall be assumed that, at the point of engine failure:

(1) the aeroplane is not flying at an altitude exceeding that at which the rate of climb equals 300 fpm with all engines operating within the maximum continuous power conditions specified; and

(2) the en-route gradient with OEI shall be the gross gradient of descent or climb, as appropriate, respectively increased by a gradient of 0,5 %, or decreased by a gradient of 0,5 %.

4.3.4.2 *En-route - Single-Engine Aeroplanes*

CAT.POL.A.320 En-route — single-engined aeroplanes

(a) In the meteorological conditions expected for the flight, and in the event of engine failure, the aeroplane shall be capable of reaching a place at which a safe forced landing can be made.

(b) It shall be assumed that, at the point of engine failure:

(1) the aeroplane is not flying at an altitude exceeding that at which the rate of climb equals 300 fpm, with the engine operating within the maximum continuous power conditions specified; and

(2) the en-route gradient is the gross gradient of descent increased by a gradient of 0.5 %.

4.3.5 *Selection of Cruising Speed*

The takeoff mass of an aeroplane is influenced by the following factors:
* Expected traffic load
* Runway length available
* Weight-altitude-temperature limit
* Obstacle limit; and
* Landing runway length

Varying cruising speed will affect overall performance. For example, cruising at a high speed will reduce flight time but depending on aeroplane mass and the outside air temperature at cruising altitude, this may result in higher fuel consumption. Consequently, the cruising speed selected is based on a compromise of the various operational requirements to be met.

4.3.6 *Selection of Cruising Altitudes*

The higher a turbo-prop or turbo-jet flies the lower the fuel consumption will be due to the less dense air. Therefore all long-range IFR flights are planned and operated at the highest available flight level commensurate with aeroplane mass and forecast en-route outside air temperature.

For turbo-prop aeroplanes these altitudes are in the region of 18000-22000' and for turbo-jets 28000-41000'. The actual altitude / flight level selected will be dictated by the direction of the flight in accordance with the semi-circular rule and possibly the forecast en-route weather.

For flights operating on the North Atlantic Organised Track Structure, the levels for turbo-jet aircraft will be dictated by the flight levels specified for the particular track on which the aeroplane is operating.

The selection of the optimum cruising altitude is always dictated at the outset by the estimated mass of the aeroplane at the top of climb compared to the forecast outside air temperature at this point in the flight.

> The best fuel / mileage ratio for a given speed schedule is always achieved at the optimum altitude and a fuel / mileage penalty will ensue from any operation at an off-optimum altitude

ALTITUDE CAPABILITY LRC/.80 MACH

WEIGHT 1000 KG	OPTIMUM ALTITUDE FEET	CRUISE THRUST LIMIT PRESS ALT FT		
		ISA + 10 C & COLDER	ISA + 15 C	ISA + 20 C
110	32600	36900	36400	35700
105	33600	37800	37200	36600
100	34600	38700	38200	37500
95	35700	39700	39200	38500
90	36800	40800	40200	39500
85	38000	41900	41300	40600
80	39300	42000	42000	41700
75	40600	42000	42000	42000
70	42000	42000	42000	42000

Figure 4.1 Cruising altitudes

Consider the figure above for an aeroplane with an estimated takeoff mass 110000 kg and a forecast outside air temperature at top of climb of ISA + 7°C. The table of altitude capability at a long range cruise (LRC) Mach number of 0.8 shows that the optimum altitude is 32600' but the aeroplane would be capable of climbing to 36900'. It is normal to request the cruising level that is nearest to the optimum level; preferably the one above the optimum since, as the weight decreases with fuel burn, the optimum level will increase.

4.3.6.1 Establishment of minimum flight altitudes

(a) An operator shall establish minimum flight altitudes and the methods to determine those altitudes for all route segments to be flown which provide the required terrain clearance taking into account the requirements and conditions.

(b) Every method for establishing minimum flight altitudes must be approved by the Authority.

(c) Where minimum flight altitudes established by States overflown are higher than those established by the operator, the higher values shall apply.

(d) An operator shall take into account the following factors when establishing minimum flight altitudes:

(1) The accuracy with which the position of the aeroplane can be determined;

(2) The probable inaccuracies in the indications of the altimeters used;

(3) The characteristics of the terrain (e.g. sudden changes in the elevation) along the routes or in the areas where operations are to be conducted.

(4) The probability of encountering unfavourable meteorological conditions (e.g. severe turbulence and descending air currents); and

(5) Possible inaccuracies in aeronautical charts.

(e) In fulfilling the requirements prescribed in sub-paragraph (d) above due consideration shall be given to:

(1) Corrections for temperature and pressure variations from standard values;

(2) The ATC requirements; and

(3) Any foreseeable contingencies along the planned route.

4.3.7 Selection of Alternate Aerodromes

An operator shall specify any required alternate(s) in the operational flight plan

4.3.7.1 Take-off Alternates

CAT.OP.MPA.180 Selection of aerodromes — aeroplanes

(a) Where it is not possible to use the departure aerodrome as a take-off alternate aerodrome due to meteorological or performance reasons, the operator shall select another adequate take-off alternate aerodrome that is no further from the departure aerodrome than:

(1) for two-engined aeroplanes:

(i) one hour flying time at an OEI cruising speed according to the AFM in still air standard conditions based on the actual take-off mass; or

(ii) the ETOPS diversion time approved in accordance with Annex V (Part-SPA), Subpart F, subject to any MEL restriction, up to a maximum of two hours, at the OEI cruising speed according to the AFM in still air standard conditions based on the actual take-off mass;

(2) for three and four-engined aeroplanes, two hours flying time at the OEI cruising speed according to the AFM in still air standard conditions based on the actual take-off mass.
If the AFM does not contain an OEI cruising speed, the speed to be used for calculation shall be that which is achieved with the remaining engine(s) set at maximum continuous power.

(b) The operator shall select at least one destination alternate aerodrome for each instrument flight rules (IFR) flight unless the destination aerodrome is an isolated aerodrome or:

(1) the duration of the planned flight from take-off to landing or, in the event of in-flight replanning in accordance with CAT.OP.MPA.150(d), the remaining flying time to destination does not exceed six hours; and

(2) two separate runways are available and usable at the destination aerodrome and the appropriate weather reports and/or forecasts for the destination aerodrome indicate that, for the period from one hour before until one hour after the expected time of arrival at the destination aerodrome, the ceiling will be at least 2000' or circling height + 500', whichever is greater, and the ground visibility will be at least 5 km.

(c) The operator shall select two destination alternate aerodromes when:

(1) the appropriate weather reports and/or forecasts for the destination aerodrome indicate that during a period commencing one hour before and ending one hour after the estimated time of arrival, the weather conditions will be below the applicable planning minima; or

(2) no meteorological information is available.

(d) The operator shall specify any required alternate aerodrome(s) in the operational flight plan.

4.3.7.1.1 Planning minima for take-off alternates

CAT.OP.MPA.185 Planning minima for IFR flights — aeroplanes

(a) Planning minima for a take-off alternate aerodrome

The operator shall only select an aerodrome as a take-off alternate aerodrome when the appropriate weather reports and/or forecasts indicate that, during a period commencing one hour before and ending one hour after the estimated time of arrival at the aerodrome, the weather conditions will be at or above the applicable landing minima specified in accordance with CAT.OP.MPA.110. The ceiling shall be taken into account when the only approach operations available are non-precision approaches (NPA) and/or circling operations. Any limitation related to OEI operations shall be taken into account.

(b) Planning minima for a destination aerodrome other than an isolated destination aerodrome

The operator shall only select the destination aerodrome when:

(1) the appropriate weather reports and/or forecasts indicate that, during a period commencing one hour before and ending one hour after the estimated time of arrival at the aerodrome, the weather conditions will be at or above the applicable planning minima as follows:

(i) RVR/visibility (VIS) specified in accordance with CAT.OP.MPA.110; and

(ii) for an NPA or a circling operation, the ceiling at or above MDH;

or

(2) two destination alternate aerodromes are selected.

(c) Planning minima for a destination alternate aerodrome, isolated aerodrome, fuel en-route alternate (fuel ERA) aerodrome, en-route alternate (ERA) aerodrome

The operator shall only select an aerodrome for one of these purposes when the appropriate weather reports and/or forecasts indicate that, during a period commencing one hour before and ending one hour after the estimated time of arrival at the aerodrome, the weather conditions will be at or above the planning minima in Table 1.

Table 1

Planning minima

Destination alternate aerodrome, isolated destination aerodrome, fuel ERA and ERA aerodrome

Type of approach	Planning minima
CAT II and III	CAT I RVR
CAT I	NPA RVR/VIS Ceiling shall be at or above MDH
NPA	NPA RVR/VIS + 1 000 m Ceiling shall be at or above MDH + 200 ft
Circling	Circling

4.3.7.2 Destination Alternates

An operator must select at least one destination alternate for each IFR flight unless:
(1) Both:
(i)   The duration of the planned flight from take-off to landing does not exceed 6 h; and
(ii) Two separate runways are available and useable at the destination and the meteorological conditions prevailing are such that, for the period from one hour before until one hour after the expected time of arrival at destination, the approach from the relevant minimum sector altitude and the landing can be made in VMC; or
(2) The destination is isolated and no adequate destination alternate exists.

An operator must select two destination alternates when:

(1) The appropriate weather reports or forecasts for the destination, or any combination thereof, indicate that during a period commencing 1 hour before and ending 1 h after the estimated time of arrival, the weather conditions will be below the applicable planning minima; or

(2) No meteorological information is available.

4.3.7.2.1   *Planning minima for destination and destination alternate aerodromes*

An operator shall only select the destination aerodrome and/or destination alternate aerodrome(s) when the appropriate weather reports or forecasts, or any combination thereof, indicate that, during a period commencing 1 h before and ending 1 h after the estimated time of arrival at the aerodrome, the weather conditions will be at or above the applicable planning minima as follows:

(1) Planning minima for a destination aerodrome except isolated destination aerodromes:

(i) RVR/visibility specified; and

(ii) For a non-precision approach or a circling approach, the ceiling at or above MDH; and

(2) Planning minima for destination alternate aerodrome(s) and isolated destination aerodromes:

Planning minima - En-route and destination alternates

Type of Approach	Planning Minima
Cat II and III	Cat I (Note 1)
Cat I	Non-precision (Notes 1 & 2)
Non-precision	Non-precision (Notes 1 & 2) plus 200' / 1000 m
Circling	Circling

Note 1 RVR

Note 2 The ceiling must be at or above the MDH.

4.3.7.2.2   *Planning minima for an en-route alternate aerodrome*

An operator shall not select an aerodrome as an en-route alternate aerodrome unless the appropriate weather reports or forecasts, or any combination thereof, indicate that, during a period commencing 1 h before and ending 1 h after the expected time of arrival at the aerodrome, the weather conditions will be at or above the planning minima in accordance with the table above.

4.3.7.2.3   *Planning minima for an ETOPS en-route alternate*

SPA.ETOPS.110 ETOPS en-route alternate aerodrome

(a) An ETOPS en-route alternate aerodrome shall be considered adequate, if, at the expected time of use, the aerodrome is available and equipped with necessary ancillary services such as air traffic services (ATS), sufficient lighting, communications, weather reporting, navigation aids and emergency services and has at least one instrument approach procedure available.

(b) Prior to conducting an ETOPS flight, the operator shall ensure that an ETOPS en-route alternate aerodrome is available, within either the operator's approved diversion time, or a diversion time based on the MEL generated serviceability status of the aeroplane, whichever is shorter.

(c) The operator shall specify any required ETOPS en-route alternate aerodrome(s) in the operational flight plan and ATS flight plan.

SPA.ETOPS.115 ETOPS en-route alternate aerodrome planning minima

(a) The operator shall only select an aerodrome as an ETOPS en-route alternate aerodrome when the appropriate weather reports or forecasts, or any combination thereof, indicate that, between the anticipated time of landing until one hour after the latest possible time of landing, conditions will exist at or above the planning minima calculated by adding the additional limits of Table 1.

(b) The operator shall include in the operations manual the method for determining the operating minima at the planned ETOPS en-route alternate aerodrome.

Table 1

Planning minima for the ETOPS en-route alternate aerodrome

Type of approach	Planning minima
Precision approach	DA/H + 200 ft RVR/VIS + 800 m[1]
Non-precision approach or Circling approach	MDA/H + 400 ft[1] RVR/VIS + 1500 m
(1) VIS: visibility; MDA/H: minimum descent altitude/height.	

4.3.8   Performance Class A Aeroplanes - Landing Requirements

4.3.8.1 Dry Runways
CAT.POL.A.230 Landing — dry runways

(a) The landing mass of the aeroplane determined in accordance with CAT.POL.A.105(a) for the estimated time of landing at the destination aerodrome and at any alternate aerodrome shall allow a full stop landing from 50' above the threshold:

(1) for turbo-jet powered aeroplanes, within 60 % of the landing distance available (LDA); and

(2) for turbo-propeller powered aeroplanes, within 70 % of the LDA.

(b) For steep approach operations, the operator shall use the landing distance data factored in accordance with (a), based on a screen height of less than 60', but not less than 35', and shall comply with CAT.POL.A.245.

(c) For short landing operations, the operator shall use the landing distance data factored in accordance with (a) and shall comply with CAT.POL.A.250.

(d) When determining the landing mass, the operator shall take the following into account:

(1) the altitude at the aerodrome;

(2) not more than 50 % of the headwind component or not less than 150 % of the tailwind component; and

(3) the runway slope in the direction of landing if greater than ± 2 %.

(e) For dispatching the aeroplane it shall be assumed that:

(1) the aeroplane will land on the most favourable runway, in still air; and

(2) the aeroplane will land on the runway most likely to be assigned, considering the probable wind speed and direction, the ground handling characteristics of the aeroplane and other conditions such as landing aids and terrain.

(f) If the operator is unable to comply with (e)(1) for a destination aerodrome having a single runway where a landing depends upon a specified wind component, the aeroplane may be dispatched if two alternate aerodromes are designated that permit full compliance with (a) to (e). Before commencing an approach to land at the destination aerodrome, the commander shall check that a landing can be made in full compliance with (a) to (d) and CAT.POL.A.225.

(g) If the operator is unable to comply with (e)(2) for the destination aerodrome, the aeroplane shall be only dispatched if an alternate aerodrome is designated that allows full compliance with (a) to (e).

4.3.8.2 Wet and Contaminated Runways

CAT.POL.A.235 Landing — wet and contaminated runways

(a) When the appropriate weather reports and/or forecasts indicate that the runway at the estimated time of arrival may be wet, the LDA shall be at least 115 % of the required landing distance, determined in accordance with CAT.POL.A.230.

(b) When the appropriate weather reports and/or forecasts indicate that the runway at the estimated time of arrival may be contaminated, the LDA shall be at least the landing distance determined in accordance with (a), or at least 115 % of the landing distance determined in accordance with approved contaminated landing distance data or equivalent, whichever is greater. The operator shall specify in the operations manual if equivalent landing distance data are to be applied.

(c) A landing distance on a wet runway shorter than that required by (a), but not less than that required by CAT.POL.A.230(a), may be used if the AFM includes specific additional information about landing distances on wet runways.

(d) A landing distance on a specially prepared contaminated runway shorter than that required by (b), but not less than that required by CAT.POL.A.230(a), may be used if the AFM includes specific additional information about landing distances on contaminated runways.

(e) For (b), (c) and (d), the criteria of CAT.POL.A.230 shall be applied accordingly, except that CAT.POL.A.230(a) shall not be applied to (b) above.

4.3.9   Performance Class B Aeroplanes – Landing Requirements

4.3.9.1 Dry Runways

CAT.POL.A.330 Landing — dry runways

(a) The landing mass of the aeroplane determined in accordance with CAT.POL.A.105(a) for the estimated time of landing at the destination aerodrome and at any alternate aerodrome shall allow a full stop landing from 50' above the threshold within 70 % of the LDA taking into account:

(1) the altitude at the aerodrome;

(2) not more than 50 % of the headwind component or not less than 150 % of the tailwind component;

(3) the runway surface condition and the type of runway surface; and

(4) the runway slope in the direction of landing.

(b) For steep approach operations, the operator shall use landing distance data factored in accordance with (a) based on a screen height of less than 60', but not less than 35', and comply with CAT.POL.A.345.

(c) For short landing operations, the operator shall use landing distance data factored in accordance with (a) and comply with CAT.POL.A.350.

(d) For dispatching the aeroplane in accordance with (a) to (c), it shall be assumed that:

(1) the aeroplane will land on the most favourable runway, in still air; and

(2) the aeroplane will land on the runway most likely to be assigned considering the probable wind speed and direction, the ground handling characteristics of the aeroplane and other conditions such as landing aids and terrain.

(e) If the operator is unable to comply with (d)(2) for the destination aerodrome, the aeroplane shall only be dispatched if an alternate aerodrome is designated that permits full compliance with (a) to (d).

4.3.9.2 Wet and Contaminated Runways

CAT.POL.A.335 Landing — wet and contaminated runways

(a) When the appropriate weather reports and/or forecasts indicate that the runway at the estimated time of arrival may be wet, the LDA shall be equal to or exceed the required landing distance, determined in accordance with CAT.POL.A.330, multiplied by a factor of 1,15.

(b) When the appropriate weather reports and/or forecasts indicate that the runway at the estimated time of arrival may be contaminated, the landing distance shall not exceed the LDA. The operator shall specify in the operations manual the landing distance data to be applied.

(c) A landing distance on a wet runway shorter than that required by (a), but not less than that required by CAT.POL.A.330(a), may be used if the AFM includes specific additional information about landing distances on wet runways.

4.3.10   Minimum Time Routes

A minimum time route is the route giving the shortest flight time from departure to destination adhering to all ATC and airspace restrictions. In zero wind, the shortest route between two points will be a Great Circle but, due to the few occasions when there is "nil wind", the minimum time route (MTR) must be constructed taking cognisance of wind effect. The pure MTR must then be adjusted to take in the requirements of ATS reporting points and any airway routings at the beginning or the end and this adjustment produces the final "optimum" MTR.

Self Assessment Test 03

1   The operator's responsibility regarding choice of route is to ensure that:
   1. appropriate maps and charts are available
   2. single engine aircraft are used on routes regardless of the surfaces over which they are flown
   3. aircraft must be able to comply with minimum flight altitude requirements only if the route is more than 200 NM long
A) 1, 2 correct
B) 1, 2, 3 correct
C) 1 correct
D) 1, 3 correct

2   The commander may commence a flight if:
A) A defect entered in the technical log has been deferred and a maintenance release issued
B) The aeroplane cannot be operated in accordance with the Mel provided all the crew agree to the operation
C) Available maps and charts have expired by 24 h
D) None of the above are correct

3   An operational flight plan is required for:
A) Every IFR flight
B) Every VFR flight
C) Every intended flight and must be signed by the commander
D) Flights in controlled airspace only

4   A non-ETOPS approved operator should not operate a 2-engined performance Class A aircraft with a passenger seating configuration of 30 more than:
A) 120 min at the 1-engine inoperative cruising speed from an adequate aerodrome
B) 180 min at the 1-engine inoperative cruising speed from an adequate aerodrome
C) 60 min at the all engines operative cruising speed from an adequate aerodrome
D) 60 min at the 1-engine inoperative cruising speed from an adequate aerodrome

5   For an ETOPS flight to be operated:
A) The aircraft must have at least 3 engines
B) An en-route alternate must be available
C) The aircraft must have no unserviceable equipment
D) The forecast destination weather at the estimated time of arrival must be VMC

6   What is the maximum distance from land at which an aircraft with a passenger configuration of 60 seats may be operated without having to comply with ditching requirements?
A) 120 min at the 1-engine inoperative cruising speed
B) 60 min at cruising speed
C) 180 min at cruising speed
D) 120 min at cruising speed

7   For a performance Class A aircraft, the en-route one-engine inoperative net flight path must:
A) Have a positive gradient 1000' above the landing aerodrome
B) Have appositive gradient 1500' above the landing aerodrome
C) Have a positive gradient at 1000' above all terrain within 5 NM either side of track when the navigation accuracy does not meet the 95% containment level
D) Clear all terrain within 5 NM either side of track by 1000'

8   A performance Class A aircraft with four engines must not be operated more than 90 min at long range cruise speed away from a suitable aerodrome unless, in the event of failure of two of the engines, the:
A)   Net flight path clears all terrain within 5 NM either side of track by 2000'
B)   Net flight path clears all terrain within 5 NM either side of track by 4000'
C)   Net flight path has a positive gradient at 1000' above the aerodrome of assumed landing
D)   Aircraft can fly level for a further 30 min after arriving overhead the landing aerodrome

9   The maximum altitude at which the performance limitations for Class B aircraft are considered is:
A)   Where the all engines operating rate of climb is 100 fpm
B)   Where the all engines operating rate of climb is 300 fpm
C)   Where the all engines operating rate of climb is 0 fpm
D)   A fixed value of 15000'

10   In order to achieve the optimum fuel/mileage ratio an aircraft should be flown:
A)   At its service ceiling
B)   At its single-engine service ceiling
C)   At its optimum altitude
D)   Above its optimum altitude because the fuel/mileage ration will gradually increase with time

11   When considering minimum flight altitudes an operator must take into account:
       1.   the accuracy with which the aircraft's position can be determined
       2.   the possibility of encountering severe turbulence
       3.   possible inaccuracies in aeronautical charts
A)   1, 2 correct
B)   2, 3 correct
C)   1, 2, 3 correct
D)   1, 2 correct

12   For a 2-engined aircraft which is not ETOPS approved, a takeoff alternate:
A)   Must be located within 1 h flight time at the 1-engine inoperative cruising speed
B)   Must be located within 2 h flight time at the 1-engine inoperative cruising speed
C)   Must be located within 1 h flight time at the long range cruising speed
D)   Is never required

13   A destination alternate need not be selected for an IFR flight if:
A)   The flight is less than 6 h long
B)   One useable runway is available at destination
C)   Two separate runways are available and useable at destination at it is expected that during the period from 1 h before to 1 h after ETA, the landing can be made in VMC
D)   Conditions (a) and (c) are met

14   Two destination alternates are required if:
A)   At ETA the weather is expected to be VMC
B)   No meteorological forecast for the destination has been obtained
C)   The commander makes such a request
D)   None of the above are correct

15   Your aircraft and crew are approved for Cat III operations. The planning minima you would use for the destination alternate would be:
A)   Cat III
B)   Cat II
C)   Cat I
D)   Non-precision

16 The planning minima for an en-route alternate aerodrome should be:
A) Non-precision planning minima for a Cat III approach at destination
B) Cat I planning minima for a circling approach at destination
C) Cat II planning minima for a Cat II approach at destination
D) The same as for a destination alternate

17 A performance Class A turbo-jet aircraft must be capable of landing within what percentage of the landing distance available?
A) 70%
B) 60%
C) 50%
D) 115%

18 When a runway is contaminated, the landing distance available must be what percentage of the landing distance required?
A) 70%
B) 60%
C) 50%
D) 115%

19 When calculating the landing requirements for an aircraft, the operator must take into account:
A) 100% of the headwind component
B) 100% of the tailwind component
C) Not more than 50% of the wind
D) Not more than 50% of the headwind component

Self Assessment Test 03 Answers

1	C
2	A
3	C
4	D
5	B
6	D
7	B
8	A
9	B
10	C
11	C
12	A
13	D
14	B
15	C
16	D
17	B
18	D
19	D

CHAPTER 5

Transoceanic and Polar Flight

5.1   Introduction

Flying across inhospitable areas such as an ocean or a polar area have many things in common in that each has extensive areas within which there may be little or no surface radio navigation or radar facilities available. As a consequence of this a more stringent formal navigation procedure maintaining a record of position, track, speed and time is required. For operation in such areas, there is usually a requirement for a minimum level of navigation equipment to be carried on an aeroplane. Most modern aeroplanes are equipped with sophisticated computerised navigation systems such as, Inertial Navigation Systems (INS), Inertial Reference Systems (IRS) and Global Navigation Satellite Systems (GNSS). In spite of this sophisticated equipment it is absolutely essential, and is a sign of good airmanship, to maintain a manual plot on a chart. This provides a fall back in the event of failure of equipment. In addition to potential navigation problems, there may be problems associated with communications. Most of these are conducted on HF and are prone to interference, especially at dawn or dusk. Selection of frequencies is critical to effective communications; poor communications means that ATC may not be as effective as normal.

5.2   Monitoring Navigation System Accuracy

The first action prior to commencing a trans-oceanic / polar long-range flight is for the crew to prepare the navigation computer, loading in the latitude and longitude co-ordinates of the gate or ramp position on which the aircraft is parked at the airport of departure. This is then followed by the insertion of a number of en-route navigation / reporting points, called waypoints, to instruct the computer where to take the aeroplane after the ramp position is vacated. The procedure by which the waypoints are loaded into the navigation computer is dictated by equipment software combined with State rules or company procedures. In some cases all of the en-route waypoints including the destination are loaded into the system at this stage. In other cases an initial number of waypoints are loaded to get airborne and the remainder, including the destination is included further along the route. The operations manual will dictate the procedure to be adopted. Whatever procedure is applied, this activity demands the greatest care, as the computer will only do what is programmed into it. During the first portion of the route the accuracy of the automated systems must be cross-checked by reference to ground based aids such as VOR/DME before the aircraft enters the oceanic / polar sector. Where duplicate systems are fitted, the system showing the most accurate position (with reference to the ground based aids) will then be used as the primary navigation aid for the oceanic / polar crossing. Once established in the oceanic / polar sector a running plot is kept of progress along the track by fixing the aircraft position at regular intervals. These intervals may be by time, every 20 / 30 min or by fixing at compulsory reporting points, such as, every 10° of longitude. The information monitored in the primary system will be compared with that of the secondary system or systems, in the case of more than two. Where a triple fit is available, comparison between the units makes it easy to establish that one unit is in error. Where a twin IRS is used the decision as to which unit is in error is slightly more difficult if there are no external references. The pilot must decide on the basis of good dead reckoning (DR) and common sense. Possibly the best combination is the use of a hybrid system consisting of a GNSS and an IRS. This provides an external reference with which to check the IRS and, at the same time, provides an excellent DR system to cover the eventuality of GNSS failure. Should a large discrepancy begin to appear then action must be taken to resolve the anomaly. If a large cross track error becomes apparent then action must be taken to regain the track within the next 100 NM. Should any doubts arise as to potential software error then it may be necessary, in the absence of any ground reference, to revert to manual dead reckoning mode, or to solicit the assistance of nearby aircraft.

5.3   *Aircraft unable to continue flight in accordance with its ATC clearance*

Another possible navigation anomaly is the case of where the aeroplane is unable to proceed according to the last ATC clearance. This may be caused by a significant difference in ambient conditions being experienced against that forecast prior to departure, en-route weather such as severe or heavy turbulence or a reduction in available engine power. These non-routine scenarios are catered for in the ICAO document 7030/4, Regional Supplementary Procedures. If these are followed the safety of the flight, and any others in the immediate vicinity which could be directly or indirectly affected, is assured.

> If an aircraft is unable to continue flight in accordance with its air traffic control clearance, a revised clearance shall, whenever possible, be obtained prior to initiating any action. This shall also apply to aircraft, which are unable to maintain the accuracy of navigation on which the safety of the separation minima applied by air traffic control (between it and adjacent aircraft) depends

This shall be accomplished using the radiotelephony distress (Mayday) or urgency signal (PAN), as appropriate. Subsequent air traffic control action with respect to that aircraft shall be based on the intentions of the pilot and the over-all air traffic situation. If prior clearance cannot be obtained, an air traffic control clearance shall be obtained at the earliest possible time and, in the meantime, the pilot shall:

• broadcast position (including the ATS route designator or the track code, as appropriate) and intentions on frequency 121.5 MHz at suitable intervals until air traffic control clearance is received

• make maximum use of aircraft lights to make the aircraft visible

• maintain a watch for conflicting traffic, and if unable to comply with the foregoing provisions the aircraft should climb or descend 500' then leave its assigned route or track by turning 90° to the right or the left whenever this is possible

The direction of the turn should, where possible, be determined by the position of the aircraft relative to any organised route or track system e.g. whether the aircraft is outside, at the edge of, or within the system. Other factors, which may affect the direction of the turn, are the direction to an alternate airport, terrain clearance and levels allocated to adjacent routes or tracks.

5.4   *Navigation in Polar Areas*

The principle difficulty with navigating in polar areas is proximity to the Pole. The magnetic compass takes its datum by reference to the Earth's magnetic pole and its operation depends on the strength of the horizontal component of the Earth's magnetic field (H). The magnetic compass becomes virtually useless when flying in close proximity to the magnetic pole where the H force becomes weak. These areas in close proximity to the magnetic poles are known as Compass Unreliable Areas (or 6 microtesla zones). Polar areas are almost devoid of ground based navigation facilities so ground based position updating becomes difficult.

The shortest routes from Europe to the Western seaboard of the USA, Japan and other Far Eastern destinations cross polar areas. To benefit from the performance capability of new generation turbo-jet aircraft and the shorter distances offered by following great circle routes, polar routes become the routes of choice.

Polar Air cargo, Atlas Air Worldwide Holdings

5.4.1 *Navigation Techniques*

Navigation in Polar Regions requires some highly specialised techniques. The basic techniques were developed decades ago but are still applicable and their practice is considerably improved by the use of modern solutions.

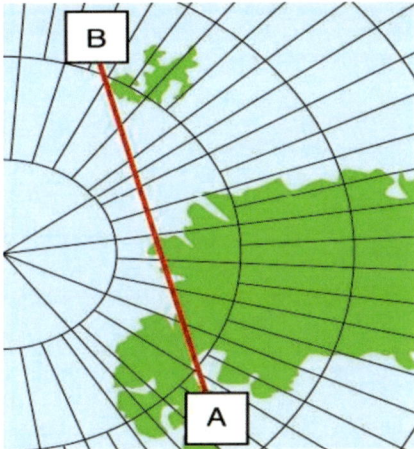

Straight line track on a polar chart

Near the pole, Earth convergency causes big differences in true direction when flying east-west because the true North reference datum changes at a greater rate than at lower latitudes.

Due to convergency of the meridians, the true track of an aeroplane (flying from A to B) increases greatly requiring continuous re-setting of the navigational course.

Difficulties in polar navigation are compounded by:

Determination of direction: Magnetic datum compasses cannot be relied upon.

Variation: Even where the horizontal component of Earth flux is strong enough to provide a magnetic reference datum, the value of variation may change rapidly with position giving a problem similar to that of convergence.

Determination of position: Where there is a lack of ground based facilities, alternative sources of position information are required.

5.5 *Grid North*

To visualise the pole on charts, polar stereographic projections are typically used although transverse or oblique Mercator charts may also be used in these areas. To overcome the problem of convergence, a different navigational datum is devised called Grid North which is depicted by a series of lines parallel to that datum to form a grid. The reference datum selected can be any meridian but is normally a meridian with Grid North (G) as the zero reference lined up parallel to the Greenwich Meridian based on True North. The difference between Grid North and True North, at any point, is equal to the convergence of the reference datum meridian and the meridian through that point and is called grid convergence.

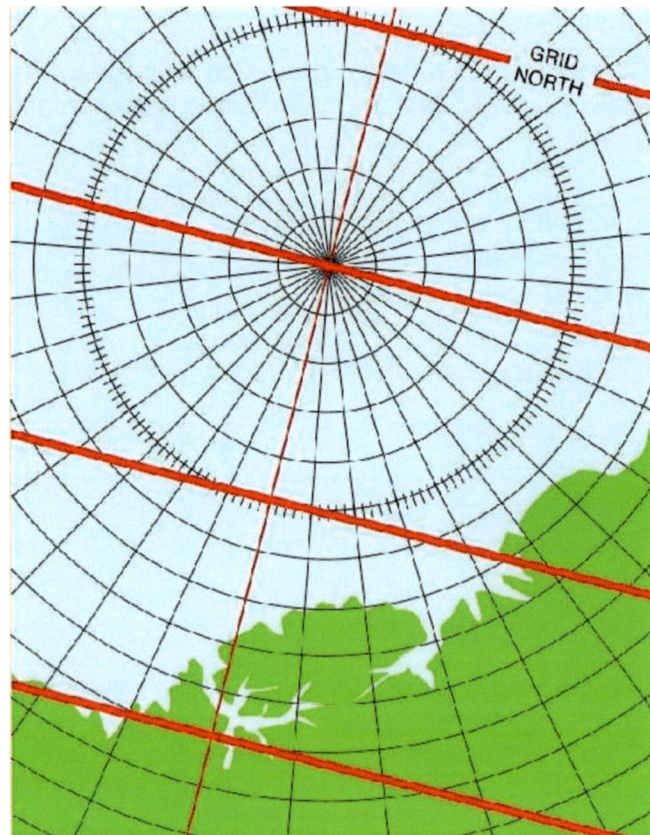

Figure 5.1 Polar chart

In order to convert between True and Grid directions convergence must be added or subtracted in the correct sense.

Grid direction = Direction (T) ± Convergence

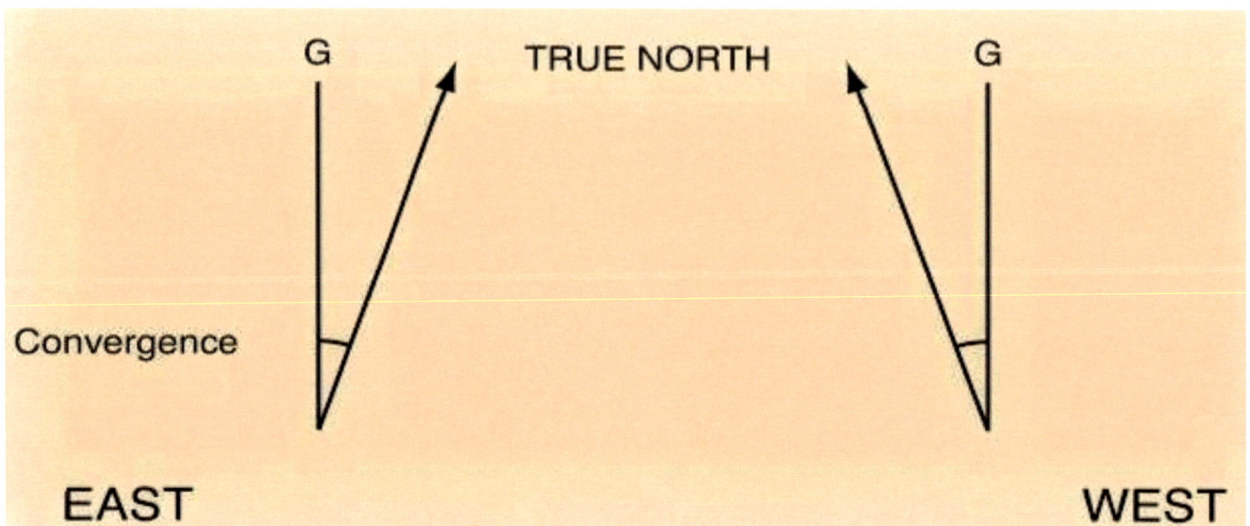

Figure 5.2 Grid direction is true direction ± convergence

Grid Convergence is East if True North (T) lies to the East of Grid North (G)

Grid Convergence is West if True North (T) lies to the West of Grid North (G)

So an aircraft track may be defined by magnetic North, true North or by a third reference datum: grid North.

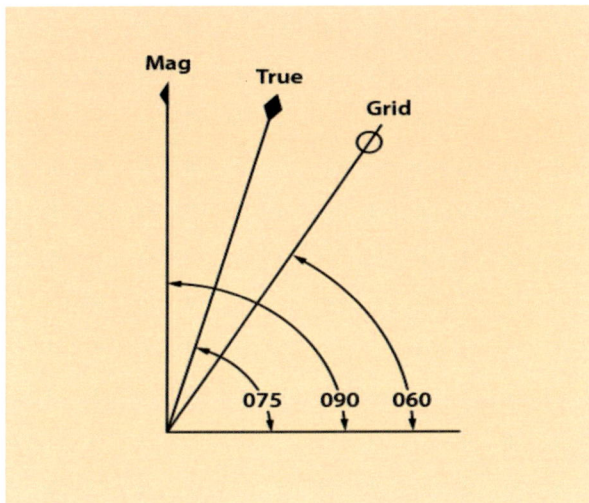

In this diagram:

Three different reference datums are used to denote direction

Magnetic direction is 090°
True direction is 075°
and Grid direction is 060°

The overall direction is the same but the reference datums are different.

Grid direction

Convergence is the term used to describe the angular difference between true North and grid North. Convergence is East if true north lies to the East of Grid north. Convergence is West if true north lies to the West of Grid north.

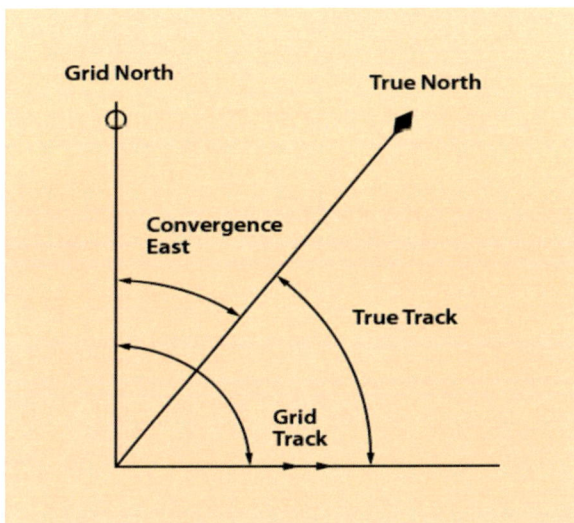

Easterly Convergence
True North lies East of Grid North

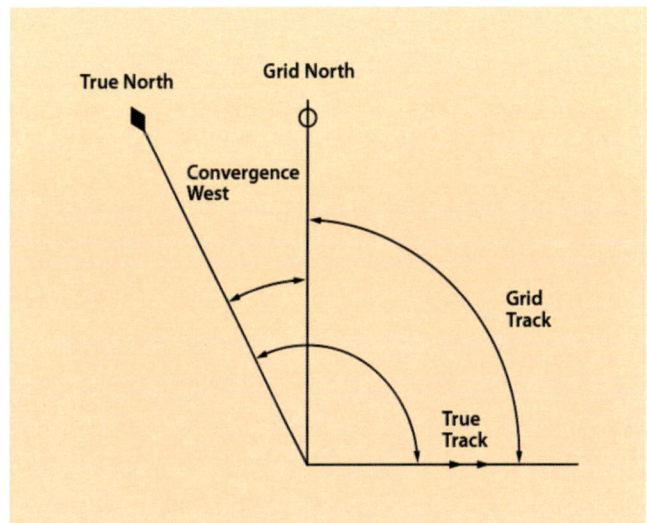

Westerly Convergence
True North lies West of Grid North

Convergence and the relationship between true and grid direction

If a magnetic directional reference is available it is important to be able to relate magnetic North (M) to Grid North (G). The combination of grid convergence and magnetic variation is known as grivation.

Grivation is East if Magnetic North (M) lies to the East of Grid North (G)

Grivation is West if Magnetic North (M) lies to the West of Grid North (G)

GRIVATION is the angular difference between grid and magnetic north

A simple rule exists when convergence and variation are both east or are both west, their sum will give the value of grivation. It is often safer, however, to draw a simple diagram.

Determination of direction is the next problem to be resolved.

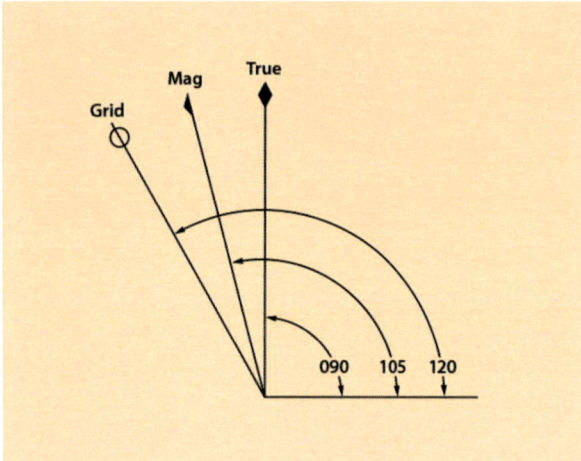

In this diagram True North lies to the East of Grid North so convergence is Easterly with a value of 30°. Variation is 15W.
Grivation is the angular difference between grid and magnetic north with a value of 15E.

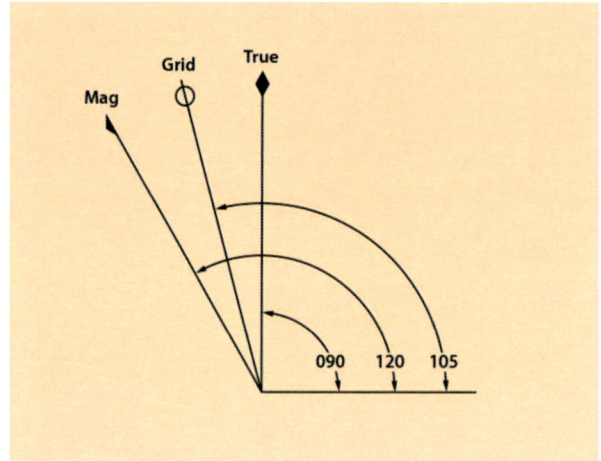

In this diagram True North lies to the East of Grid North so convergence is Easterly with a value of 15°. Variation is 30W.
Grivation is the angular difference between grid and magnetic north with a value of 15E.

When the magnetic datum is available no problem exists. Grivation is applied to the indicated magnetic heading to obtain the grid heading or the value of grivation is set on to the compass variation setting control aligning the axis of the remote indicating compass to Grid North.

For example:
Indicated magnetic heading = 010° M, grivation 25° E required grid direction 035° G.
Indicated magnetic heading = 010° M, grivation 25° W required grid direction 345° G.

The values of grivation may be shown on polar and other high latitude charts by lines joining places having the same value of grivation. These lines are called isogrivs. Like isogonals, they will require redrawing periodically by cartographers in order to account for the annual change in variation.

An ISOGRIV is a line joining places with the same value of grivation

As a flight approaches the magnetic pole the compass unusable area will be reached and an alternative method of navigation is required. Until the development of modern Inertial Reference Systems and Global Positioning Systems, this was done by using a sophisticated directional gyro, which had the property of a comparatively low mechanical drift rate. Such a gyro could be aligned with the grid meridian and was corrected for Earth rate at its current position. Because of its properties of rigidity in space it would remain aligned to the grid meridian in spite of the Earth's rotation around its axis or the movement of the aeroplane across the meridians. Unfortunately, no matter how carefully manufactured, directional gyros seldom give zero mechanical drift. It was the task of the navigator to establish and maintain a check on the mechanical drift rate of the compass. This was achieved using celestial bodies such as the Sun, Moon or stars as datums. From data in an air almanac, the navigator could establish the correct bearing (azimuth) of the chosen celestial body and then would use the periscopic sextant to measure a bearing of that body as referenced to the gyro. Comparing the two and taking into account convergence, the gyro error could be determined. By repeating this at regular intervals an error trend could be built up so that heading could be compensated accordingly.

The calculation of drift rates importantly provides an appreciation of what is involved as an emergency means of maintaining a heading reference in the event of equipment failure.

For these calculations there are two sources of drift, namely:
• Real (mechanical) drift, which is a result of mechanical imperfections such as:- slight imbalance of the rotor / gimbal system, bearing friction, mechanical or electrical latitude correction
• Apparent drift which results from the fact that the Earth directional reference system rotates in space while the directional gyro maintains a constant direction in space – i.e. the meridians change alignment with respect to the gyro datum. There are two accountable factors that cause this:
o Earth rotation, known as Earth Rate (with a formula ER = 15 sin lat)
o East / West transport, known as Transport Wander

Consider this example
An aeroplane is operating a route by reference to a grid system. It is following a constant grid heading of 290° G. This heading is being maintained by reference to the No. 1 compass system stabilised to the earth's magnetic field and compensated by application of current grivation values. No. 2 compass system is operating in DG mode (free gyro) with the latitude correction set to compensate for Earth Rate at 50° N.

The following observations are made:
1) At 0700 position 58°N 06°W, No. 1 compass 290° G, No. 2 compass 290°
2) At 0740 position 59N 16°W, No. 1 compass 290° G, No. 2 compass 293°

Calculate the overall drift rate of the gyro:
Working:
Latitude nut = 15 sin latitude
Latitude nut = +15 sin 50°
Latitude nut – +15 x 0.766
Latitude nut = +11.5° / h

Earth rate = -15 sin (mean lat)
Earth rate = -15 Sin 58° 30'
Earth rate = -15 x 0.853
Earth rate = -12.8° / h
Anticipated Drift Rate = + 11.5 - 12.8 = -1.3° / h
For 40 min = - 0.87°
Gyro calculated heading 290 - 0.9 = 289.1
Gyro actual heading 293
Actual drift (40 min) + 3.9
Drift rate + 5.9° / h
Readings increasing.

Because we are referring this to a grid we do not need to consider transport wander as this is virtually the same as convergence and that is removed by the use of the grid datum. (In fact, at this latitude there is about a 1° heading error in this assumption but, as you move towards the poles, the error becomes very small). Another simple trick to remember is that, if you are near the pole, the true bearing of any celestial body is 180° (T) (approximately) at any time.

Imagine you are heading straight towards the Sun and it 1800 UTC. If the grid north is based on the Greenwich Meridian, what is your approximate grid heading?

At 1800 UTC the Sun must be approximately in longitude 90°W (6 h after transiting the Greenwich meridian at ≈ 15° / h = 90°):

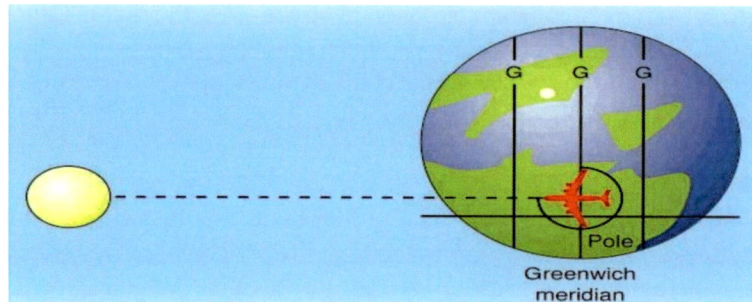

Figure 5.3 The approximate Position of the Sun at 1800 UTC

It can be instantly visualised that your grid heading is 270°.

On today's polar flights, the IRS or GPS provide heading references. These are normally at least duplicated and sometimes triplicated units to allow for redundancy. But do not believe, because they are electronic devices, that nothing can go wrong. Keep a check on them even if you only use a simple technique as just explained. Your company operations manual may even require you to operate one directional gyro in "free gyro" mode when entering and within a compass unreliable area. By comparison with the IRS heading information, you would then be able to build up a picture of gyro drift error which, in the event of IRS failure, could provide you with the basis for establishing a heading reference. It has to be said that a total IRS failure is a most unlikely scenario as the most likely cause of total IRS failure is total electrical power failure and this would probably leave you without a gyro (or anything much else) anyway.

The most likely problem is the failure or, more difficult, the loss of reference of one system which will cause divergence of the displayed navigational information. You must determine which of the systems is faulty.

In a triple IRS fit this is no problem as the one that is diverging from the other two will, statistically, be the unit at fault. In a twin fit, however, you must use every tool and piece of information available to make the correct selection.

Solving the problem of position has almost gone full circle. We used to do it by using the stars then we used long-range navigation systems such as Loran or Omega. In polar regions however, these radio aids were frequently severely affected by propagation interference. The next step forward was the development of the highly accurate Inertial Navigation System which, although inherently accurate, suffered from being a DR system in which the errors are cumulative. Now we are witnessing a return to using references in space – this time man-made ones. The increased use of GNSS and the continuing improvement in its performance through Satellite Based Augmentation Systems is providing us with ever improving position data, which, when used in association with twin IRS, provides a highly reliable monitored system.

5.5.1   Determination of Tracks on Polar Routes

5.5.1.1 Track structure – polar areas

A Polar Track Structure (PTS), consisting of 10 fixed tracks in Reykjavik CTA and 5 fixed tracks through Bodo OCA has been established. The PTS tracks through Bodo OCA constitute a continuation of relevant PTS tracks in Reykjavik CTA.

Although not mandatory, flights planning to operate on the Europe-Alaska axis at FL 310 to FL 390 inclusive are recommended to submit flight plans in accordance with one of the promulgated PTS tracks.

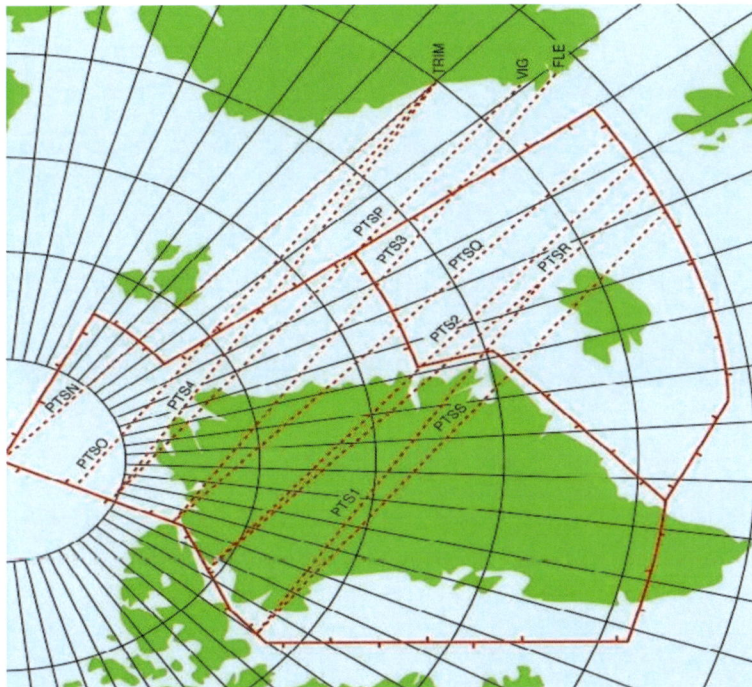

Figure 5.4 Polar Track Structure (PTS)

5.5.2   Abbreviated Clearances

An abbreviated clearance may be used when clearing an aircraft to follow one of the polar tracks throughout its flight within the Reykjavik CTA and/or the Bodo OCA. When an abbreviated clearance is issued it shall include:
- the cleared track specified by the track code;
- the cleared flight level(s); and
- the cleared Mach Number. (if required)

On receipt of an abbreviated clearance the pilot shall read back the contents of the clearance message and in addition the full details of the track specified by the track code.

5.5.3   Abbreviated Position Reports

When operating on the PTS within the Reykjavik CTA and/or Bodo OCA, position reports may be abbreviated by replacing the normal latitude co-ordinate with the word "Polar" followed by the track code.
E.g. "Trollair" 016 Position Polar Romeo 20W/1620 FL 330 Mach .84 estimating Polar Romeo 40W/1718, next Polar Romeo 60W.
Unless otherwise required by air traffic services a position report shall be made at the significant points listed in the appropriate AIP for the relevant PTS track.

5.6   MNPS AIRSPACE

MNPS is a Minimum Navigation Performance Specification, which is applied to certain areas known as Minimum Navigation Performance Specification Areas (MNPSA). These are areas within which the concentration of traffic coupled with limitations of the current communications, navigation and control systems, make it necessary to ensure that certain requirements should be fulfilled in order that an aeroplane can be considered safe to fly.

NAT HLA Airspace (North Atlantic High Level Airspace)

NAT HLA specifically refers to the North Atlantic region.

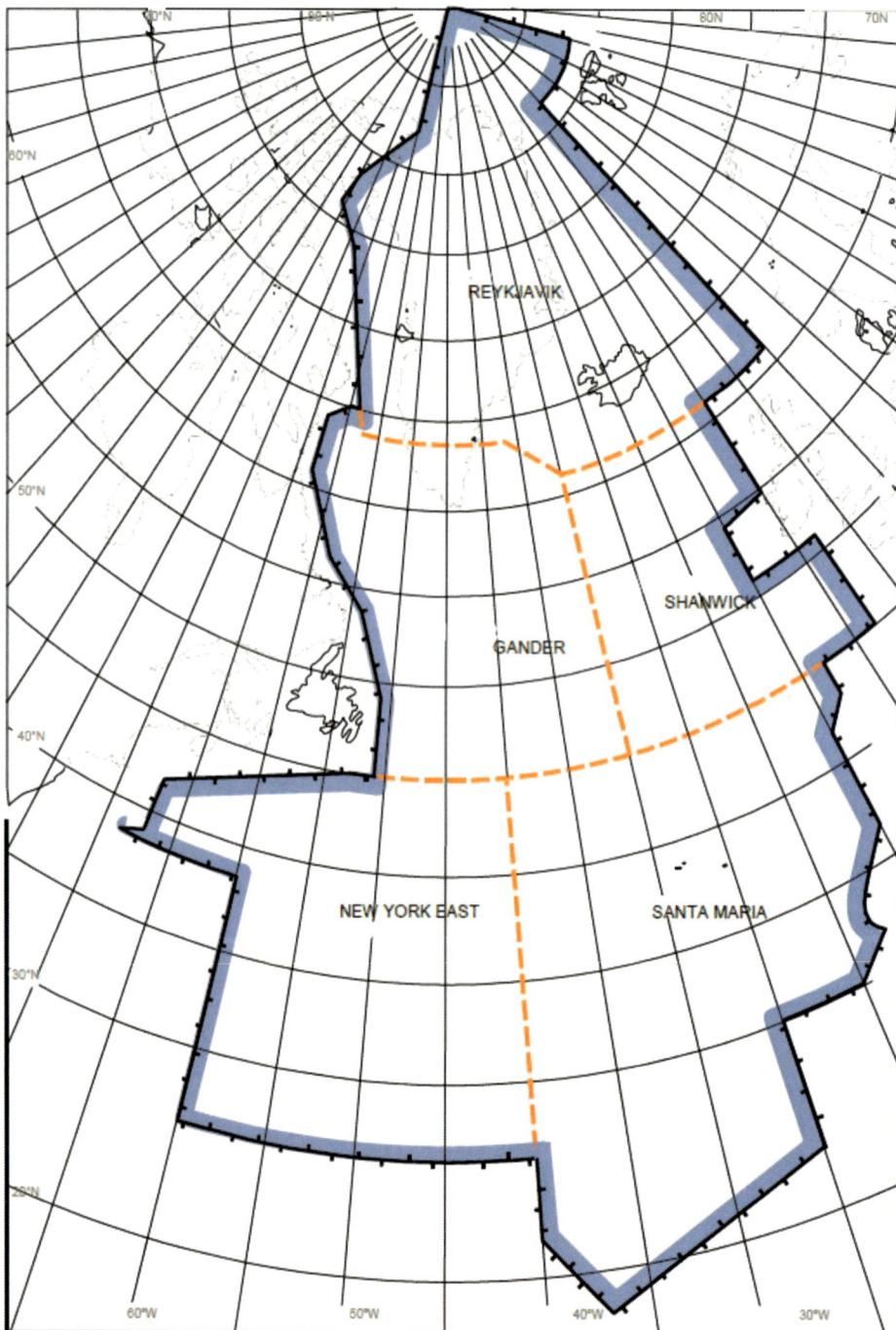

The airspace of the North Atlantic which links Europe and North America is the busiest oceanic airspace in the world. In 2012 approximately 460,000 flights crossed the North Atlantic. For the most part in the North Atlantic, Direct Controller Pilot Communications (DCPC) and ATS Surveillance are unavailable. Aircraft separation assurance and hence safety are nevertheless ensured by demanding the highest standards of horizontal and vertical navigation performance/accuracy and of operating discipline.

The vast majority of North Atlantic flights are performed by commercial jet transport aircraft in the band of altitudes FL290 – FL410. To ensure adequate airspace capacity and provide for safe vertical separations, Reduced Vertical Separation Minima (RVSM) is applied throughout the ICAO NAT Region.

A large portion of the airspace of the North Atlantic Region, through which the majority of these North Atlantic crossings route between FLs 285 and 420 inclusive, is designated as the NAT High Level Airspace (NAT HLA). Within this airspace a formal Approval Process by the State of Registry of the aircraft or the State of the Operator ensures that aircraft meet defined NAT HLA Standards and that appropriate crew procedures and training have been adopted. The lateral dimensions of the NAT HLA airspace include the following Control Areas (CTAs):

REYKJAVIK, SHANWICK (excluding SOTA & BOTA), GANDER, SANTA MARIA OCEANIC, BODO OCEANIC and the portion of NEW YORK OCEANIC EAST which is north of 27°N.

Note that "NAT HLA Airspace" is a re-designation of the airspace formerly known as the "North Atlantic Minimum Navigational Performance Specifications Airspace (NAT MNPSA)" but excludes those portions of SHANWICK OCA which form the SOTA and BOTA areas and includes the BODO OCEANIC FIR. This re-designation is the third of the milestones of the "MNPS to PBN Transition Plan" for the North Atlantic Region and is effective from 04 February 2016. However, recognizing that ICAO Annex 6 allows for a "minimum navigation performance specification" to be regionally specified in Regional Supplementary Procedures Doc 7030, it has been determined to maintain reference to a "MNPS" in the NAT Region within NAT Doc 7030 and in Doc 007, within particular contexts. Thus, approvals initially issued to operate in the NAT MNPSA are referred to as "NAT MNPS" approvals and approvals issued to operate in the NAT HLA are referred to as "NAT HLA MNPS" approvals.

Pilots MUST NOT fly across the North Atlantic within NAT HLA airspace, nor at flight levels 290 to 410 inclusive anywhere within the NAT Region, unless they are in possession of the appropriate Approval(s) issued by the State of Registry or the State of the Operator. It should be noted that State Approvals for NAT MNPSA operations granted prior to 04 February 2016 will be valid for NAT HLA operations. Except that those Approvals issued prior to 01 January 2015 and based upon the earlier "6.3 NMs" MNPS standard, will not be valid beyond January 2020.

Although aircraft and pilots may fly above the NAT HLA without the requisite of a NAT HLA MNPS Approval, it is important that crews of such aircraft have both an understanding of the operational procedures and systems employed in the NAT HLA and specific knowledge of any active organized route structures.

Aircraft without NAT HLA MNPS or RVSM Approvals may, of course, also fly across the North Atlantic below FL285. However, due consideration must be given to the particular operating environment. Especially by pilots/operators of single and twin engine aircraft. Weather conditions can be harsh; there are limited VHF radio communications and ground-based navigation aids; and the terrain can be rugged and sparsely populated. International General Aviation (IGA) flights at these lower levels constitute a very small percentage of the overall NAT traffic but they account for the vast majority of Search and Rescue operations.

5.6.1   The North Atlantic Organised Track System (NAT OTS)

As a result of passenger demand, time zone differences and airport noise restrictions, much of the North Atlantic (NAT) air traffic contributes to two major alternating flows: a westbound flow departing Europe in the morning, and an eastbound flow departing North America in the evening. The effect of these flows is to concentrate most of the traffic uni-directionally, with peak westbound traffic crossing the 30W longitude between 1130 UTC and 1900 UTC and peak eastbound traffic crossing the 30W longitude between 0100 UTC and 0800 UTC.

Due to the constraints of large horizontal separation criteria and a limited economical height band (FL310–400) the airspace is congested at peak hours. In order to provide the best service to the bulk of the traffic, a system of organised tracks is constructed to accommodate as many flights as possible within the major flows on or close to their minimum time tracks and altitude profiles. Due to the energetic nature of the NAT weather patterns, including the presence of jet streams, consecutive eastbound and westbound minimum time tracks are seldom identical. The creation of a different organised track system is therefore necessary for each of the major flows. Separate organised track structures are published each day for eastbound and westbound flows. These track structures are referred to as the Organised Track System or OTS.

It should be appreciated, however, that use of OTS tracks is not mandatory. Currently about half of NAT flights utilise the OTS. Aircraft may fly on random routes which remain clear of the OTS or may fly on any route that joins or leaves an outer track of the OTS. There is also nothing to prevent an operator from planning a route which crosses the OTS. However, in this case, operators must be aware that whilst ATC will make every effort to clear random traffic across the OTS at published levels, re-routes or significant changes in flight level from those planned are very likely to be necessary during most of the OTS traffic periods.

Over the high seas, the NAT Region is primarily Class A airspace (at and above FL60) (See ICAO Doc. 7030 - NAT Regional Supplementary Procedures), in which Instrument Flight Rules (IFR) apply at all times. Throughout the NAT Region, below FL410, 1000 feet vertical separation is applied. However, airspace utilisation is under continual review, and within the HLA portion of NAT airspace, in addition to the strategic and tactical use of 'opposite direction' flight levels during peak flow periods the Mach Number Technique is applied.

Construction of the North Atlantic Organised Track System

The appropriate OAC constructs the OTS after determination of basic minimum time tracks; with due consideration of airlines' preferred routes and taking into account airspace restrictions such as danger areas and military airspace reservations. The night-time OTS is produced by Gander OAC and the day-time OTS by Shanwick OAC (Prestwick), each incorporating any requirement for tracks within the New York, Reykjavik, Bodø and Santa Maria Oceanic Control Areas (OCAs). OAC planners co-ordinate with adjacent OACs and domestic ATC agencies to ensure that the proposed system is viable. They also take into account the requirements of opposite direction traffic and ensure that sufficient track/flight level profiles are provided to satisfy anticipated traffic demand. The impact on domestic route structures and the serviceability of transition area radars and navaids are checked before the system is finalised.

5.6.2   *Interpretation of the NAT OTS Message*

5.5.6 Interpretation of the NAT OTS Message

The agreed OTS is promulgated by means of the NAT Track Message via the AFTN to all interested addressees. A typical time of publication of the day-time OTS is 2200 UTC and of the night-time OTS is 1400 UTC.

This message gives full details of the co-ordinates of the organised tracks as well as the flight levels that are expected to be in use on each track. In most cases there are also details of domestic entry and exit routings associated with individual tracks (e.g. NAR .....'). In the westbound (day-time) system the track most northerly, at its point of origin, is designated Track 'A' (Alpha) and the next most northerly track is designated Track 'B' (Bravo) etc. In the eastbound (night-time) system the most southerly track, at its point of origin, is designated Track 'Z' (Zulu) and the next most southerly track is designated Track 'Y' (Yankee), etc.. Examples of both eastbound and westbound systems and Track Messages are shown below in this Chapter.

The originating OAC identifies each NAT Track Message, within the Remarks section appended to the end of the NAT Track message, by means of a 3-digit Track Message Identification (TMI) number equivalent to the Julian calendar date on which that OTS is effective. For example, the OTS effective on February 1st will be identified by TMI 032. (The Julian calendar date is a simple progression of numbered days without reference to months, with numbering starting from the first day of the year.) If any subsequent NAT Track amendments affecting the entry/exit points, route of flight (co-ordinates) or flight level allocation are made, the whole NAT Track Message will be re-issued. The reason for this amendment will be shown in the Notes and a successive alphabetic character, i.e. 'A', then 'B', etc., will be added to the end of the TMI number (e.g. TMI 032A).

The remarks section is an important element of the Track Message. The Remarks may vary significantly from day to day. They include essential information that Shanwick or Gander need to bring to the attention of operators. These Remarks sometimes include details of special flight planning restrictions that may be in force. For example, with effect from 05 February 2015 Phase 2A of the NAT Data Link Mandate was implemented. From that date all NAT OTS Tracks in the revised altitude band FL350-390 are subject to the FANS equipage requirement. The Remarks section carries such notification. Also since the implementation of RLatSM Tials in December 2015 The Remarks section of the Track Message identifies two core OTS tracks and a ½ Degree spaced central track, on which to flight plan or fly in the DLM altitude band FL350-390 inclusive, aircraft must also be RNP 4 certified. The Remarks section of the Night-time Eastbound OTS Message also includes important information on appropriate clearance delivery frequency assignments.

The hours of validity of the two Organised Track Systems (OTS) are normally as follows:

> Day-time OTS 1130 UTC to 1900 UTC at 30°W
> Night-time OTS 0100 UTC to 0800 UTC at 30°W

Changes to these times can be negotiated between Gander and Shanwick OACs and the specific hours of validity for each OTS are indicated in the NAT Track Message. For flight planning, operators should take account of the times as specified in the relevant NAT Track Message(s). Tactical extensions to OTS validity times can also be agreed between OACs when required, but these should normally be transparent to operators.

Correct interpretation of the track message by airline dispatchers and aircrews is essential for both economy of operation and in minimising the possibility of misunderstanding leading to the use of incorrect track co-ordinates. Oceanic airspace outside the published OTS is available, subject to application of the appropriate separation criteria and NOTAM restrictions. It is possible to flight plan to join or leave an outer track of the OTS. If an operator wishes to file partly or wholly outside the OTS, knowledge of separation criteria, the forecast upper wind situation and correct interpretation of the NAT Track Message will assist in judging the feasibility of the planned route. When the anticipated volume of traffic does not warrant publication of all available flight levels on a particular track, ATC will publish only those levels required to meet traffic demand. However, the fact that a specific flight level is not published for a particular track does not necessarily mean that it cannot be made available if requested. Nevertheless, it should be recognised that the actual availability of an unpublished flight level for planning on an OTS Track may be subject to constraints of the NAT Flight Level Allocation Scheme (FLAS) agreed between NAT ATS Providers.

Example 1 — Example of Westbound NAT Track Message

```
FF CYZZWNAT
102151 EGGXZOZX
(NAT-1/3 TRACKS FLS 310/390 INCLUSIVE
JAN 14/1130Z TO JAN 14/1900Z
PART ONE OF THREE PARTS-
A PIKIL 57/20 58/30 59/40 58/50 DORYY
EAST LVLS NIL
WEST LVLS 310 320 330 340 350 360 370 380 390
EUR RTS WEST NIL
NAR -
B RESNO 56/20 57/30 58/40 57/50 HOIST
EAST LVLS NIL
WEST LVLS 310 320 330 340 350 360 370 380 390
EUR RTS WEST NIL
NAR -
C DOGAL 55/20 56/30 57/40 56/50 JANJO
EAST LVLS NIL
```

WEST LVLS 310 320 330 340 350 360 370 380 390
EUR RTS WEST NIL
NAR -
END OF PART ONE OF THREE PARTS)

FF CYZZWNAT
102151 EGGXZOZX
(NAT-2/3 TRACKS FLS 310/390 INCLUSIVE
JAN 14/1130Z TO JAN 14/1900Z
PART TWO OF THREE PARTS-
D NEBIN 5430/20 5530/30 5630/40 5530/50 KODIK
EAST LVLS NIL
WEST LVLS 350 360 370 380 390
EUR RTS WEST NIL
NAR -
E MALOT 54/20 55/30 56/40 55/50 LOMSI
EAST LVLS NIL
WEST LVLS 310 320 330 340 350 360 370 380 390
EUR RTS WEST NIL
NAR -
F LIMRI 53/20 54/30 55/40 54/50 NEEKO
EAST LVLS NIL
WEST LVLS 310 320 330 340 350 360 370 380 390
EUR RTS WEST NIL
NAR -
G BEDRA 49/20 48/30 45/40 43/50 42/60 DOVEY
EAST LVLS NIL
WEST LVLS 310 320 330 350 360 390
EUR RTS WEST NIL
NAR -
H ETIKI 48/15 48/20 47/30 44/40 42/50 41/60 JOBOC
EAST LVLS NIL
WEST LVLS 310 320 330 350 360 390
EUR RTS WEST REGHI
NAR -
END OF PART TWO OF THREE PARTS)
FF CYZZWNAT
102152 EGGXZOZX
(NAT-3/3 TRACKS FLS 310/390 INCLUSIVE
JAN 14/1130Z TO JAN 14/1900Z
PART THREE OF THREE PARTS-
J 41/50 39/60 MUNEY
EAST LVLS NIL
WEST LVLS 320 340 360 380
EUR RTS WEST
NAR -
REMARKS.
1. TMI IS 014 AND OPERATORS ARE REMINDED TO INCLUDE THE
TMI NUMBER AS PART OF THE OCEANIC CLEARANCE READ BACK.
2. ADS-C AND CPDLC MANDATED OTS ARE AS FOLLOWS
TRACK A 350 360 370 380 390
TRACK B 350 360 370 380 390
TRACK C 350 360 370 380 390
TRACK D 350 360 370 380 390
TRACK E 350 360 370 380 390
TRACK F 350 360 370 380 390
TRACK G 350 360 370 380 390
TRACK H 350 360 370 380 390

CRANFIELD AVIATION TRAINING SCHOOL LTD. PART-FCL GBR.ATO-0136
CATS INNOVATION CENTRE, LUTON, Bedfordshire LU2 8DL U.K.
5-14

www.catsaviation.com

Operational Procedures

END OF ADS-C AND CPDLC MANDATED OTS
3. RLATSM OTS LEVELS 350-390. RLATSM TRACKS AS FOLLOWS
TRACK C
TRACK D
TRACK E
END OF RLATSM OTS
4. FOR STRATEGIC LATERAL OFFSET AND CONTINGENCY PROCEDURES RELATED TO OPS
IN NAT FLOW PLEASE REFER TO THE NAT PROGRAMME COORDINATION WEB SITE AT
WWW.NAT PCO.ORG. SLOP SHOULD BE USED AS A STANDARD PROCEDURE AND NOT JUST
AS WEATHER TURBULENCE AVOIDANCE.
5. EIGHTY PERCENT OF GROSS NAVIGATION ERRORS RESULT FROM POOR COCKPIT
PROCEDURES. ALWAYS CARRY OUT PROPER WAY POINT CHECKS.
6. OPERATORS ARE REMINDED THAT THE CLEARANCE MAY
DIFFER FROM YOUR
FLIGHT PLAN, FLY YOUR CLEARANCE.
7. UK AIP. ENR 2.2.4.2 PARA 5.2 STATES THAT NAT
OPERATORS SHALL FILE PRM'S.
8. FLIGHTS REQUESTING WESTBOUND OCEANIC CLEARANCE VIA
ORCA DATALINK SHALL
INCLUDE IN THE RMK/ FIELD THE HIGHEST
ACCEPTABLE FLIGHT LEVEL WHICH CAN BE
MAINTAINED AT THE OAC ENTRY POINT.-
END OF PART THREE OF THREE PARTS ...

5.6.3 *Collaborative Decision Making Process*

Operators proposing to execute NAT crossings during the upcoming OTS period are encouraged to contribute to the OTS planning process. A comprehensive set of Collaborative Decision Making (CDM) procedures for NAT track design is now employed.

This CDM process commences with the Preferred Route Message (PRM) system, which has been used in the NAT Region for many years. To enable oceanic planners to take into consideration operators' preferred routes in the construction of the OTS, all NAT operators (both scheduled and non- scheduled) are urged to provide information by AFTN message to the appropriate OACs regarding the optimum tracks of any/all of their flights which are intended to operate during the upcoming peak traffic periods. Such information should be provided, in the correct format, as far in advance as possible, but not later than 1900 UTC for the following day-time OTS and 1000 UTC for the following night-time OTS. The requirement and schedule for submitting PRMs in respect of day-time westbound flights are specified in the UK AIP in Section ENR 2.2 at paragraph 3.5.2, and the addresses and formats for these westbound PRMs are specified in paragraph 3.24. The filing of night-time eastbound preferred routings is an element of the NavCanada Traffic Density Analyser (TDA) tool. Access to the TDA requires a password which can be requested from NAV CANADA Customer Service. The TDA can then be accessed directly from a computer server site

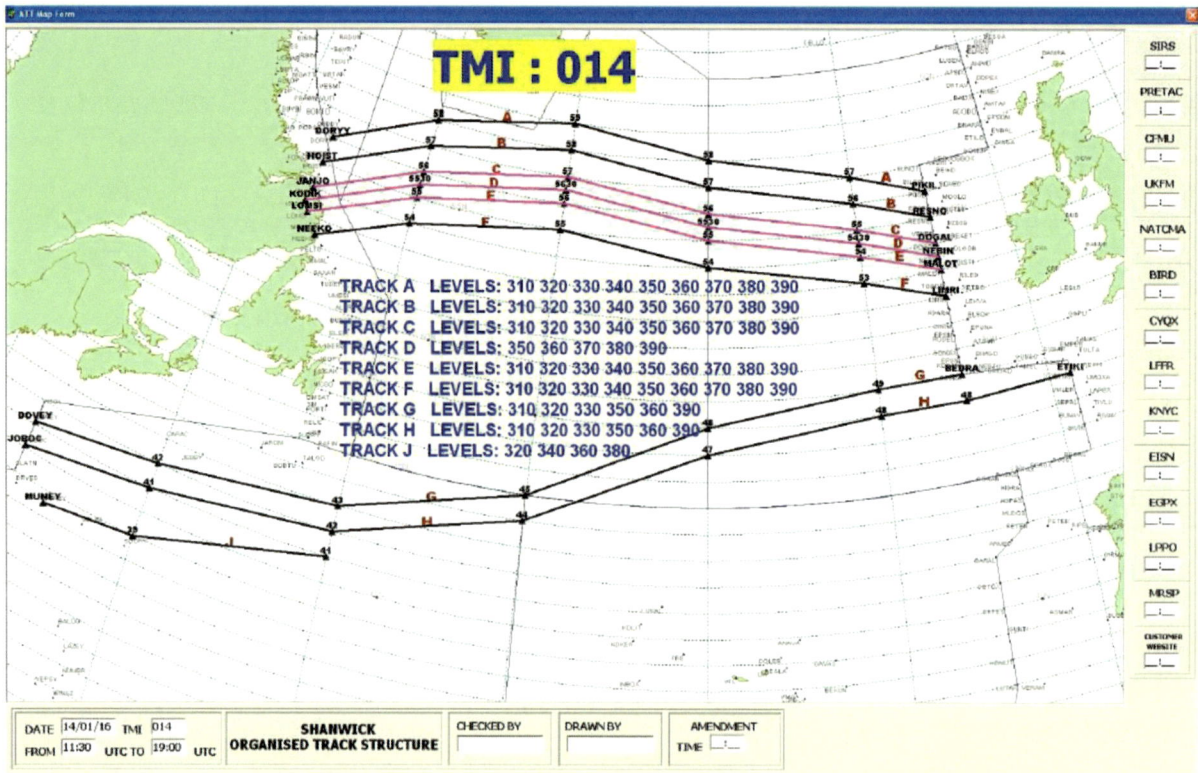

NAT Doc 007 V.2016-1 Figure 2 — Example of Day-Time Westbound NAT Organised Track System

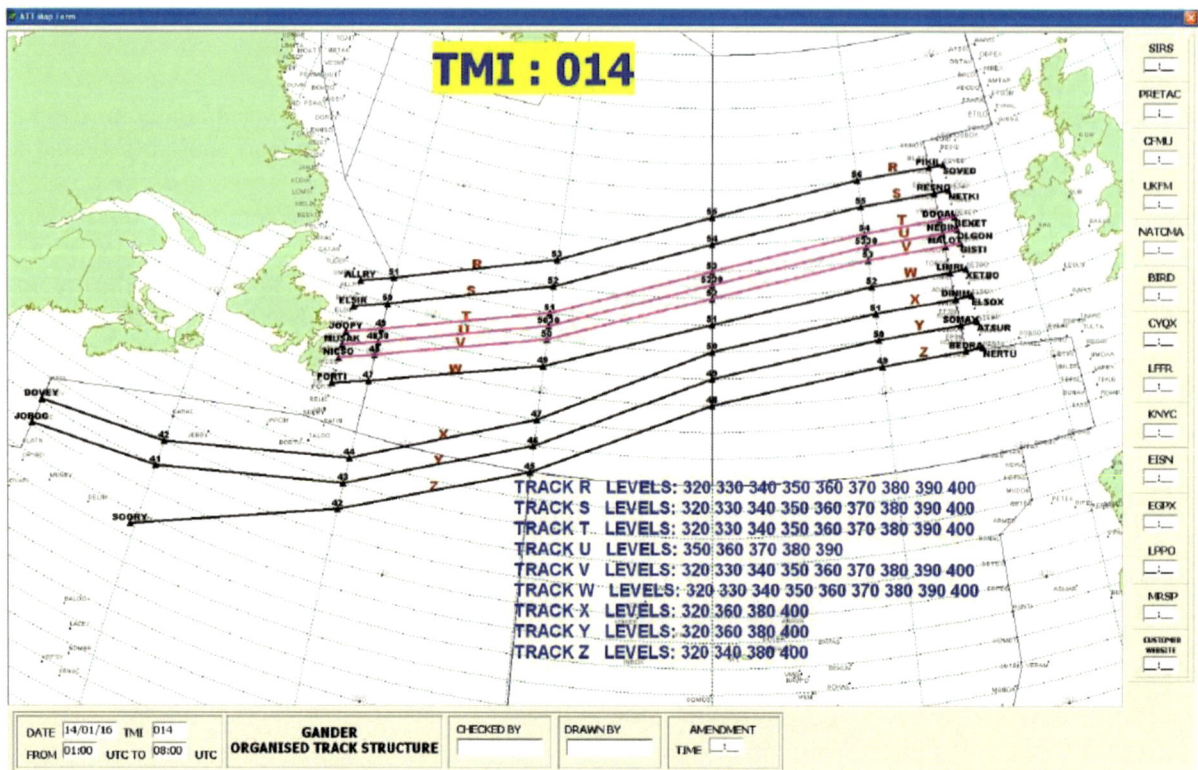

NAT Doc 007 V.2016-1 Figure 3 — Example of Night-Time Eastbound NAT Organised Track System

5.6.4 Flights Planning on the Organised Track System

4.2.1 If (and only if) the flight is planned to operate along the entire length of one of the organised tracks, from oceanic entry point to oceanic exit point, as detailed in the NAT Track Message, should the intended organised track be defined in Item 15 of the flight plan using the abbreviation 'NAT' followed by the code letter assigned to the track.

4.2.2 Flights wishing to join or leave an organised track at some intermediate point are considered to be random route aircraft and full route details must be specified in the flight plan. The track letter must not be used to abbreviate any portion of the route in these circumstances.

4.2.3 The planned Mach Number and flight level for the organised track should be specified at either the last domestic reporting point prior to oceanic airspace entry or the organised track commencement point.

4.2.4 Each point at which a change of Mach Number or flight level is planned must be specified by geographical co-ordinates in latitude and longitude or as a named waypoint and followed in each case by the next significant point..

4.2.5 For flights operating along the whole length of one of the organised tracks, estimates are only required for the commencement point of the track and Oceanic FIR boundaries.

4.2.6 Phase 2A of the NAT data Link Mandate was implemented 05 February 2015. In this phase all OTS tracks will be designated as DLM airspace at Flight Levels 350 to 390 inclusive. Aircraft/crews which are not DLM compliant are not permitted to plan/fly on, or to join or cross, any OTS track at these levels. For such aircraft, however, continuous climb or descent through the specified levels (FL350-390) may be available, on request, subject to traffic. When a "Split" westbound structure is published, although eastbound flights which are not DLM compliant may flight plan in the airspace between the branches of the Split OTS they should not plan any route which results in a partial back-tracking of a westbound OTS track.
Flights Planning on Random Route Segments in a Predominantly East - West Direction

4.2.7 For flights operating at or south of 70°N, the planned tracks shall normally be defined by significant points formed by the intersection of half or whole degrees of latitude with meridians spaced at intervals of 10 degrees from the Greenwich meridian to longitude 70°W.

4.2.8 For flights operating north of 70°N and at or south of 80°N, the planned tracks shall normally be defined by significant points formed by the intersection of parallels of latitude expressed in degrees and minutes with meridians normally spaced at intervals of 20 degrees from the Greenwich meridian to longitude 60°W, using the longitudes 000W, 020W, 040W and 060W.

4.2.9 For flights operating at or south of 80°N, the distance between significant points shall, as far as possible, not exceed one hour's flight time. Additional significant points should be established when deemed necessary due to aircraft speed or the angle at which the meridians are crossed, e.g.:

a) at intervals of 10 degrees of longitude (between 5°W and 65°W) for flights operating at or south of 70°N; and

b) at intervals of 20 degrees of longitude (between 10°W and 50°W) for flights operating north of 70°N and at or south of 80°N.

4.2.10 When the flight time between successive significant points referred to in 4.2.10 is less than 30 minutes, one of these points may be omitted.

4.2.11 For flights operating north of 80°N, the planned tracks shall normally be defined by significant points formed by the intersection of parallels of latitude expressed in degrees and minutes with meridians expressed in whole degrees. The distance between significant points shall normally equate to not less than 30 and not more than 60 minutes of flying time. (The 30 minute minimum was introduced in the Iceland AIP in 2014) .

Flights Planning on Random Routes in a Predominantly North - South Direction

Note: The ICAO Regional Supplementary Procedures for the NAT Region (Doc.7030) state that flights operating between North America and Europe shall generally be considered as operating in a predominantly east-west direction. However, flights planned between these two continents via the North Pole shall be considered as operating in a predominantly north-south direction.

4.2.12 For flights whose flight paths at or south of 80°N are predominantly oriented in a north- south direction, the planned tracks shall normally be defined by significant points formed by the intersection of whole degrees of longitude with specified parallels of latitude which are spaced at intervals of 5 degrees.

4.2.13 For flights operating north of 80°N, the planned tracks shall be defined by points of intersection of parallels of latitude expressed in degrees and minutes with meridians expressed in whole degrees. The distance between significant points shall normally equate to not less than 30 and not more than 60 minutes of flying time. (N.B.: This 30 minute minimum was introduced in the Iceland AIP in 2014).

Flights Planning to Enter or Leave the NAT Region via the North American Region

4.2.14 To provide for the safe and efficient management of flights to/from the NAT Region, a transition route system is established in the NAM Region (North American Routes - NARs). This system details particular domestic routings associated with each oceanic entry or landfall point. These routes are promulgated to expedite flight planning; reduce the complexity of route clearances and minimize the time spent in the route clearance delivery function. The NAR System is designed to accommodate major airports in North America where the volume of North Atlantic (NAT) traffic and route complexity dictate a need to meet these objectives. It consists of a series of pre-planned routes from/to coastal fixes and identified system airports. Most routes are divided into two portions —

Common Portion — that portion of the route between a specified coastal fix and specified Inland Navigation Fix (INF). (Note: Eastbound NARS only have a common portion).

Non-common Portion — that portion of the route between a specified INF and a system airport.

4.2.15 The routes are prefixed by the abbreviation "N," with the numbering for the common portions orientated geographically from south to north. The odd numbers have eastbound application while the even numbers apply to westbound. Following a one-to-three-digit number, an alpha character indicates the validation code and forms part of the route identifier. Validation codes are associated to amendments to the common routes only and not to non-common route portions.

4.2.16 The use of NARs is, however, not compulsory. The East-bound Track Message includes recommended NARs for access to each OTS Track. Since 01 October 2012 the West-bound Track Message routinely carries the annotation "NAR Nil" for each OTS Track. West-bound NAR details are still listed in the Canada Flight Supplement and Moncton FIR issues daily NOTAMS showing "recommended NARs". Operators may file them if desired. The only exception is in respect of West-bound OTS Tracks terminating at CARAC, JAROM or RAFIN for which a NAR must be filed. Here operators may file on any one of the destination appropriate NARs published from that relevant coastal fix.

4.2.17 Canadian Domestic route schemes and the US East Coast Link Routes are also published. Flights entering the NAM Region north of 65N must be planned in accordance with the NCA and/or NOROTS as appropriate. All of these linking structures are referenced in Chapter 3 of this Manual and account must be taken of any such routing restrictions when planning flights in this category.

Flights Planning to Operate Without Using HF Communications

4.2.18 The carriage of functioning HF communications is mandatory for flight in the Shanwick OCA, even if the pilot intends using alternative media for regular ATS air-ground contacts. Aircraft with only functioning VHF communications equipment should plan their route outside the Shanwick OCA and ensure that they remain within VHF coverage of appropriate ground stations throughout the flight. Theoretical VHF coverage charts are shown in Attachment 5. Such strict routing restriction may not apply in all NAT Oceanic Control

Areas. Some may permit the use of SATCOM Voice to substitute for or supplement HF communications. Details of communication requirements by individual NAT ATS Providers are published in State AIPs. However, it must also be recognised that the Safety Regulator of the operator may impose its own operational limitations on SATCOM Voice usage. Any operator intending to fly through NAT HLA Airspace without fully functional HF communications or wishing to use an alternative medium should ensure that it will meet the requirements of its State of Registry and those of all the relevant ATS Providers throughout the proposed route.

Flights Planning to Operate with a Single Functioning LRNS

4.2.19 Within the NAT HLA airspace only those routes identified with an asterisk in sub paragraphs (1), (2), (3) and (4) of paragraph 3.2.1 may be flight planned and flown by aircraft equipped with normal short-range navigation equipment (VOR, DME, ADF) and at least one approved fully operational LRNS. Specific State Approval for such NAT HLA operations must, however, be obtained from the State of the Operator or the State of Registry of the aircraft.
Flights Planning to Operate with Normal Short-Range Navigation Equipment Only.

4.2.20 Two routes providing links between Iceland and the ICAO EUR Region (G3 and G11) (see Chapter 3) are designated as special routes of short stage lengths where it is deemed that aircraft equipped with normal short-range navigation equipment can meet the NAT HLA track-keeping criteria. Nevertheless, State Approval for NAT HLA operations is still required in order to fly along these routes.

5.6.5 *Random routings during the operating times of the NAT OTS*

While it is not mandatory that flights must plan on one of the specified tracks appropriate to its direction of flight and at one of the assigned flight levels it is highly recommended. Operators who habitually plan flights on "random routes" will obviously pose a difficulty by wishing to fly across the published tracks at the same levels as the aircraft using the tracks. However, due to commercial requirements, company policy, or a destination lying outside the general group of destinations being served by aeroplanes using the NAT OTS system, a random route flight may be necessary. Such a route will not be refused clearance but, in the majority of cases, will be assigned an uneconomic flight level below those of the aeroplanes on the tracks or will be re-routed to avoid the track system altogether. Either of these will incur a large economic penalty.

5.6.5.1 *Selection of routes*

Notwithstanding the existence and operation of the NAT OTS system there will be times when flights will be operating in the opposite direction and causing a potential conflict. There are three scenarios for consideration here:

5.6.5.1.1 *Flights wholly outside the NAT OTS*

Flights operating wholly outside the NAT OTS obviously do not cause any conflict and therefore may file any route at any flight level the operator wishes.

5.6.5.1.2 *Flights joining the OTS from a point outside the NAT OTS*

Two typical examples of this situation are flights from the west coast of North America or Canada to Europe, and flights from Latin America or the Caribbean. In both these cases the departure point of these flights is well outside the westerly entry / exit points to the NAT OTS system.

In the Polar flight case the aeroplane is coming down from the far northern areas of Canada to a point approximately south of the southern tip of Greenland and then continuing in a south-easterly or easterly direction towards the European Continent.

Somewhere around 40°W these flights will come in contact with the northern extremities of the NAT OTS system. The recommendation from the Oceanic Control Authorities is that these flights join the NAT OTS at the closest major reporting point of the most northerly NAT OTS, at an appropriate flight level.

In the case of the flights from the Caribbean/Latin America the recommendation is that they plan to join the most southerly NAT OTS track at an appropriate major reporting point, and flight level.

5.6.5.1.3   *Flights leaving the NAT OTS*

Flights leaving Europe and heading towards the Caribbean / Latin America or towards western Canada/USA will, in most cases, due to the geographical location of their departure point, find it most efficient to commence their operation along the most southerly or northerly NAT OTS. They will then leave this route at an appropriate major reporting point when turning away towards their destination.

There are always exceptions and the exceptions in these cases are Polar Flights. On many occasions the Great Circle or optimum flight route "on the day" will take them across the NAT OTS system at a very early point in their oceanic crossing. In this case the recommended procedure is that they stay below the published flight levels of the NAT OTS (on their optimum route) until clear of the most northerly track.

The same applies to flights to the southern Caribbean islands, Latin America and South America where a low level transit is made until clear of the most southerly NAT OTS at which point the aeroplane then can climb without any restriction to its optimum cruising altitude.

5.6.5.1.4   *Cruising levels for random routings*

Any flights not operating within the NAT OTS system i.e. from published entry point to published exit point along the full length of the published track, are known as random routings

Therefore the selection of cruising levels for these flights must also be considered in three scenarios:

• Flights joining the NAT OTS at some point along that track (Polar / Caribbean) initially may plan/file at the most optimum flight level achievable in the initial stages of the cruise portion. Upon joining the NAT OTS the flight must then expect to conform to the published levels operational within the active track system.

• Flights leaving the NAT OTS must initially plan/file and operate at one of the published levels until the point where the flight departs out of the NAT OTS system whereupon it may cruise at whatever level is desirable or achievable at that point.

• Flights that fly north or south of the active NAT OTS system and maintain the minimum lateral separation may plan/file and operate at their own achievable optimum flight level(s) as these flights do not come in conflict with the traffic operating within the track system.

5.6.5.2 Compliance with MNPS

There is a discrete code letter that is used to advise the ATS authorities that the aeroplane operators, their flight crews and aeroplanes are suitably certificated to operate in particular types of designated airspace such as the MNPS. In the case of MNPS the code used and internationally recognised is the letter "X" entered in item 10 of the ATS flight plan.

5.6.6   *Aircraft separation within MNPSA*

Regarding aircraft separation within the MNPSA there are several situations which must be considered, the three essential ones being vertical, lateral and longitudinal.

5.6.6.1 Vertical separation

Since its inception vertical separation within the MNPS area including when the NAT OTS system is operative, has been 4000' between aircraft flying in the same direction and 2000' between aircraft flying in opposite directions on the same track. Separation is based on the standard barometric subscale setting of 1013.25 hPa.

5.6.6.1.1   *Reduced vertical separation minima (RVSM)*

Since 1997 a system of reduced vertical separation has been operational within the MNPS including the NAT OTS where traffic travelling in the same direction are now separated by only 2000' on the same track and by

1000' between opposite direction traffic. This is only available to aircraft that are suitably equipped and are RVSM approved between FL290 - FL410.

5.6.6.2 Lateral separation

Originally the lateral separation was 2° of latitude (120 NM) but, because of improved navigation equipment, this has now been reduced to 1° of latitude (60 NM).

5.6.6.3 Longitudinal separation

Minimum longitudinal separation between turbojet aircraft meeting the MNPS provided that a portion of the route of the aircraft is within, above, or below MNPS airspace shall be:

(1) 10 min, provided the Mach number technique is applied and whether in level, climbing or descending flight:

(a) the aircraft concerned have reported over a common point and follow the same track or continuously diverging tracks until some other form of separation is provided; and

(i) at least 10 min longitudinal separation exists at the point where the tracks diverge;

(ii) at least 5 min longitudinal separation will exist where 60 NM lateral separation is achieved; and

(iii) at least 60 NM lateral separation will be achieved at or before

- the next significant point (normally ten degrees of longitude along track(s) or
- within 90 min of the time the second aircraft passes the common point or
- within 60 NM of the common point, whichever is estimated to occur first; or

(b) If the aircraft have <u>not</u> reported over a common point, it is possible to ensure, by radar or other means approved by the State, that the appropriate time interval will exist at the common point from which they either follow the same track or continuously diverging tracks;

(2) Between 10 and 5 minutes inclusive, <u>only</u> when it is possible to ensure, by radar or other means approved by the State, that the required time interval exists and will exist at the common point. Additionally, the preceding aircraft is maintaining a greater Mach number than the following aircraft in accordance with the following:

9 min, if the preceding aircraft is Mach 0.02 faster than the following aircraft

8 min, if the preceding aircraft is Mach 0.03 faster than the following aircraft

7 min, if the preceding aircraft is Mach 0.04 faster than the following aircraft

6 min, if the preceding aircraft is Mach 0.05 faster than the following aircraft

5 min, if the preceding aircraft is Mach 0.06 faster than the following aircraft

Note:- When a preceding aircraft is maintaining a greater Mach number than the following aircraft, in accordance with the above, and the aircraft will follow continuously diverging tracks so that 60 NM lateral separation will be achieved by the next significant point, the requirement stated in (1)(a)(ii) above to have at least 5 minutes longitudinal separation where 60 NM lateral separation is achieved may be disregarded.

(3) 15 minutes between turbojet aircraft meeting the MNPS provided that a portion of the route of the aircraft is within, above, or below MNPS airspace but not covered by (1) or (2) above.

5.6.7   ATS Flight Plan – Cruising Speeds

As we have seen the longitudinal separation within the MNPSA and on the NAT OTS system is done by using the Mach number technique (MNT) and on the high-level airways system by use of the true airspeed. Therefore, we have again three separate sections of our flight through the MNPSA namely the initial cruise on airways over Europe or Canada/North America, the oceanic transit and the final cruise to destination again on airways.

To cater for this difference the flight plan is filed with regard to cruise airspeed information as follows:

- TAS expressed in knots – e.g. N0465
- Mach number in MNPS – e.g. M080
- TAS expressed in knots – e.g. N0470

A typical oceanic ATC flight plan for a B767 with regard to airspeed would be as follows:

N0465F310 WOD UG1 SHA/M080F350 NATA YQX/N0470F390 N162

This entry is decoded as – TAS 465 knots – FL310 – Woodley NDB – Airway UG1 – Shannon VOR - Then Speed Mach.80 - FL350 - NAT OTS Alpha – To Oceanic Exit Point Gander VOR – Then Speed 470 knots – Flight Level 390 – North American (Airways Route) No. 162 to Destination.

5.6.8   *Oceanic ATC clearance*

After obtaining and reading back an oceanic clearance, the pilot should monitor the forward estimate for oceanic entry and if this changes by 3 min or more should pass a revised estimate to ATC

As planned longitudinal spacing by the oceanic area control centre (OAC) is based solely on the estimated times over the oceanic entry fix or boundary, failure to adhere to this ETA amendment procedure may jeopardise planned separation between aircraft, thus resulting in re-clearance to a less economical track/flight level for the complete crossing; any such failure may also penalise following aircraft.

5.6.8.1 ATC System Loop Error

One of the most significant navigation errors associated with Oceanic Clearances is the ATC System Loop error. This is basically any error caused by a misunderstanding between the pilot and the controller regarding the assigned flight level, Mach number or route to be followed. Such errors can arise from incorrect interpretation of the NAT Track Message by dispatchers, errors in co-ordination between OACs, or misinterpretation of Oceanic Clearances or re-clearances by pilots. Errors of this nature, which are detected by ATC from pilot position reports, will normally be corrected. However, timely ATC intervention cannot always be guaranteed, especially as it may depend on HF communications.

5.6.9   *Clearance Read-Back*

Whether flying eastbound or westbound some form of "clearance read-back" must be observed, the content being dependent upon the type of oceanic clearance received.

In the event that the flight is cleared along the full length of its filed NAT OTS track then the read-back need only include; the NAT OTS track by "letter name", flight level, Mach No, and oceanic entry point

Example: Polaris 007 is cleared to the Boston Airport via track Delta Flight level 350, Mach .80 via 53N15W.

If however, the flight is re-routed onto a different track the read-back must include this new track name and the NAT track signal number

Example
Jumbo 456 is cleared to the Shannon Airport via track X-ray
Flight level 320, Mach .79, via Ramea track message number 135.

Quoting the track message number indicates to the oceanic controller that the flight knows the co-ordinates of the new, re-routed, track. If the flight is not in possession of the track message number then a full read-back of the co-ordinates of, in this case track X-ray is required.

If filed / cleared on a random route then the full co-ordinates must always be read-back

Example
Yellowstone 2311 is cleared to Antigua via random track 51N15W 49N20W 36N30W 28N40W 23N50W 18N60W Flight level 370, Mach .82.

5.7 Communications in MNPS airspace

Notwithstanding the development of VHF and satellite communications the primary method of air/ground communication in MNPS airspace is by way of high frequency long-range radio with its attendant potential for atmospheric interference. When out of range use 123.45 MHz.

During its transit through domestic airspace on either side of the MNPS area the flight will communicate with ATC by way of VHF. Once some 200 miles west of the Continent of Europe / British Isles and the Republic of Ireland communication must be by way of HF with contacts made to "Shanwick Aeradio" east of 030W. Communication will be with "Gander Radio" west of this meridian until within some 200 miles of the east of Canada or the United States of America where voice communication on VHF becomes possible again.

5.7.1 Position Reports

Position reports in MNPSA and on the NAT OTS, flying in an eastbound or westbound direction will be made at every 10° of longitude i.e. 50°W, 40°W, 30°W and 20°W, and the reverse in a westbound direction.

20 degrees longitude North of 70N
10 degrees longitude South of 70N

5.7.1.1 Contents of Position Reports

The position report must contain certain essential elements:

- The word position
- Flight number/company call sign
- Position by latitude and longitude
- Time overhead this position
- Flight level
- Mach number
- 'Next position" in latitude and longitude
- Estimated time of arrival at the next position
- The following position after the next position

Example
'Shanwick Aeradio – Trollair 007 – Position
Trollair 007 – Shanwick Aeradio pass your message
Shanwick Aeradio Trollair 007 was by 53N20W at time 1655 Flight Level 350 Mach decimal 80 Estimating 52N30W at time 1729 51N40W next.'

5.7.1.2 Copy of Position Reports

The six national authorities controlling traffic within the MNPS airspace share the HF communications network. Therefore, it is recommended but not mandatory that flights crossing the boundary points from one Oceanic control area to the next should ask that this position report be "copied" by or to the next controlling authority.

5.7.2 Meteorological Reports

Despite latter day satellite technology replacing the earlier Radio sonde balloon analyses, "spot" weather reports from aeroplanes are still considered to be valuable sources of this type of data. The information requested is the actual (spot) wind direction and speed value along with the temperature observed at the Reporting point position, plus any other significant weather in view or being experienced, such as cumulonimbus clouds/thunderstorms, lightning, or clear air turbulence and its degree of severity. Also if any significant vertical wind shear is being experienced. For flights operating within the MNPS area but outside the NAT OTS system there is a requirement that each position report include a weather report giving the "spot" wind and temperature at the flight level at the flight position. During the period of activity of the NAT

OTS one flight every hour is requested to send the weather report by ATC adding on to the end of the Oceanic clearance the words "send met reports'.

5.7.3 SELCAL

Check before NAT entry.

When using HF communications, pilots should maintain a listening watch on the assigned frequency, unless SELCAL is fitted, in which case they should ensure the following sequence of actions:

- provision of the SELCAL code in the flight plan; (any subsequent change of aircraft for a flight will require passing the new SELCAL information to the OAC);
- checking the operation of the SELCAL equipment, at or prior to entry into Oceanic airspace, with the appropriate aeradio station. (This SELCAL check must be completed prior to commencing SELCAL watch); and
- maintenance thereafter of a SELCAL watch.

5.7.4 VHF in MNPSA

The international VHF distress/emergency frequency is 121.5 Mhz and all aircraft transiting through the MNPS whether the NAT OTS is active or not must maintain a listening watch on this frequency.

To allow exchanges of operational information such as weather being encountered by aeroplanes without adding to the workload of the ground station, there is a second VHF frequency in place on 131.8 Mhz for this purpose within the MNPS area, for aircraft/aircraft communications.

5.7.5 Communications Failure

5.7.5.1 HF communications failure procedures

As we have seen in our text the communications scenario within the MNPS area is made up of a combination of VHF and HF communications. Additionally, while within the oceanic sectors, a listening watch must be maintained on the emergency VHF frequency, 121.5 Mhz, with the availability of a secondary operational frequency on 131.8 Mhz and 123.45 MHz as well. In the event of a complete loss of both HF radio communication units the initial procedure for the crew would be to make contact on 121.5 and request an alternative discrete frequency. If no such frequency was available, the crew should advise that position reports and communications would be made on 131.8 Mhz to an aircraft within VHF range. This aeroplane would relay the information to the OCA authorities by HF radio. In the unlikely event of there being no aeroplane within VHF range then position reports would be made on 121.5 Mhz or alternatively the flight would proceed according to its acknowledged oceanic clearance and resume contact when within VHF range.

5.7.5.1.1 Communications Failure Occurs Before Entry into NAT Oceanic Airspace

There are a number of contingency situations to be considered here.
(1) Loss of VHF communications ability.
(2) Loss of HF communications ability.
(3) Loss of both VHF and HF communications ability.

Regarding 1) above the prudent course of action here would be to follow the rules for loss of radio contact by selecting SSR code 7600 and diverting to the nearest available adequate airport to have the problem rectified. Additionally, attempts could be made to contact Shanwick Radio or Gander Radio or other appropriate HF radio station on one of the published North Atlantic Telephone / Radio Links (NARTEL) frequencies as dictated by the area of registration of the aeroplane and advising of the intentions of the commander. Finally, and this would be a "last resort", though legally correct the flight could proceed in accordance with its last acknowledged clearance and follow its assigned NAT OTS track, or Random route Mach No. and Flight Level according to its filed ATC flight plan. The SSR loss of radio contact code would advise the ATS and communications stations of the situation with regard to the radio failure. Regarding 2) above, the prudent but again not mandatory procedure would be for the flight to re-route on the published "radio routes" through Icelandic and Greenland airspace where there would be continuous VHF coverage available. Regarding 3) above, this forms part of 1) where the flight would continue according to its last acknowledged ATC clearance or failing this then according to its filed ATS flight plan while maintaining the radio failure SSR code.

5.7.5.1.2 *Communications failure before leaving MNPS Airspace*

Here we have a similar scenario to that considered in the previous section.

• Having crossed the Atlantic using the standard VHF communications system, any degradation in this equipment would obviously be picked up and dealt with by reverting to 121.5 Mhz or 131.8 Mhz, and if unable then proceeding according to its last acknowledged clearance and setting up the 7600 SSR code.

• Having changed back to the received ATS VHF frequency for contact with the domestic controllers should a VHF radio failure then occur it would be a matter of re-establishing contact on HF or following the loss of radio procedure and proceeding in accordance with the last received clearance.

5.7.6 *MNPS SSR Codes*

Regulatory procedures within MNPS require that aircraft set up an SSR code of A2000 from a point 30 min after entry into this airspace until a point 30 min prior to exiting

5.7.7 *Miscellaneous MNPS procedures*

5.7.7.1 *Step climb*

The request for a step climb to a higher level while within MNPSA can be made either at the end of the normal position report or as a separate request between compulsory position reporting points.

5.7.7.2 *Change of Mach Number.*

We have three situations here. The rules for longitudinal separation dictate that if the aeroplane is not able to maintain the Mach No. agreed in the oceanic clearance by 0.03 of that Mach No. then OCA must be advised and an achievable Mach No. agreed.

Secondly, should the commander wish to adjust the agreed Mach No. by more than 0.03 Mach due to weather or ambient conditions then any such change must be similarly agreed with OCA.

Finally, OCA may request the aeroplane to slow down or speed up due to potential conflicts arising in the longitudinal separation as the flight progresses.

5.7.7.3 *Alternative use of flight levels*

The semi-circular rule dictates that above FL 290 the eastbound levels will be 330, 370, and 410 and in the reverse direction 310, 350, and 390.

Due to the amount of aeroplanes transiting MNPS at peak times the necessity arose to utilise "eastbound" levels in a westbound direction and "westbound" levels in an eastbound direction in order to safely accommodate and separate the traffic existing. This is done by assigning and publishing the allocation of levels as part of the daily NAT OTS track messages.

On the example NAT OTS message (**Error! Reference source not found.**) track Alpha has flight levels 330 and 370 assigned.

It will also be seen on studying this attached NAT OTS track message that "even" flight levels are also assigned now. This is due to the introduction of Reduced Vertical Separation Minima (RVSM) between FL290 – FL410 (1000' separation).

5.7.8   *Navigation System Requirements and Failure Procedures*

In order to receive authority for unrestricted operations within the MNPS area an operator must ensure that the aeroplane types to be used are equipped with two independent long-range navigation systems such as Inertial Navigation System (INS), Inertial Reference System (IRS) or Global Positioning System (GPS)

These must be capable of providing the required navigational accuracy without any reference to ground stations or radar assistance.

5.7.8.1 System failures

In the event of a single long-range navigation system failure before takeoff then the takeoff should be delayed while the degraded system is repaired.

Suffering a single failure before the oceanic boundary is reached – then the commander should consider:

- landing at an adequate aerodrome or returning to the departure airfield,
- divert to and re-route via the radio route through Iceland and Greenland airspace,
- obtain a re-clearance above or below MNPS airspace.

5.7.8.1.1   *System failure within MNPS airspace*

Once in oceanic airspace continue to operate the aircraft in accordance with the oceanic clearance already received. However, OCA should be advised that total navigation system reliability has been reduced.

The commander should continually assess the prevailing circumstances with regard to the second navigation system's performance, distance remaining with MNPS airspace and any significant differences in across track, wind drift or significant changes in ground speed from those forecast on the operational flight plan experienced.

Consult with OCA with regard to possible mutually acceptable alternative actions such as:

- Climb
- Descend
- Re-route
- Turn back
- Turn out of the MNPS area
- Obtain clearance prior to any deviation from the original oceanic clearance.

5.7.8.1.2   *Failure of the remaining system after entering MNPS airspace*

- Notify ATC
- Make best use of the procedures specified for a "one system" failure while endeavouring to attempt visual sightings and the establishment of VHF contact on 121.5 Mhz or 131.8 Mhz to obtain any useful information.
- See and be seen – maintain an extra vigilant lookout for conflicting traffic and switch on all external lights.
- Broadcast any actions being seriously considered or taken on 121.5 Mhz and 131.8 Mhz.
- If no instructions are received directly from OCA or via a "relay" aircraft, and if operating within the NAT OTS the commander should consider leaving the NAT OTS. This should be achieved by making a 90 degree turn to the right or left as dictated by the existing circumstances and climbing or descending 500 feet to position the aeroplane between the tracks and between the flight levels being used.

5.7.9   *Gross Navigation Error (GNE)*

A gross navigation error is defined as a deviation from cleared track of 25 NM or more

These errors are normally detected by means of long range radar as aircraft leave oceanic airspace. 80% of such errors occur after re-routing. You should always carry out a waypoint cross check after loading the FMS with the re-route data.

5.7.10   *Diversion across the NAT OTS*

Should an event occur in flight necessitating a diversion to the nearest adequate en-route alternate while the aeroplane is flying within the NAT OTS, such diversionary action will necessitate a diversion across the NAT OTS system. As a consequence of the reduced vertical separation minima it will be necessary for the commander to initiate a descent to 500' below its cruising altitude and turn towards the alternate aerodrome to acquire a track separated by 30 NM from its assigned route or track. This action will put the aeroplane "between" the NAT OTS tracks on either side and between the flight levels being used. E.g. had the aeroplane initially been at 3500' with traffic above and below at 36000 and 34000' respectively the aeroplane will now be at 34500' between the tracks. A descent can now be continued to a level below the MNPS whereupon the flight can then route direct with no level restriction to the en-route alternate.

If below FL410 climb / descend 500'
If at FL410 climb 1000' / descend 500'
If above FL410 climb or descend 1000'

Self Assessment Test 04

1   The lateral limits of MNPS airspace extend from:
A)   The equator to the North pole
B)   The equator to 27°N
C)   27°N to the North pole
D)   0°W to 180°W

2   The vertical limits of MNPS airspace are:
A)   FL290 – FL410
B)   FL310 – FL390
C)   FL285 – FL420
D)   FL180 – FL420

3   To operate in MNPS airspace:
    1.   specific crew training must be given
    2.   authorisation by the State of Registry of the aircraft is required
    3.   cruising speed must be by reference to TAS
A)   1, 2, 3 correct
B)   1, 3 correct
C)   2, 3 correct
D)   1, 2 correct

4   The minimum vertical separation in RVSM airspace is:
A)   500'
B)   1000'
C)   2000'
D)   4000'

5   When operating south of 70°N significant points used to define east/west tracks should be:
A)   Spaced 5° of longitude apart
B)   Spaced 10° of longitude apart
C)   Spaced 20° of longitude apart
D)   Spaced 10° of latitude apart

6   When operating north of 70°N significant points used to define east/west tracks should be:
A)   Spaced 5° of longitude apart
B)   Spaced 10° of longitude apart
C)   Spaced 20° of longitude apart
D)   Spaced 10° of latitude apart

7   The westbound OTS operates during the period:
A)   0100 – 0800 UTC at 30°W
B)   1130 – 1800 UTC at 30°W
C)   0000 – 0700 UTC at 30°W
D)   1130 – 1800 UTC at 0°W

8   The eastbound OTS operates during the period:
A)   0100 – 0800 UTC at 30°W
B)   1130 – 1800 UTC at 30°W
C)   0000 – 0700 UTC at 30°W
D)   1130 – 1800 UTC at 0°W

9   In case of HF communications failure in MNPSA, the VHF air to air frequency to be used is:
A)   131.8 MHz
B)   121.8 MHz
C)   118.5 MHz
D)   128.8 MHz

10   Lateral separation in MNPS airspace is:
A)   120 NM
B)   90 NM
C)   60 NM
D)   30 NM

11   If flying to Europe in MNPS airspace at 0800 UTC you would be:
A)   Out of the OTS
B)   In the day time OTS
C)   In the night time OTS
D)   In random airspace

12   When using Mach number technique, what is the minimum separation between two aircraft which are travelling at the same speed?
A)   15 min
B)   10 min
C)   5 min
D)   More than 15 min

13   A minimum time route may be defined as:
Λ)   The route which uses the least amount of fuel
B)   A great circle route
C)   The route which has the closest diversion
D)   The shortest time between departure and destination whilst adhering to all ATC restrictions

14   A SELCAL check for entry into oceanic airspace should be completed:
A)   Before obtaining oceanic clearance
B)   Before the OCA boundary
C)   At or before the OCA boundary
D)   It is not required

15   What SSR code should an aircraft squawk once established within MNPS airspace?
A)   A1200
B)   A2000
C)   A7000
D)   C2000

Self Assessment Test 04 Answers

1	C
2	C
3	D
4	B
5	B
6	C
7	B
8	A
9	A
10	C
11	A
12	B
13	D
14	C
15	B

CRANFIELD AVIATION TRAINING SCHOOL LTD. PART-FCL GBR.ATO-0136
CATS INNOVATION CENTRE, LUTON, Bedfordshire LU2 8DL U.K.

www.catsaviation.com

5-30

Operational Procedures

CHAPTER 6

Special Operations Procedures and Hazards

6.1   Minimum Equipment List (MEL)

If some deviation from the aircraft certification requirements of a State was not permitted an aircraft could not be flown unless all of its systems and equipment were operative. However, experience has shown that some unserviceable items can be accepted (for short periods of time) as long as the operative systems and equipment provide for safe operations. The MEL lists systems and items of equipment which may be inoperative for certain flight conditions and allows for operation of aircraft under strict guidelines. The MEL is consulted prior to pushback / taxi. After pushback / taxi has commenced the Abnormal / Emergency procedures should be consulted.

The MEL is compiled by the operator but must be approved by the State of the Operator. It is based on a Master Minimum Equipment List (MMEL) which itself is established for the aircraft type by the organisation responsible for the type design (usually the manufacturer) in conjunction with State of Design (usually the State of the Manufacturer). Note that the MEL cannot be less restrictive than the MMEL

The MEL must be included in the Operations Manual and operators must:
• ensure that no flight is commenced unless the effect of multiple MEL inoperative items is analysed; and
• not operate aircraft other than in accordance with MEL unless permitted by the authority; in no circumstances will this permission be outside the constraints of the MMEL
In addition, the commander must operate the aircraft in accordance with the constraints of the MEL.
The Aeroplane Flight Manual is associated with the Certificate of Airworthiness and contains limitations within which the aircraft is considered to be airworthy; it also gives instructions and information necessary to the flight crew for the safe operation of the aircraft. The Flight Manual must be carried on board aircraft and contains operating limitations, procedures (normal and abnormal), performance data, etc.

6.2   Aeroplane De-icing / Anti-icing

Ice or snow on the critical surfaces forming part of the wings and tail areas can reduce aerodynamic lift by disturbing the airflow. Takeoff distance will be greater, stalling speed will be increased and climb gradient will be reduced. Ice and snow may get into the hinge areas and prevent sufficient control movement and in addition the total aeroplane weight may exceed that at which the power output of the engines is capable of "lifting" the aeroplane off the ground. Icing can be expected when the outside air temperature (OAT) is plus 10°C or below and there is visible moisture in the air such as fog, rain or wet snow, and the dewpoint is within 3°C of the OAT. When such conditions exist at the aerodrome and if there is visible ice or snow material deposits adhering to any of the control surfaces then these must be removed by the use of de icing fluid being sprayed at high pressure on to the surfaces.

6.2.1   Definitions

De-icing – a procedure by which frost, ice or snow is removed from an aircraft in order to provide clean surfaces

Anti-icing – a precautionary procedure which provides protection against the formation of frost or ice and accumulation of snow on the treated surfaces of an aircraft for a limited period of time

Hold-over time (HOT) – the estimated time period during which the de-icing / anti-icing fluid will be effective. It begins when final application of fluid commences and expires when the fluid applied loses its effectiveness

6.2.2   Operators responsibilities

There shall be no aircraft operations in icing conditions unless certified. An operator shall establish procedures to be followed when ground de-icing and anti-icing and related inspections of the aeroplane(s) are necessary. An operator shall not operate an aeroplane in expected or actual icing conditions unless it is certified and equipped to operate in icing conditions. An operator shall not operate an aeroplane in expected or actual icing conditions at night unless it is equipped with a means to illuminate or detect the formation of ice. Any illumination that is used must be of a type that will not cause glare or reflection that would handicap crewmembers in the performance of their duties.

6.2.3   Commander's responsibilities

A commander shall not commence takeoff unless the external surfaces are clear of any deposit, which might adversely affect the performance and/or controllability of the aeroplane, except as permitted in the AFM. A commander shall not commence a flight under known or expected icing conditions unless the aeroplane is certified and equipped to cope with such conditions. Rules and procedures for operating in ice and snow are available in either the Aeroplane Flight Manual, Operations Manual or Route Manual, depending upon what system the operator uses to disseminate this type of information to the flight crews.

6.2.4   De-icing / Anti-icing Ground Procedures

De-icing/anti-icing may be carried out by the use of fluids, hot air, sweeping or taxi through facilities. It is of utmost importance to realise that fluids used during ground de-icing are not intended for and do not provide ice protection during flight.
Where fluids are used the de-icing/anti-icing procedures may be:
• one step – carried out with anti-icing fluid where the fluid is used to deice the aircraft and remains on it to provide limited anti-ice capability; or
• two step – the first step (de-icing) is followed by a second step (anti-icing) as separate fluid application; the provides the maximum possible HOT
In cases where the HOT is exceeded an aircraft must be de-iced/anti-iced before it may be considered safe for further operation. Note however that takeoff with under-wing frost (caused by cold-soaked fuel) may be permitted within limits established by the aircraft manufacturer.
Two common types of fluid used the de-icing / anti-icing procedures are classified as Type I and Type II fluids. The Type I fluid is un-thickened, has limited HOT capability and forms a thin liquid film on the aircraft surface. Type II fluid is thickened, has a longer HOT capability than a Type I fluid and forms a thick gel-like film on the aircraft surface. The wind flow over the aircraft causes the fluid to progressively flow off during the takeoff.
De-icing fluids are normally heated water, a heated mixture of water and a Type I fluid or a heated mixture of water and a Type II fluid. These fluids should be applied heated.
Anti-icing fluids are normally a mixture of water and Type I fluid (should be heated and diluted for application), Type II fluid or a mixture of water and Type II fluid (normally applied cold but may also be heated). However cold application provides longer anti-ice protection.

The holdover time of fluids varies with atmospheric and other conditions as follows:
- Type II fluid gives a longer holdover time than Type I
- Holdover time reduced during intense weather conditions, strong winds, jet blasts
- Where fluid is mixed with water, the greater the water content the shorter the holdover time

Weather condition	Effect on hold over time
Hoar frost	Longest holdover time
Freezing fog	↓
Snow	↓
Freezing rain	↓
Rain on cold soaked surface	Shortest holdover time

6.3   Bird Strikes

This is a serious hazard at any aerodrome and is a difficult problem to solve. Birds will congregate in large numbers near wet or marshy ground, near rivers, woods, and harbours. Consequently aerodromes in close proximity to these areas will experience the presence of birds in large numbers. Birds take approximately 2 s to react to an oncoming aircraft approaching at a typical speed of 100 - 150 KT.

> Bird strikes are most frequent from the surface to 500 m
> The highest risk is between 0-150 m

Garbage disposal dumps (especially open tip) or any other source, such as the cargo / freight or refuse disposal areas at the aerodrome, can be another point for birds to gather.

6.3.1   Risk assessment of bird strikes

The risk assessment of bird strikes should be done through:
- The establishment of a national procedure for the recording and reporting of bird strikes to aeroplanes;
or
- The collection of information from aeroplane operators and aerodrome personnel on the presence of birds on or around the aerodrome.

ICAO has instituted a system known as the ICAO Bird Strike Information System (IBIS) designed to collect and disseminate information on bird strikes to aircraft. Information on the system is included in the manual on the ICAO Bird Strike Information System (IBIS). When a bird strike hazard is identified at an aerodrome, the appropriate authority should take action to decrease the number of birds constituting a potential hazard to aircraft operations by adopting measures for discouraging their presence on, or in the vicinity of, an aerodrome. Birds are least likely to congregate in areas of long grass. Guidance on effective measures for establishing whether or not birds, on or near an aerodrome, constitute a potential hazard to aircraft operations, and on methods for discouraging their presence, is given in the ICAO Airport Services Manual, Part 3.

> Referring back to the conditions that attract birds, garbage disposal dumps or any such other source attracting bird activity on, or in the vicinity of, an aerodrome should be eliminated or their establishment prevented, unless an appropriate study indicates that they are unlikely to create conditions conducive to a bird hazard problem

6.3.2   Sources of information on bird strikes

Aerodromes at which there is persistently a large bird population publish this information in that State's Aeronautical Information Publication (AIP) and on the enclosed Aeronautical Charts in that publication.

Additionally, further information will be provided in the Aeronautical Information Service Bulletins and NOTAMS.

6.3.3   *Reporting of bird strikes*

The commander of any aeroplane involved in a bird strike must report the occurrence to the Authority by use of the appropriate forms. The initial report may be made on the appropriate VHF radio frequency being used at the time of the incident.

6.4   *Noise Abatement*

6.4.1   *Operator's Responsibilities*

An operator shall establish operating procedures for noise abatement during instrument flight operations in compliance with ICAO PANS-OPS and takeoff climb procedures for noise abatement specified by the operator for any one aeroplane type should be the same for all aerodromes.

In general, noise abatement procedures can comprise any one or more of the following:

• Noise preferential runways – the initial departure and final approach paths are directed away from noise sensitive areas

• Noise preferential routes – the departure and final approach paths are directed away from noise sensitive areas

• Noise abatement takeoff or approach procedures – these minimise the overall exposure to noise on the ground and maintain the required level of safety.

6.4.2   *Noise preferential runways*

In general terms a noise preferential runway is one that permits aeroplanes to avoid noise-sensitive areas during the initial departure and final approach phases of flight.

> Runways should not normally be selected for preferential use for landing unless they are equipped with suitable glide path guidance, e.g. ILS, or visual approach slope indicator (VASI) system for operations in instrument meteorological conditions (IMC)

> Noise abatement should not be the determining factor in runway nomination under the following circumstances:
>
> • If the runway is not clear and dry, i.e. it is adversely affected by snow, slush, ice or water, or by mud, rubber, oil or other substances;
>
> • For landing in conditions when the ceiling is lower than 150 m (500') above aerodrome elevation, or for takeoff and landing when the horizontal visibility is less than 1.9 km;
>
> • When the cross-wind component, including gusts, exceeds 28 kph (15 KT);
>
> • When the tail-wind component, including gusts, exceeds 9 kph (5 KT);
>
> • When wind shear has been reported or forecast or when thunderstorms are expected to affect the approach or departure.

6.4.3   Noise preferential routes

Noise preferential routes are established to ensure that departing and arriving aeroplanes avoid over-flying noise-sensitive areas in the vicinity of the aerodrome as far as is practicable.

In establishing noise preferential routes:
- Turns during takeoff and climb should not be required unless:
- The aeroplane has reached (and can maintain throughout the turn) a height of not less than 150 m (500') above terrain and the highest obstacles under the flight path.
- The bank angle for turns after takeoff is limited to 15° except where adequate provision is made for an acceleration phase permitting attainment of safe speeds for bank angles greater than 15°. (PANS-OPS permits turns after takeoff at 120 m (400') and obstacle clearance of at least 90m (300') during the aeroplane's turn. These are minimum requirements for noise abatement purposes.)
- No turns should be required coincident with a reduction of power associated with a noise abatement procedure
- Sufficient navigational guidance should be provided to permit aeroplanes to adhere to the designated route

PANS-OPS also states that the aeroplane should not be diverted from its assigned noise preferential route unless:
- In the case of the departure, it has attained an altitude or height which represents the upper limit for noise abatement procedures; or
- It is necessary for the safety of the aeroplane (e.g. avoidance of severe weather)

One of the main ways whereby the airport authorities guide the operators to observe local noise abatement procedures is the use of pre-determined "low-noise level" departure and arrival routes. These are adjustments to the original instrument departure and arrival routes known as standard instrument departure (SID) procedures, and standard instrument arrival route (STAR) procedures. In establishing these noise preferential routes the safety criteria of the SID and the STAR regarding obstacle clearance climb gradients and other factors, will be taken into full consideration. Where noise preferential routes are established, these routes when interfaced with the SID and STAR routes should be compatible.

6.4.4   Aeroplane Operating Procedures

This section provides the aeroplane operating procedures to be taken into account when developing noise abatement takeoff and climb procedures. Two examples of noise abatement climb procedures are given, one which alleviates noise close to the aerodrome, Noise Abatement Departure Procedure 1 (NADP 1) and one which alleviates noise more distant from the aerodrome, Noise Abatement Departure Procedure 2 (NADP 2). The State in which the aerodrome is located is responsible for ensuring that noise abatement objectives are specified by aerodrome operators and the noise abatement objectives should enable operators to develop safe procedures in accordance with ICAO Procedures for Air Navigation Services – Aircraft Operations (PANS-OPS). The State of the Operator is responsible for the approval of safe flight procedures, developed by the aircraft operators.

6.4.4.1 Operational Limitations

Noise abatement procedures based on ICAO PANS-OPS should not be selected if noise benefits cannot be expected. Noise abatement climb procedures which do not comply with the minimum requirements of the procedures in the relevant section of ICAO PANS-OPS shall not be approved by the State of the Operator. The pilot-in-command has the authority to decide not to execute a noise abatement departure procedure if conditions preclude the safe execution of the procedure.

6.4.4.1.1   *Takeoff*

Noise abatement procedures in the form of reduced power takeoff should not be required in adverse operating conditions such as:

a) if the runway surface conditions are adversely affected (e.g. snow, slush, ice or water, or by mud, rubber, oil or other substances);

b) when the horizontal visibility is less than 1.9 km (1 NM);

c) when the cross-wind component, including gusts, exceeds 28 kph (15 KT);

d) when the tail-wind component, including gusts, exceeds 9 kph (5 KT); and

e) when wind shear has been reported or forecast or when thunderstorms are expected to affect the approach or departure.

Note: Some operating manuals (or Flight Manuals) may impose restrictions to the use of reduced takeoff power while engine anti-ice systems are operating.

6.4.4.1.2   *Departure Climb*

Aeroplane operating procedures for the departure climb shall ensure that the safety of flight operations is maintained while minimizing exposure to noise on the ground. The following requirements need to be satisfied:

a) Noise abatement procedures shall not be executed below a height of 240 m (800') above aerodrome elevation;

b) The noise abatement procedure specified by an Operator for any one aeroplane type should be the same for all aerodromes;

c) To minimize the impact on training while maintaining some flexibility to address variations in the location of noise sensitive areas, sufficient commonality shall exist between the departure procedures specified by the Operator. There will be no more than two departure procedures to be used by one Operator for an aeroplane type, one of which should be identified as the normal departure procedure, and the other as the noise abatement departure procedure;

d) Normal departure procedures typically include general noise reduction measures which encompass one of the two examples shown in Appendix A - Noise Abatement Departure Climb Guidance;

e) Conduct of noise abatement climb procedures is secondary to the satisfaction of obstacle requirements;

f) All necessary obstacle data shall be made available to the operator and the Procedure Design Gradient shall be observed;

g) The power settings to be used subsequent to the failure or shut-down of an engine or any other apparent loss of performance, at any stage in the takeoff or noise abatement climb are at the discretion of the pilot-in-command and noise abatement considerations no longer apply.

h) The minimum level of thrust for the flap/slat configuration, after power reduction, is defined as the lesser of the maximum climb power and that level necessary to maintain the specified engine inoperative minimum net climb gradient (1.2%, 1.5% or 1.7% for 2, 3 or 4 engines) for the flaps/slats configuration of the aeroplane, in the event of loss of an engine, without a throttle position increase by the pilot in command. The minimum thrust level varies as a function of flap setting, altitude, and aeroplane weight, therefore, this information must be provided in the aircraft operating manual;

i) The power settings specified in the aircraft operating manual are to take account of the need for engine anti-icing when applicable;

j) Noise abatement climb procedures are not to be used in conditions where windshear warnings are extant or the presence of windshear or downburst activity is suspected; and

k) The maximum acceptable body angle specified for an aeroplane type shall not be exceeded.

A noise abatement procedure shall be developed for each aeroplane type by the operator (with advice from the aeroplane manufacturer, as needed), and agreed to by the State of the Operator. The departure procedure to be used on a specific departure should satisfy the noise objectives of the State of the aerodrome.

6.4.4.2 Noise Abatement Departure Climb Guidance

Aeroplane operating procedures for the takeoff climb shall ensure that the necessary safety of flight operations is maintained whilst minimising exposure to noise on the ground. The following two examples of operating procedures for the climb have been developed as guidance.

> The first procedure (NADP 1) is intended to provide noise reduction for noise sensitive areas in close proximity to the departure end of the runway. The second procedure (NADP 2) provides noise reduction to areas more distant from the runway end

The two procedures differ by whether the acceleration segment for flap/slat retraction is initiated prior to reaching the maximum prescribed height or initiated at the maximum prescribed height. To ensure optimum acceleration performance, thrust reduction may be initiated at an intermediate flap setting.

Note 1: For both procedures, intermediate flap transitions required for specific performance related issues may be initiated prior to the prescribed minimum height; however, no power reduction can be initiated prior to attaining the prescribed minimum altitude.
Note 2: The indicated airspeed for the initial climb portion of the departure prior to the acceleration segment is to be flown at a climb speed of V2 + 20 to 40 kph (10 to 20 KT).

6.4.4.2.1   *Example of a procedure alleviating noise close to the aerodrome (NADP 1)*

This procedure involves a power reduction at or above the prescribed minimum altitude and delaying flap/slat retraction until the prescribed maximum altitude is attained. At the prescribed maximum altitude, accelerate and retract flaps / slats on schedule while maintaining a positive rate of climb and complete the transition to normal en-route climb speed.

The noise abatement procedure is not to be initiated at less than 240 m (800') above aerodrome level.

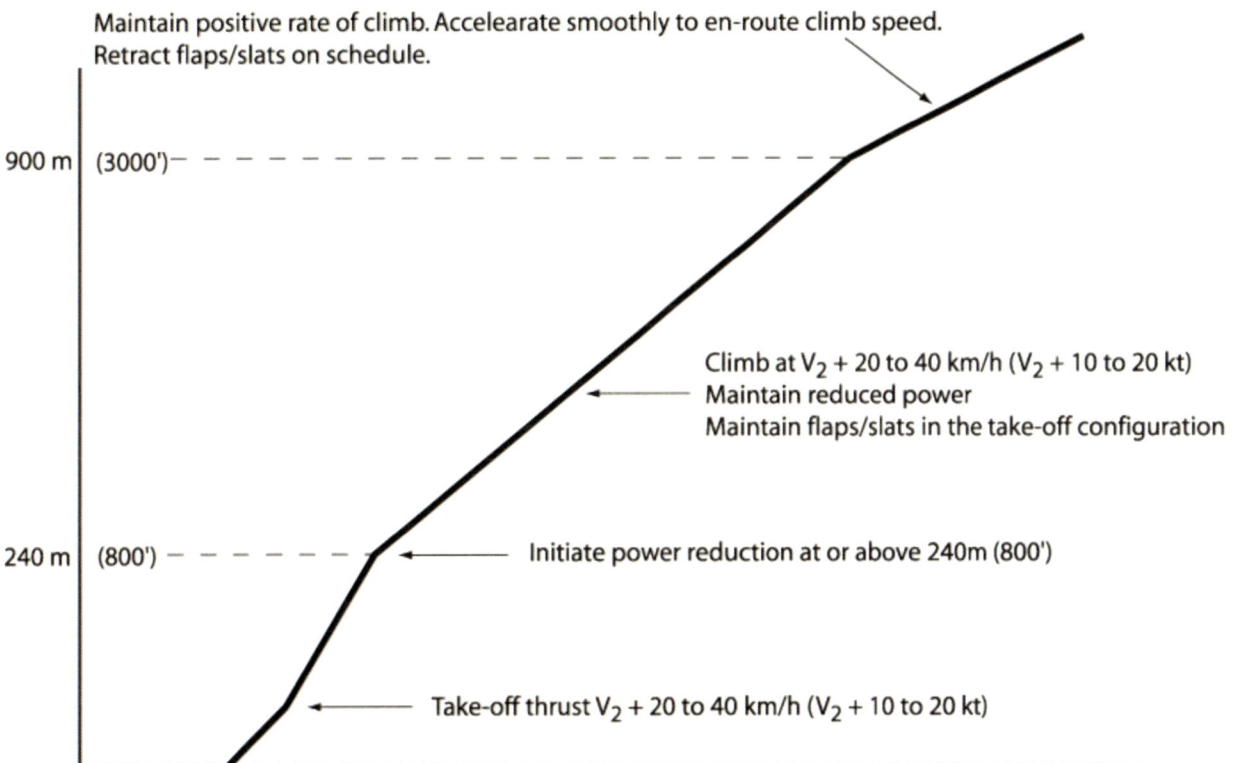

Figure 6.1 NADP 1

The initial climbing speed to the noise abatement initiation point shall not be less than V_2 + 20 kph (10 KT).
- on reaching an altitude at or above 240 m (800') above aerodrome level, adjust and maintain engine power / thrust in accordance with the noise abatement power/thrust schedule provided in the aircraft operating manual. Maintain a climb speed of V_2 plus 20 to 40 kph (10 to 20 KT) with flaps and slats in the takeoff configuration;
- at no more than an altitude equivalent to 900 m (3000') above aerodrome level, while maintaining a positive rate of climb, accelerate and retract flaps/slats on schedule; and
- at 900 m (3000') above aerodrome level, accelerate to en-route climb speed.

6.4.4.2.2 *Example of a procedure alleviating noise more distant from the aerodrome (NADP 2)*

This procedure involves initiation of flap / slat retraction on reaching the minimum prescribed altitude. The flaps / slats are to be retracted on schedule while maintaining a positive rate of climb. The power reduction is to be performed with the initiation of the first flap / slat retraction or when the zero flap / slat configuration is attained. At the prescribed altitude, complete the transition to normal en-route climb procedures.

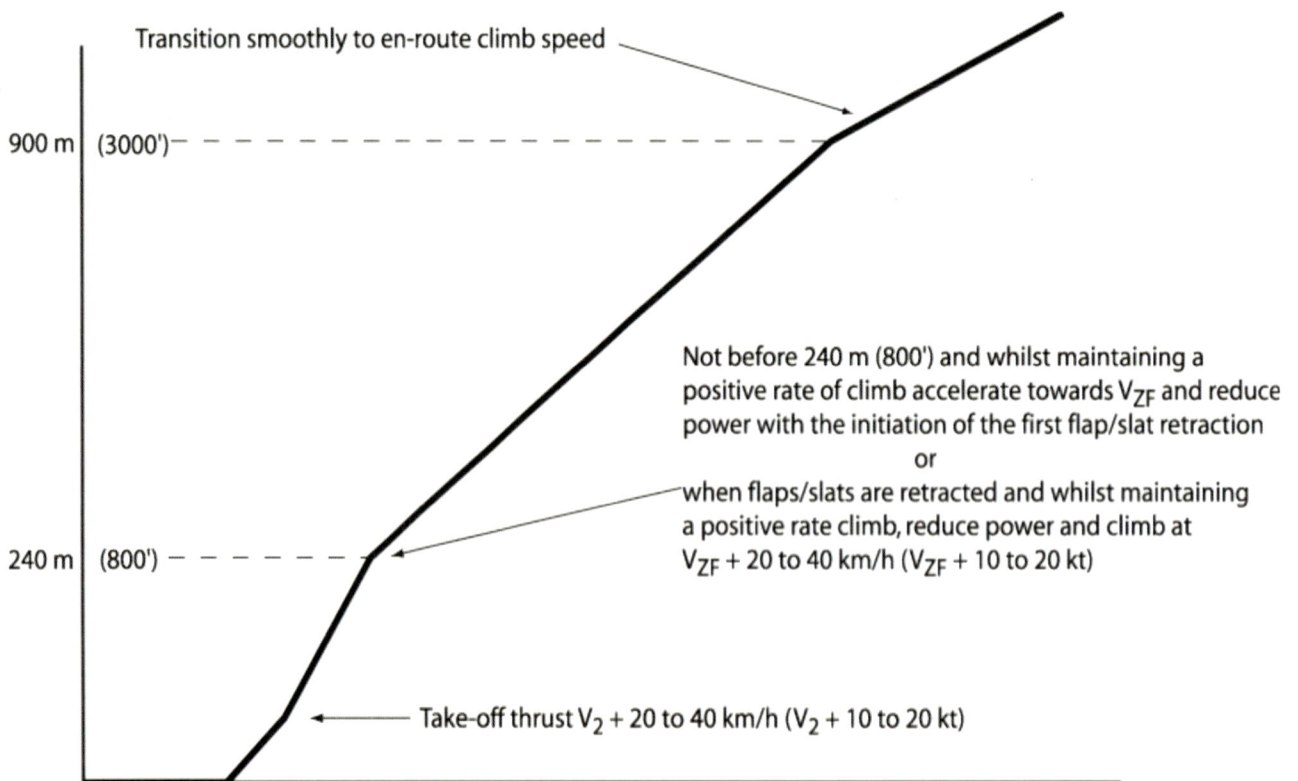

Transition smoothly to en-route climb speed

900 m (3000')

Not before 240 m (800') and whilst maintaining a positive rate of climb accelerate towards V_{ZF} and reduce power with the initiation of the first flap/slat retraction

or

when flaps/slats are retracted and whilst maintaining a positive rate climb, reduce power and climb at V_{ZF} + 20 to 40 km/h (V_{ZF} + 10 to 20 kt)

240 m (800')

Take-off thrust V_2 + 20 to 40 km/h (V_2 + 10 to 20 kt)

Figure 6.2 NADP 2

The noise abatement procedure is not to be initiated at less than 240 m (800') above aerodrome level.
The initial climbing speed to the noise abatement initiation point is V_2 + 20 to 40 kph (10 to 20 KT).
On reaching an altitude equivalent to at least 240 m (800') above aerodrome level, decrease aircraft body angle/angle of pitch whilst maintaining a positive rate of climb, accelerate towards V_{ZF} and either:
a) reduce power with the initiation of the first flaps/slats retraction; or
b) reduce power after flaps/slats retraction.
Maintain a positive rate of climb and accelerate to and maintain a climb speed of V_{ZF} + 20 to 40 kph (10 to 20 KT) to 900 m (3000') above aerodrome level.
On reaching 900 m (3000') above aerodrome level, transition to normal en-route climb speed.

6.4.4.3 Noise Abatement Approach Procedures

- The minimum range from the threshold at which the final landing configuration takes precedence over noise abatement is 5 NM, or after passing the outer marker, whichever is earlier;
- Excessive rates of descent are not required;
- Glide path / approach angles should not require an approach to be made:
- above the ILS glide path angle
- above the glide path angle of the VASI system
- above the normal PAR final approach angle
- above 3° except where the ILS glide path angle is greater than 3°
- Pilots should not be required to turn on to final approach at distances less than those which:
- in visual operations, will permit an adequate period of stabilised flight on final approach before crossing the threshold
- in instrument approaches, will permit the aircraft to be established on final prior to interception of the glide path

Continuous descent and reduced power / reduced drag techniques (or combination of both) may be used. These are achieved by delaying flap and gear extension until the final stages of the approach; speeds therefore tend to be higher than normal.

Compliance with noise abatement approach procedures is not required when:
- the runway is not clear and dry (i.e. adversely affected by snow, slush, ice, water, mud, rubber, oil);
- ceiling < 500' above aerodrome elevation or horizontal visibility < 1.9 km
- crosswind, including gusts > 15 KT
- tailwind, including gusts > 5 KT
- windshear reported or forecast or when adverse weather conditions are expected to affect the approach

6.4.4.4 Noise Abatement Landing Procedures

Noise abatement procedures shall not prohibit the use of reverse thrust during landing

A displaced threshold may be used as a noise abatement measure provided aircraft noise is significantly reduced by displacing the threshold and the runway length remaining is safe and sufficient for all operating requirements.

6.5   Fire and Smoke

For most flight deck crewmembers of modern-day commercial aeroplanes the only area of concern is the risk of a cabin fire while en route, particularly with regards to ETOPS operations. A number of aeroplanes have been lost with many fatalities from this cause. Consequently many operators have now completely banned smoking on all their flights.

'Fire and Smoke", (and how to deal with them), is a mandatory training qualification requirement for all flight deck and cabin crewmembers. It forms an important part of their initial training, and is regularly re-emphasised in subsequent Recurrent/Refresher training seminars.

We have two elements of this topic to review:
- On the ground with regard to what are currently known as the "Emergency Services' at the aerodrome
- On board the aeroplane with the crew

6.5.1 Nature of Fire

Fire is rapid oxidisation (i.e. heat combined with oxygen) which corrodes the combustible material that acts as a fuel. Fire normally produces a number of visible and invisible by-products namely:
- Flames from the volatile gases
- Glowing carbon residues. (Soot and embers)
- Gases (both toxic and non toxic)

Fire needs 3 elements: air (oxygen), fuel and ignition. Take away one of these elements by blanketing the air, removing the ignition, or removing the fuel and the fire will be automatically extinguished.

The most common methods of controlling or extinguishing fire endeavour to initially blanket the flames to remove the supply of oxygen. Subsequent steps are to reduce the temperature so that risk of further ignition is reduced. Europe uses the European Standard "Classification of fires" (EN 2:1992, incorporating amendment A1:2004). Fires are classified as follows:

Class	Combustible Material
A	Solid Fuel - Carpets, coats, seats, paper, etc.
B	Liquid Fuel - Kerosene, Avgas, petrol, spirits (Duty Free), etc.
C	Gaseous Fuel - Propane, butane (Camping Gaz), etc.
D	Metal - Aircraft alloy wheels etc.
E	Electrical - Wiring insulation, (when current is OFF fire may continue as Class A fire)
F	Fats and oils – cooking fat fires

6.5.2 Rescue & Fire fighting Categories

Aerodrome rescue and fire fighting (RFF) capabilities are divided into "categories" from Category 1, the least, to Category 10, the most capable. The level of protection normally available at an aerodrome is expressed in these terms and in accordance with the types and amounts of extinguishing agents available at the aerodrome to support the types of aeroplanes that normally frequent it. The level of protection at an aerodrome for rescue and fire fighting shall also be appropriate to the aerodrome category determined.

The determination of this category is usually based upon the longest, in fuselage length, of the aeroplane(s) using that aerodrome, the width of the fuselage(s) and the frequency of their movements at the aerodrome

Aerodrome category	Aeroplane overall length (metres)	Maximum Fuselage Width (metres)
1	0 m up to but not including 9 m	2
2	9m up to but not including 12 m	2
3	12 m up to but not including 18 m	3
4	18 m up to but not including 24 m	4
5	24 m up to but not including 28 m	4
6	28 m up to but not including 39 m	5
7	39 m up to but not including 49 m	5
8	49 m up to but not including 61 m	7
9	61 m up to but not including 76 m	7
10	76 m up to but not including 90 m	8

6.5.3 Extinguishing agents

As we above, combustible materials are many and varied and the type of fire they produce is equally variable. An essential component of effective fire fighting is the correct selection of the agent(s) required to extinguish particular types of fire. The use of foam provides an effective and rapid coverage of a fire and excludes air from the flames. It does not react badly with any fire and is therefore widely used as a *first line of attack* on the fire. However its effectiveness can be considerably enhanced by the use of other extinguishing agents. These complimentary extinguishing agent(s) should be:

- Carbon dioxide (CO_2);
- Dry chemical powders;
- Halogenated hydrocarbons (halons); and
- Combinations of these agents

When selecting dry chemical powders for use with foam care must be exercised to ensure compatibility. Dry chemical powders and halons are normally considered more efficient than CO_2 for aircraft rescue and fire fighting operations. Airfield crash services may also use fine wide sprays of water.

6.5.4 Fire extinguishers

The following table summarises the types of extinguisher most likely to be available on an aeroplane and illustrates the effect and the type of fire for which each is suitable.

Type	Colour code	Effect on Fire	Most Efficient on Classes	Disadvantages
Water	Red	Cools / Blankets	A	Limited use without experience and training
Foam	Red with a cream panel		A, B	
CO_2	Red with a black panel	Blankets / Cools	B, E	Asphyxiant
Dry powder	Red with a blue panel	Blankets / Cools	A, B, C, E	Incapacitation and reduced visibility
Class D powder	Red with a blue panel		D	
Halon 1211 / BCF		Blankets flames	A, B, E	Irritant / toxic, needs follow up with water

Fire extinguisher classification according to European Standard EN 3.

All types of aeroplanes carry some form or type of fire extinguisher. A basic pilot trainer such as the Piper PA38 - Tomahawk carries a fire extinguisher (normally BCF) located in the small baggage compartment behind the two pilots' seats. A large aeroplane will have a more comprehensive complement of extinguishers, each type of aeroplane having its own specific number and types. The location and types of extinguisher for each aeroplane will be found in the Aircraft Operating Manual.

6.5.4.1 EASA Requirements

6.5.4.1.1 Fire Extinguishers

An operator shall not operate an aeroplane unless hand fire extinguishers are provided for use in crew, passenger and, as applicable, cargo compartments and galleys in accordance with the following:

- The type and quantity of extinguishing agent must be suitable for the kinds of fires likely to occur in the compartment where the extinguisher is intended to be used and, for personnel compartments, must minimise the hazard of toxic gas concentration;
- At least one hand fire extinguisher, containing Halon 1211 or equivalent as the extinguishing agent, must be conveniently located on the flight deck for use by the flight crew;
- At least one hand fire extinguisher must be located in, or readily accessible for use in, each galley not located on the main passenger deck;
- At least one readily accessible hand fire extinguisher must be available for use in each Class A or Class B cargo or baggage compartment and in each Class E cargo compartment that is accessible to crew members in flight; and

- At least the following number of hand fire extinguishers must be conveniently located in the passenger compartment(s):

Maximum approved passenger seating configuration	Number of Extinguishers
7 to 30	1
31 to 60	2
61 to 200	3
201 to 300	4
301 to 400	5
401 to 500	6
501 to 600	7
601 or more	8

When two or more extinguishers are required, they must be evenly distributed in the passenger compartment.

- At least one of the required fire extinguishers located in the passenger compartment of an aeroplane with a maximum approved passenger seating configuration of at least 31, and not more than 60, and at least two of the fire extinguishers located in the passenger compartment of an aeroplane with a maximum approved passenger seating configuration of 61 or more must contain Halon 1211 or equivalent as the extinguishing agent.

6.5.4.1.2   *Crash Axes and Crowbars*

An operator shall not operate an aeroplane with a maximum certificated takeoff mass exceeding 5700 kg or having a maximum approved passenger seating configuration of more than 9 seats unless it is equipped with at least one crash axe or crowbar located on the flight deck. If the maximum approved passenger seating configuration is more than 200 an additional crash axe or crowbar must be carried and located in or near the most rearward galley area

Crash axes and crowbars located in the passenger compartment must not be visible to passengers.

6.5.4.1.3   *Protective Breathing Equipment*

An operator shall not operate a pressurised aeroplane or, after 1 April 2000, an unpressurised aeroplane with a maximum certificated takeoff mass exceeding 5700 kg or having a maximum approved seating configuration of more than 19 seats unless:

(1) It has equipment to protect the eyes, nose and mouth of each flight crew member while on flight deck duty and to provide oxygen for a period of not less than 15 min. The supplemental oxygen required by OPS 1 may provide the supply for Protective Breathing Equipment (PBE). In addition, when the flight crew is more than one and a cabin crew member is not carried, portable PBE must be carried to protect the eyes, nose and mouth of one member of the flight crew and to provide breathing gas for a period of not less than 15 minutes; and

(2) It has sufficient portable PBE to protect the eyes, nose and mouth of all required cabin crew members and to provide breathing gas for a period of not less than 15 min.

PBE intended for flight crew use must be conveniently located on the flight deck and be easily accessible for immediate use by each required flight crew member at their assigned duty station.

PBE intended for cabin crew use must be installed adjacent to each required cabin crew member duty station. An additional, easily accessible portable PBE must be provided and located at or adjacent to the hand fire extinguishers except that, where the fire extinguisher is located inside a cargo compartment, the PBE must be stowed outside but adjacent to the entrance to that compartment.

PBE while in use must not prevent communication where required.

6.5.5 Fire detection and protection Systems

Different types of aeroplanes have different types of Fire detection systems according to the type of aeroplane, the regulatory requirements, the manufacturer's philosophy, and the customer's desires. The engine chosen and its maker's manufacturing processes will also come into consideration. Let us consider two common types, a turbo-prop, and a twin jet medium range transport

6.5.5.1 Turbo-Prop Aeroplane

The fire detection system for this aeroplane is located in the engine compartment and is divided into four separate zones.

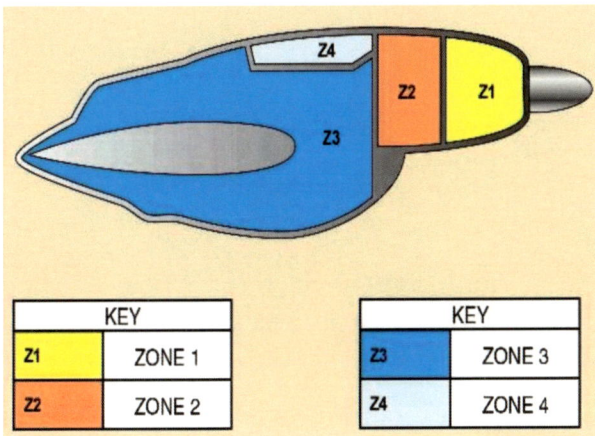

Zone 1   -   Extends from the propeller to the engine fireproof bulkhead

Zone 2   -   Extends from the engine fireproof bulkhead to the next bulkhead

Zone 3   -   All the nacelle area below & aft of the accessory drive gearbox bay.

Zone 4   -   The accessory drive gearbox bay

KEY	
Z1	ZONE 1
Z2	ZONE 2

KEY	
Z3	ZONE 3
Z4	ZONE 4

Figure 6.3 Fire zones

Two firewire systems are fitted - one in each nacelle complex. Each firewire is routed around zones 1, 2, and 4 and is connected to a control unit. When a fire is present the temperature increase alters the capacitive impedance between the outer and inner electrodes of the firewire; this results in a current flow, which closes a relay in the control unit. Relay operation enables an electrical circuit to operate a fire-warning bell in the cockpit and a fire warning light on the pilots' emergency panel.

Each engine has its own fire extinguishing fire bottle but the operation of each is arranged in such a way that one or both bottles can be discharged into an engine.

When the fire is extinguished the fire detection system is reset automatically.

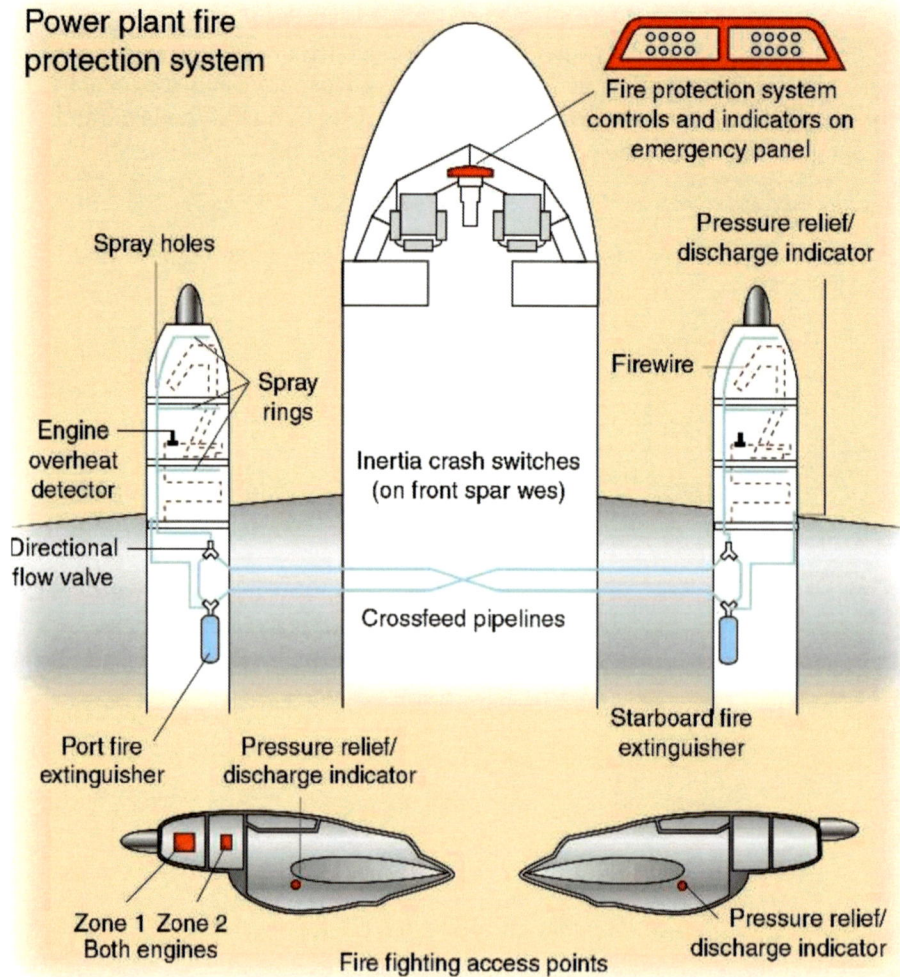

Figure 6.4

6.5.5.2 Engine Internal Overheat Detection

An overheat condition inside an engine is sensed by a detector fitted in an extension of the engine breather pipe. If an engine overheats, the temperature increase actuates the detector which completes a circuit to operate an associated engine overheat warning light on the emergency panel. Each warning light has a press-to-test facility.

6.5.6   Medium Twin Jet Aeroplane

Fire protection consists of overheat and fire detection sensors and fire extinguishers. Detection provides visual and aural indications of overheat and fire conditions in the engines, and fire conditions in the Auxiliary Power Unit (APU) and main wheel well areas. The extinguishers provide a means of extinguishing engine and APU fires.

6.5.6.1 Engine overheat and fire detection

Four dual element overheat/fire detection loops are installed in each engine nacelle. The detectors are the Kidde sensor element types. As the temperature of an element increases, electrical resistance decreases. At a predetermined temperature, the element signals an overheat condition. At a higher temperature, the element signals a fire condition.

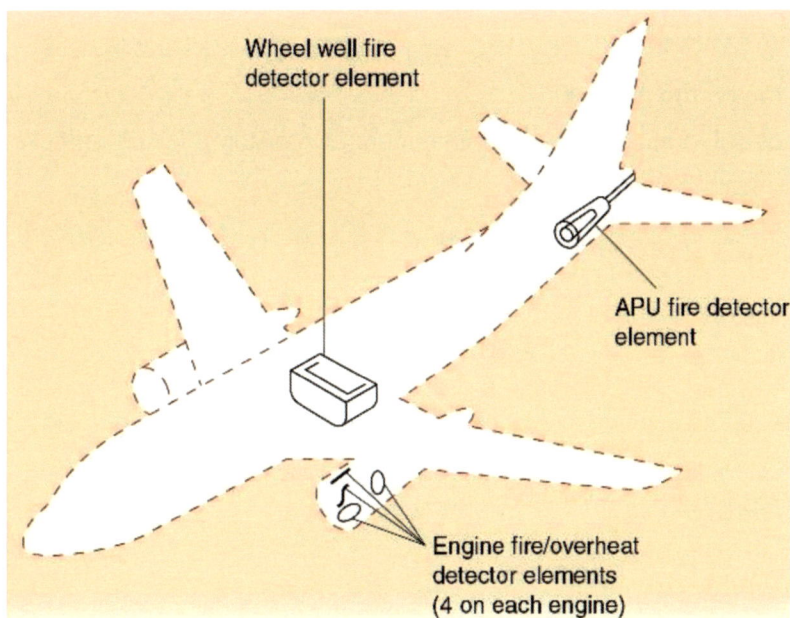

Figure 6.5

The two elements of each detector are labelled A and B. The "A" elements of each detector are connected in series and are called Loop A. The "B" elements of each detector are called Loop B. An Overheat Detection (OVHT DET) Switch for each engine, labelled A, B, and NORMAL, permits selection of Loop A, B, or both A and B as the active detecting elements. During normal operation as a dual loop system, with the OVHT DET Switch in NORMAL, an alert is initiated only if both elements of a detector signal an overheat or fire condition. Engine overheat alert indications result from dual loop indications of overheat/overheat, overheat/fire overheat/fault. An engine overheat condition is indicated by the illumination of the MASTER CAUTION Lights, OVHT/DET System Annunciator Light and the associated ENG OVERHEAT Light. The ENG OVERHEAT Light remains illuminated until the temperature drops below the onset temperature.

Engine Fire alert indications result from dual loop indications of fire/fire or fire/fault. An engine fire condition is indicated by the illumination of the FIRE WARN Lights and the associated Engine Fire Warning Switch Light and the sound of the alarm bell. The bell may be silenced and the FIRE WARN Lights extinguished by pressing either Master Fire Warning Switch or the Bell Cut-out Switch on the fire panel. The Engine Fire Warning Switch remains illuminated until the temperature drops below the onset temperature.

6.5.6.2 APU Fire Detection

A Kidde sensor element fire detection loop is installed on the APU. At a predetermined alarm temperature, the electrical resistance of the sensor decreases to a point where it actuates the warning signals.

The FIRE WARN Lights illuminate, the bell sounds, the APU Fire Warning Switch illuminates and the APU shuts down. The warning horn in the main wheel well also sounds if the aeroplane is on the ground. When the FIRE WARN Lights are illuminated, a fire is assumed and should be extinguished. The APU Fire Warning Switch remains illuminated until the temperature surrounding the sensor/responder has decreased below the alarm temperature. Illumination of the amber APU Detection Inoperative (APU DET INOP) Light, located on the fire panel, indicates a failure in the APU fire detection loop.

6.5.6.3 Wheel Well Fire Detection

A fire detection loop is installed in the main wheel well. The detector is a Fenwall metallic type. There is no provision for short circuit detection. Testing for fire checks the continuity of the loop by sending an artificial electronic signal to the fire warning system. The detector is not actually heated.

6.5.7 Flight crew actions

6.5.7.1 Carburettor fire on the ground

This type of fire will be a fire in the engine compartment of a piston engined aeroplane and the following actions should be carried out:

- Cut off the source of fuel to the carburettor;
- Keep turning the engine on the starter to use up excess fuel;
- Pull the mixture control to Idle Cut-off;
- Advance the Throttle to fully open;
- Turn off the Electric pump;
- Turn off the Fuel selector

If the fire persists activate the engine fire extinguishing equipment if fitted. If the engine has started, continue cranking with the starter.

6.5.7.2 Carburettor Fire in the air

- Turn fuel selector Off Mixture to Idle cut-off;
- Activate the engine fire-extinguishing bottle if fitted;
- Turn the Electric pump off;
- Turn the Cabin heat and defroster off;
- Turn off as many non-essential sources of electrical power as possible

6.5.8 Smoke in the cockpit

This condition is indicated by an accumulation of smoke identifiable by odour or visual confirmation. The operations manual for your aeroplane will contain guidance as to the precise actions to be taken in the event of flight deck smoke but the following actions are shown as an example.

The following flight deck crew actions are prescribed for a sample aeroplane:

- Turn off as many non-essential sources of electrical power as possible;
- Oxygen masks and regulators ON 100% - (This prevents the inhalation of smoke or fumes);
- Smoke goggles ON - (If the smoke concentration affects vision, don the smoke goggles and use the oxygen regulator in the emergency position to clear the oxygen mask and goggles)

6.5.9 Smoke removal from the passenger cabin

Flight deck crew initial actions as for smoke clearance in the cockpit. Then:

1. Leave the cockpit door closed
2. Establish communications between Cockpit and Cabin
3. Select pressurisation mode to Standby
4. Cabin altitude selector select to increase maximum 10000' (Selecting a higher cabin altitude increases the ventilation rate)
5. Select cabin rate selector to Maximum increase (to around 2000 fpm)
6. Left and right air conditioning pack switched to High (this ensures maximum ventilation)
7. Engine air bleeds ON
8. Engine thrust selected to a minimum 45% N1 (at the Number one Turbo compressor) (minimum needed to provide maximum cabin ventilation)
9. Cockpit air conditioning and gasper outlets OPEN. (This ensures an adequate flow of ventilating air in the cockpit)

If the smoke condition is uncontrollable, descend to the lowest safe altitude or 10000' whichever is higher

At 14000' or below:

1. Pressurisation mode selector selected to Manual
2. Air-conditioning Outflow valve switch to Open
3. Position outflow valve to Full open. (this causes the cabin airflow to carry the smoke towards the rear)

6.5.10   *Crew precautions in dealing with fire and smoke*

As a consequence of several disasters resulting in large losses of life among crew members and passengers the relevant authorities and service providing agencies investigated in great depth ways and means of reducing the danger of on-board fires and smoke inhalation on board commercial aeroplanes.

One of the critical findings of these analyses was that most deaths result from the inhalation of smoke as distinct from the actual fire.

While general agreement could not be arrived at with regard to precautions for passengers, agreement was reached with regard to improving the survivability of crewmembers. This was determined in two ways:

a) The donning of a "smoke hood'

b) The donning of "smoke goggles" and "anti-inflammable gloves'.

The main type of smoke hood in use at the present time is the Drager Oxycrew smoke hood which once donned provides complete smoke and noxious gas protection for 20 min, by operation of chemical oxygen generation lanyard located at the front of the waistcoat assembly.

It is essential that the neck seal is properly fitted when donning the hood. Clothing or long hair should not be allowed to prevent a snug, gas tight seal around the neck.

6.5.11   *Smoke in a cargo compartment*

All cargo compartments now have "smoke detecting" equipment fitted with a Warning alert in the cockpit. The normal preventative measure is to deprive the affected area of oxygen and in addition discharge a suitable fire-extinguishing agent (halon being the most effective).

6.5.12   *Wheel well fires*

When we consider the heat and friction generated by a large aircraft during its takeoff run at heavy weight with high ambient temperature, it is obvious that the potential for a fire is high. The "trigger" for this potential fire is an abandoned takeoff where full braking is initiated suddenly and the aeroplane is forced into a sudden and hard stop with all the kinetic energy being converted into heat energy and contained within the braking system and wheel assembly. Sand has been considered to be the most effective agent for magnesium fires.

6.5.12.1   *Stops made from high speed - Takeoff*

Similarly, the technique and effects here will vary from aeroplane to aeroplane so we will once again look at our sample heavy turbo-prop. Following an accelerate-stop made from a speed of up to 90 KT and providing the aeroplane has previously been stationary for approximately one hour to allow the brakes to cool below 50 °C, a brake cooling period of ten min should be allowed before the next takeoff is attempted. If the aeroplane has carried out a quick turnaround (less than 20 min) the cooling period should be 30 min for a stop made from a speed approaching 90 KT. Following an accelerate-stop from a speed greater than 90 KT, the mandated inspection of the wheel well and under-carriage area should be observed. This requires the removal of wheels and brakes. No further time increases are necessary for hot, high airfields.

In the event of a fire, smoke or overheated brake situation on your aeroplane - you must always consult the operations manual and appropriate checklists for the aeroplane you are operating.

6.6   *Windshear and Microburst*

Two phenomena that are categorised under hazardous weather conditions for flight came to light in the late 1960's mostly as a result of "unexplainable" fatal accidents. One of the early unaccountable accidents was a Pan American B727 taking off in approaching thundery weather. The aeroplane crashed during the initial climb phase for no apparent reason. More recently a Delta Airlines Lockheed L-1011 Tri-Star endeavouring to land at Dallas, Texas in the USA, in much the same type of weather conditions, crashed short of the runway. The common factor to both of these accidents, and to many other similar accidents and/or incidents, was the weather and the associated turbulence and rapid variations in vector wind.

6.6.1   *Definitions*

Essentially windshear is a sudden and unexpected change of wind direction and speed. It can occur at any altitude. The Civil Aviation Authority of the United Kingdom defines this phenomenon as "Variations in vector wind (along the aircraft's flight path) of a pattern, intensity and duration to displace an aircraft abruptly from its intended path such that substantial control action is required'.

Low altitude windshear - Windshear along the final approach path or along the runway and along the takeoff path and initial climb-out flight path

Vertical windshear – rate of change of horizontal wind speed with altitude

Horizontal windshear – rate of change of horizontal wind speed with horizontal distance

Up and downdraught windshear – caused by rapid up and down vertical air currents

6.6.2   *Associated Meteorological Phenomena*

Upper level windshear may occur as a result of vertical draughts associated with thunderstorms or standing wave activity. It is also commonly associated, in clear air, with the rapid change of wind speed on the polar side of jet streams and in the vicinity of the standing wave activity frequently associated with flight over or downwind of mountain ranges.

Low level windshear is usually caused by some localised, or approaching, weather situations, often combined with man-made ground objects, buildings, hangars and such like. Examples are approaching fronts, some geographical features such as hills, mountains, a coastline, or high buildings in the aerodrome vicinity particularly in the approach or departure paths. Others causes can be "microbursts" and downdrafts associated with thunderstorms or mountain waves over the mountains, already mentioned. Some of these items, individually or together, can cause vertical, horizontal, or up and down draft windshear.

6.6.3   *Effect of decreasing headwind / increasing tailwind*

Consider an aircraft on the approach to land. If it encounters a sudden decrease in headwind (or increase in tailwind) it will descend below the approach path; however, due to its inertia, the groundspeed initially remains constant whilst airspeed rapidly decreases. Large amounts of power may be needed to recover. This is also known as an energy loss situation. Now consider an aircraft, which is departing. A sudden increase in headwind (or decrease in tailwind) will cause the aircraft to climb above the desired flight path; indicated airspeed increases and due to inertia groundspeed initially remains constant. This is also referred to as an energy gain situation. A good indication of windshear can be obtained from a comparison between the IRS ground speed and the readings of the ASI. In smooth conditions the difference between the two will be reasonably steady or only slow changing however, in windshear conditions, the sudden changes in airspeed will show up instantly and may give you time to act early. It is very important not to chase after short term airspeed and altitude changes, rather, try to maintain aircraft attitude.

6.6.4   *Microbursts*

Another source of windshear is the microburst weather phenomenon. This very dangerous occurrence happens usually in front of an approaching thunderstorm. The detail of how this develops is beyond the scope of this lesson but a resume reads like this. As the updrafts are developing uniformly in the cumulonimbus, (CB) cloud of the thunderstorm, the wind at altitude is normally of slow speed, or even calm with very little or no wind shear (change of speed) to break the uniform development of the updraft air currents. However, in some cases, a change of wind speed with altitude develops and the axis of the CB may become angled from the vertical. Should this occur prior to the "mature" stage of the development, then there would be a strong forward moving cold down draft, coming out of the vertical up and down movement within and without the CB cloud. This leads to the development of a very intense "downburst" (microburst) in the area immediately to the leeward side of the thunderstorm. In appearance and character, this cold downburst resembles an extremely active and intense local cold front. Should a flight crew try to land or takeoff ahead of the CB cloud and it's associated thunderstorm, they may very well be affected by the "microburst" downdrafts in front of the approaching storm, as was the case in both of the accident examples cited. These produce extremes of both horizontal and vertical wind shear and can lead to extreme control difficulty.

6.6.5   *Precautions and Recovery Actions*

We have studied how the "wind change" affects the aerodynamic lift and must now consider what precautions and recovery action(s) must be taken. In the days of piston or turbo prop aeroplanes the response time of the engine was almost instantaneous and the aeroplane immediately "flew" out of the windshear effect once power was applied, in the case of loss of speed, or reduced, in the case of increased speed. Unfortunately due to the slower response time of the pure turbo-jet engine, called "spool up" time or known to some flight crews as "throttle stagger" the flight crew must initiate a timely correct and quick response or, preferably, be proactive. In the event that an approach is being made in conditions when windshear activity is possible, you should ensure that your approach is as stable as possible. Select a higher approach speed and set the throttles and attitude as early as possible. Remember that gusts are transient. Do not chase after short-term airspeed or altitude changes but try to maintain the attitude. Monitor the IRS/ASI and only adjust the power if the speed divergence is sustained. If in doubt, do not hesitate to carry out a missed approach procedure.

In some cases it may be necessary to apply full power and pitch up until the stick shaker activates in order to fly out of the wind shear. This action allows maximum possible lift to be developed

6.7   *Decompression of a pressurised cabin*

The first sign of a sudden loss of pressure in a pressurised cabin is an explosive noise, a bang, immediately followed by a rapid and severe drop in temperature, accompanied by the cabin filling with vapour as the warm air condenses in the new cold, lower pressure atmosphere

Oxygen is required above 10000'. As our sudden "depressurisation" will most likely have taken place several thousands of feet above this altitude the commander must now initiate an emergency descent to bring the aeroplane down to 10000' within 3 min of the explosive decompression. At 40000' the time of useful consciousness is approximately 12 s. As a system response to this decompression the emergency oxygen system in the aeroplane will have operated and oxygen masks will have been automatically deployed in the cabin. The flight crew have their own individual "sweep-on" oxygen mask and all inter-crew and radio communication will now be done while wearing the oxygen mask. Once the aeroplane has been stabilised at 10000' then both flight crew and passengers can breathe normally without the need of the oxygen system

6.7.1   *Difference between slow and rapid decompression*

As described above, there is no doubting when an explosive decompression occurs. However, a slow decompression is harder to detect insofar as depending upon the rate of leakage of the pressurised air within the fuselage neither the flight crew or the passengers will be immediately aware of the loss of pressurisation. In the cockpit of most modern commercial aeroplanes and forming part of the air conditioning and pressurisation system is a gauge showing the "cabin altitude" as distinct from the altitude at which the aeroplane is flying. There may also be another gauge called the "rate of change" (of the cabin altitude) and one or other of these gauges would be the first to indicate a developing loss of cabin pressure. The "cabin altitude" would be seen to rise, and a rate of climb would begin to show on the rate of change indicator. The next indication would be a steady decrease in the air temperature within the fuselage. This would gradually become obvious to both the flight crew and passengers, or there may be a gauge showing "cabin temperature'. In addition people would start to display signs of a condition known as "hypoxia" (deprivation of oxygen). Their behaviour would become similar to the onset of alcohol intake, euphoria, a loss of inhibitions followed by impaired thinking and judgement, slow reactions, muscular and mental lack of coordination, deteriorating vision and hearing which, if not corrected, can eventually lead to unconsciousness and death. Unfortunately, hypoxia gives a feeling of well being and it is very difficult to detect in oneself. The flight crew, being trained with regard the symptoms of lack of oxygen and hypoxia, should be the first to detect (from their own behaviour and the indication from the cockpit gauges) that a slowly developing loss of cabin pressure has begun. The subsequent in-flight actions are then the same as for the explosive decompression situation. i.e. a rapid descent to 10000', unless subsequent investigation within the cockpit or cabin areas reveals the source of the leak, e.g. a faulty door lock or door seal, and the problem can be resolved.

6.7.2 Oxygen Requirements

6.7.2.1 Supplemental Oxygen - Pressurised Aeroplanes

CAT.IDE.A.235 Supplemental oxygen — pressurised aeroplanes

(a) Pressurised aeroplanes operated at pressure altitudes above 10 000' shall be equipped with supplemental oxygen equipment that is capable of storing and dispensing the oxygen supplies in accordance with Table 1.

(b) Pressurised aeroplanes operated at pressure altitudes above 25 000' shall be equipped with:

(1) quick donning types of masks for flight crew members;

(2) sufficient spare outlets and masks or portable oxygen units with masks distributed evenly throughout the passenger compartment, to ensure immediate availability of oxygen for use by each required cabin crew member;

(3) an oxygen dispensing unit connected to oxygen supply terminals immediately available to each cabin crew member, additional crew member and occupants of passenger seats, wherever seated; and

(4) a device to provide a warning indication to the flight crew of any loss of pressurisation.

(c) In the case of pressurised aeroplanes first issued with an individual CofA after 8 November 1998 and operated at pressure altitudes above 25000', or operated at pressure altitudes at, or below 25 000' under conditions that would not allow them to descend safely to 13 000' within four minutes, the individual oxygen dispensing units referred to in (b)(3) shall be automatically deployable.

(d) The total number of dispensing units and outlets referred to in (b)(3) and (c) shall exceed the number of seats by at least 10 %. The extra units shall be evenly distributed throughout the passenger compartment.

(e) Notwithstanding (a), the oxygen supply requirements for cabin crew member(s), additional crew member(s) and passenger(s), in the case of aeroplanes not certified to fly at altitudes above 25 000', may be reduced to the entire flying time between 10000' and 13 000' cabin pressure altitudes for all required cabin crew members and for at least 10 % of the passengers if, at all points along the route to be flown, the aeroplane is able to descend safely within four minutes to a cabin pressure altitude of 13 000'.

(f) The required minimum supply in Table 1, row 1 item (b)(1) and row 2, shall cover the quantity of oxygen necessary for a constant rate of descent from the aeroplane's maximum certified operating altitude to 10 000' in 10 minutes and followed by 20 minutes at 10000'.

(g) The required minimum supply in Table 1, row 1 item 1(b)(2), shall cover the quantity of oxygen necessary for a constant rate of descent from the aeroplane's maximum certified operating altitude to 10 000' in 10 minutes followed by 110 minutes at 10000'.

(h) The required minimum supply in Table 1, row 3, shall cover the quantity of oxygen necessary for a constant rate of descent from the aeroplane's maximum certified operating altitude to 15 000' in 10 minutes.

SUPPLY FOR	DURATION AND CABIN PRESSURE ALTITUDE
1. All occupants of flight deck seats on flight deck duty	Entire flight time when the cabin pressure altitude exceeds 13000' and entire flight time when the cabin pressure altitude exceeds 10000' but does not exceed 13000' after the first 30 min at those altitudes, but in no case less than: (i) 30 min for aeroplanes certificated to fly at altitudes not exceeding 25000' (Note 2) (ii) 2 h for aeroplanes certificated to fly at altitudes more than 25000' (Note 3).
2. All required cabin crew members	Entire flight time when cabin pressure altitude exceeds 13000' but not less than 30 min (Note 2), and entire flight time when cabin pressure altitude is greater than 10000' but does not exceed 13000' after the first 30 min at these altitudes.
3. 100% of passengers (Note 5)	Entire flight time when the cabin pressure altitude exceeds 15000' but in no case less than 10 min.(Note 4)
4. 30% of passengers (Note 5)	Entire flight time when the cabin pressure altitude exceeds 14000' but does not exceed 15000'.
5. 10% of passengers (Note 5)	Entire flight time when the cabin pressure altitude exceeds 10000' but does not exceed 14000' after the first 30 min at these altitudes.

Note 1: The supply provided must take account of the cabin pressure altitude and descent profile for the routes concerned.
Note 2: The required minimum supply is that quantity of oxygen necessary for a constant rate of descent from the aeroplane's maximum certificated operating altitude to 10000' in 10 min and followed by 20 min at 10000'.
Note 3: The required minimum supply is that quantity of oxygen necessary for a constant rate of descent from the aeroplane's maximum certificated operating altitude to 10000' in 10 min and followed by 110 min at 10000'. The oxygen required in OPS 1.780(a)(1) may be included in determining the supply required.
Note 4: The required minimum supply is that quantity of oxygen necessary for a constant rate of descent from the aeroplane's maximum certificated operating altitude to 15000' in 10 min.
Note 5: For the purpose of this table "passengers" means passengers actually carried and includes infants.

Figure 6.6 Minimum Requirements for Supplemental Oxygen for Pressurised Aeroplanes (Note 1)

6.7.2.2 Supplemental Oxygen - Non-Pressurised Aeroplanes

CAT.IDE.A.240 Supplemental oxygen — non-pressurised aeroplanes
Non-pressurised aeroplanes operated at pressure altitudes above 10 000' shall be equipped with supplemental oxygen equipment capable of storing and dispensing the oxygen supplies in accordance with Table 1.

SUPPLY FOR	DURATION AND PRESSURE ALTITUDE
1. All occupants of flight deck seats on flight deck duty	Entire flight time at pressure altitudes above 10000'
2. All required cabin crew members	Entire flight time at pressure altitudes above 13000' and for any period exceeding 30 min at pressure altitudes above 10000' but not exceeding 13000'
3. 100% of passengers (See Note)	Entire flight time at pressure altitudes above 13000'.
4. 10% of passengers (See Note)	Entire flight time after 30 min at pressure altitudes greater than 10000' but not exceeding 13000'.

Note: For the purpose of this table "passengers" means passengers actually carried and includes infants under the age of 2.

Figure 6.7 Supplemental Oxygen - Non-Pressurised Aeroplanes

6.7.3 Flight-deck oxygen

The flight-deck crew is provided with supplemental oxygen in the form of an individual container per pilot located on the same side or via a dual providing container located behind the co-pilot's seat. In contrast, passengers receive their oxygen via individual chemical oxygen generators located at each Passenger Service Unit (PSU). Four continuous flow masks are connected to each generator. A chemical oxygen generator with two masks is located above each attendant station and in each rest room. The system is activated automatically by a pressure switch at a cabin altitude of 14000' or when the Passenger Oxygen Switch on the aft overhead panel is positioned to the ON position. When the system is activated, the PAX

OXY ON light will illuminate and OVERHEAD will illuminate on the Master Caution System. Activating the system causes the masks to drop from the stowage compartments. The oxygen generators are activated when any mask in the unit is pulled down. Pulling one mask down causes all masks in that unit to come down and 100% oxygen flows to all masks. A green "in-line" flow indicator is visible in the transparent oxygen hose whenever oxygen is flowing to the mask. Oxygen flows for approximately 12 min and cannot be shut off. If the passenger oxygen is activated and a PSU oxygen mask compartment does not open, the masks may be dropped manually.

6.7.4   *Portable oxygen*

Portable oxygen containers strategically positioned on the flight deck and relevant sections of the passenger cabin supplement the "designed-in" supplemental oxygen system.

6.8   *Wake Turbulence*

The "wake" left behind in the water by a boat or ship is clearly visible. There is a wake behind the aeroplane which unfortunately is nearly always invisible. This creates wake turbulence. A pressure differential exists between the upper and lower surfaces of the wing which cause spill-over of air to up and over the wing tips. This results in a pair of circulating vortices trailing behind the aeroplane. The greater the lift being generated by the wings the stronger the vortices become. The amount of lift generated by the wings and their lift augmentation devices is a function of weight.

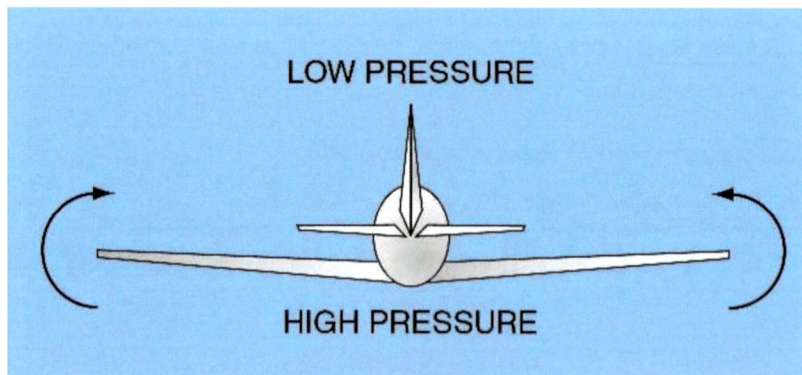

Figure 6.8 Vortex wake

Wake vortices are present behind every aeroplane and helicopter but are particularly severe when generated by large, wide-bodied jet aeroplanes. These vortices are two counter-rotating cylindrical air masses trailing behind the aeroplane. An aircraft flying into a wake vortex will experience sudden turbulence. This may result in severe vibration, sudden changes of pitch and / or roll attitude or loss of control. The degree of upset is dependent upon the size of the aeroplane affected and the intensity of the vortex. A small training aircraft would be very likely to be totally upset if caught in the vortex wake of a B747 but you should also note that an MD80 aeroplane is on record as having entered an uncontrolled 90° roll when caught in a wake vortex.

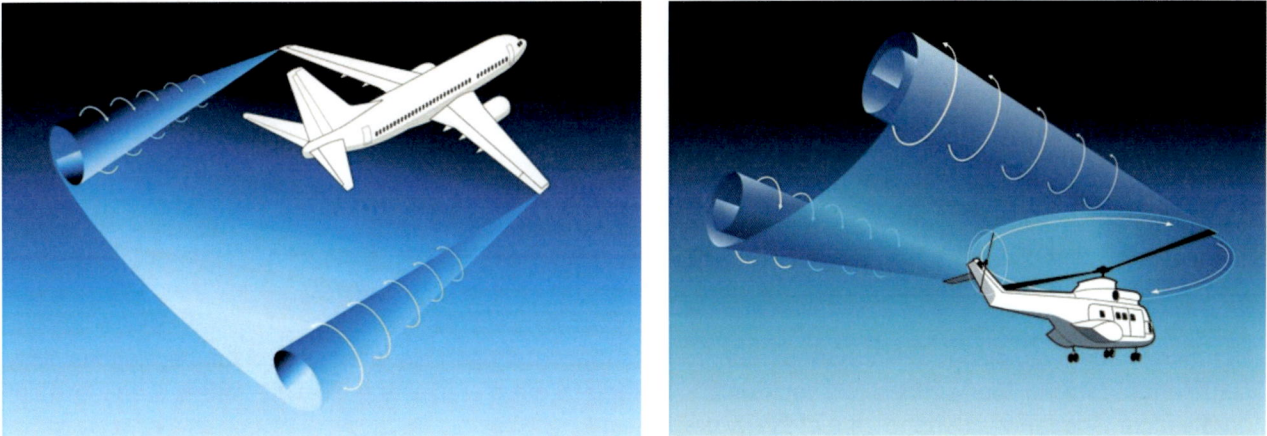

Figure 6.9 Wake vortices

Vortices are most dangerous to aircraft during the takeoff, initial climb, final approach and landing phases of flight. They tend to drift downwards and when close to the ground move sideways from the track of the generating aeroplane, occasionally rebounding upwards. Operational experience with actual in-flight wake turbulence encounters is well documented. Analysis of wake turbulence data collected by certain States has yielded yet more definitive criteria and the conflict between safety and expedition, between caution and regularity and between separation minima and runway acceptance rate has now been generally resolved.

6.8.1 Separation Minima

Wake turbulence separation minima are intended to greatly reduce the potential hazards of wake turbulence. Because wake turbulence is invisible, its presence and location cannot be determined with precision. Pilots should thoroughly understand the likely situations where hazardous wake turbulence may be encountered.
The discovery of "Wake Turbulence" followed investigation into several incidents that occurred where a "following aeroplane" suffered a significant displacement of its flight path, either in the landing or takeoff phase. As a result of these investigations, ICAO have devised "wake turbulence separation" minima to eliminate as far as possible the risk of one aeroplane being hazardously "upset" by flying through or across the turbulence wake of a larger and heavier aeroplane. These are now applied by individual member States.

6.8.2 Effects on aeroplanes

The three basic effects of wake turbulence on a following aeroplane are induced rolls, loss of height or rate of climb, and possible structural stress. The greatest danger is the roll induced on the penetrating aeroplane to the degree that it exceeds the counter control capability of the aeroplane concerned. Should the wake turbulence encounter occur in the approach area, its effect is greater because the following aeroplane is in a critical state with regard to speed, thrust, altitude and reaction time.

6.8.3 Wake turbulence characteristics

Wake vortices generated by an aeroplane in flight are related to the aeroplane gross mass, airspeed, configuration and wing span. Vortex characteristics are altered and eventually dominated by interactions between the vortices and the ambient atmosphere. The wind, wind shear, turbulence and atmospheric stability affect the motion and decay of a vortex system. The proximity of the ground significantly affects vortex movement and decay. Vortex generation begins on rotation when the nose wheel lifts off the runway and ends when the nose wheel touches down on landing. Vortex strength increases proportionally to weight and is greatest when the generating aeroplane is HEAVY and is flying slowly.

Helicopters produce vortices when in flight and there is some evidence that per kilogram of gross mass, their vortices are more intense than those of fixed-wing aeroplanes. When hovering or while hover-taxiing helicopters should be kept well clear of light aircraft.

Calm or light winds will "keep" the vortices in position in the vicinity of the runway and extra ATC spacing must be used in these circumstances, and if not then the commander must request a delay in takeoff and landing. In a cross wind situation, vortices created by aeroplanes operating on one runway can drift or be blown on to a parallel runway.

Dissipation of Vortices
Wing vortices dissipate as a result of one or more of the following three circumstances;

With the passage of time
Some disturbances along the length of the vortices become unstable and sinusoidal oscillations may commence causing the vortices to synchronize. A sudden structural change called vortex breakdown or bursting can suddenly widen the core of the vortex.

Ground effect
The effect of proximity to the ground is also a factor with respect to the development, persistence, and eventual break up of vortices. The ground acts as a 'plane of reflection'. As the trailing vortices descend downwards their vertical speed decreases and, if there are calm conditions or very little surface wind, the vortices start to move horizontally across the ground away from each other. This occurs at a height corresponding to about half the wing span measurement of the wing vortex of the generating aeroplane.

6.8.3.1 Recommended pilot actions

Takeoff
If sequenced behind a heavier turbulence category aeroplane, either delay the takeoff or plan to rotate before the point where the preceding aeroplane rotated.

Landing
Again either delay to allow the vortices to dissipate or aim to touch down beyond the point where the heavier aeroplane landed.

Approach or Climb out
Stay above the flight path of the preceding aeroplane

6.8.3.2 Aeroplane categorisation for wake turbulence

Wake turbulence separation minima is based on a grouping of all aeroplane types into "wake turbulence" three categories each of which is related to a band of maximum certificated takeoff mass values.
The following are the details of the three categories:

HEAVY (H) - all aeroplane types of 136000 kg or more
MEDIUM (M) - all aeroplane types less than 136000 kg and more than 7000 kg
LIGHT (L) - all aeroplane types of 7000 kg or less

Pilots are required to advise ATC at the airport of their aircraft's wake turbulence category. This can be done when making their first radio call,
Example: 'Manchester approach Polaris 007 HEAVY on frequency ------ with information Alpha'

6.8.4   *Application of minima versus aeroplane categorisation*

The following table gives the separation to be applied between aeroplanes.

Aeroplane Category		Separation Minima
Leading Aeroplane	Following Aeroplane	
HEAVY	HEAVY	7.4 km (4.0 NM)
	MEDIUM	9.3 km (5.0 NM)
	LIGHT	11.1 km (6.0 NM)
MEDIUM	HEAVY	5.6 km (3.0 NM)
	MEDIUM	5.6 km (3.0 NM)
	LIGHT	9.3 km (5.0 NM)
LIGHT	HEAVY	5..6 km (3.0 NM)
	MEDIUM	5.6 km (3.0 NM)
	LIGHT	5.6 km (3.0 NM)

These separation minima are applied under the following three sets of circumstances:
a) An aeroplane is operating directly behind another aeroplane at the same altitude or less than 300 m (1000') below;
b) Both aeroplanes are using the same runway or parallel runways separated by less than 760 m;
c) An aeroplane is crossing behind another aeroplane, at the same altitude or less than 300 metres (1000') below.

Time separation - landing traffic
In addition to separating flights by distances according to category there is also a system whereby aeroplanes are separated by "time".
For timed approaches the following separation minima is applied to aeroplanes landing behind HEAVY or a MEDIUM aeroplane as follows:

MEDIUM aeroplane following a HEAVY aeroplane – 2 min
LIGHT aeroplane following a HEAVY or MEDIUM aeroplane – 3 min

Time separation – departing traffic
A minimum of 2 min is applied between a LIGHT and MEDIUM aeroplane taking off behind a HEAVY aeroplane or a LIGHT aeroplane taking off behind a MEDIUM aeroplane in the case of:
The same runway
Parallel runways separated by less than 760 m
Crossing runways if the projected flight path of the following aeroplane will cross the projected flight path of the leading aeroplane at the same altitude or less than 300 m (1000') below.
Parallel runways separated by 760 m or more if the projected flight path of the following aeroplane will cross the projected flight path of the leading aeroplane at the same altitude or less than 300 m (1000') below.

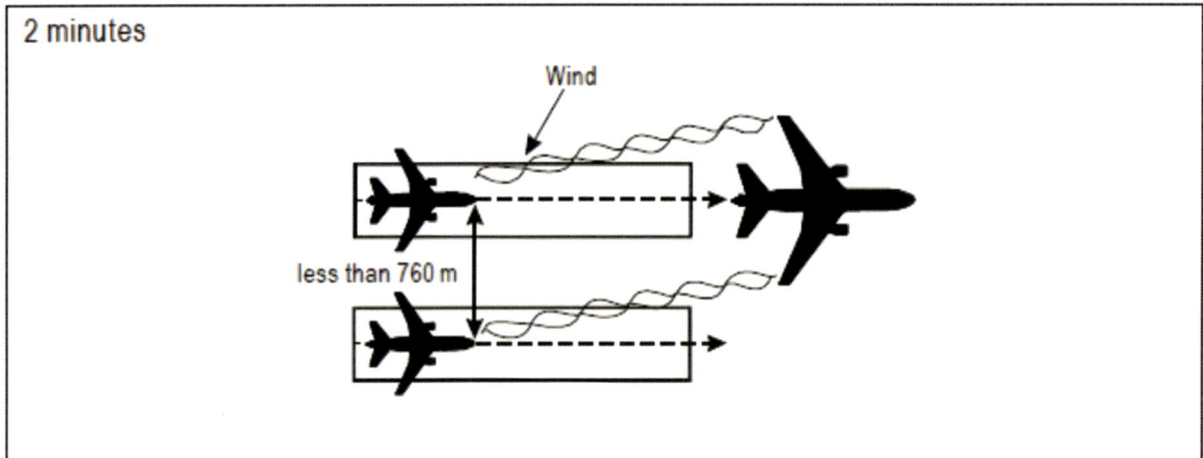

Figure 6.10 Two-minute separation for following aircraft

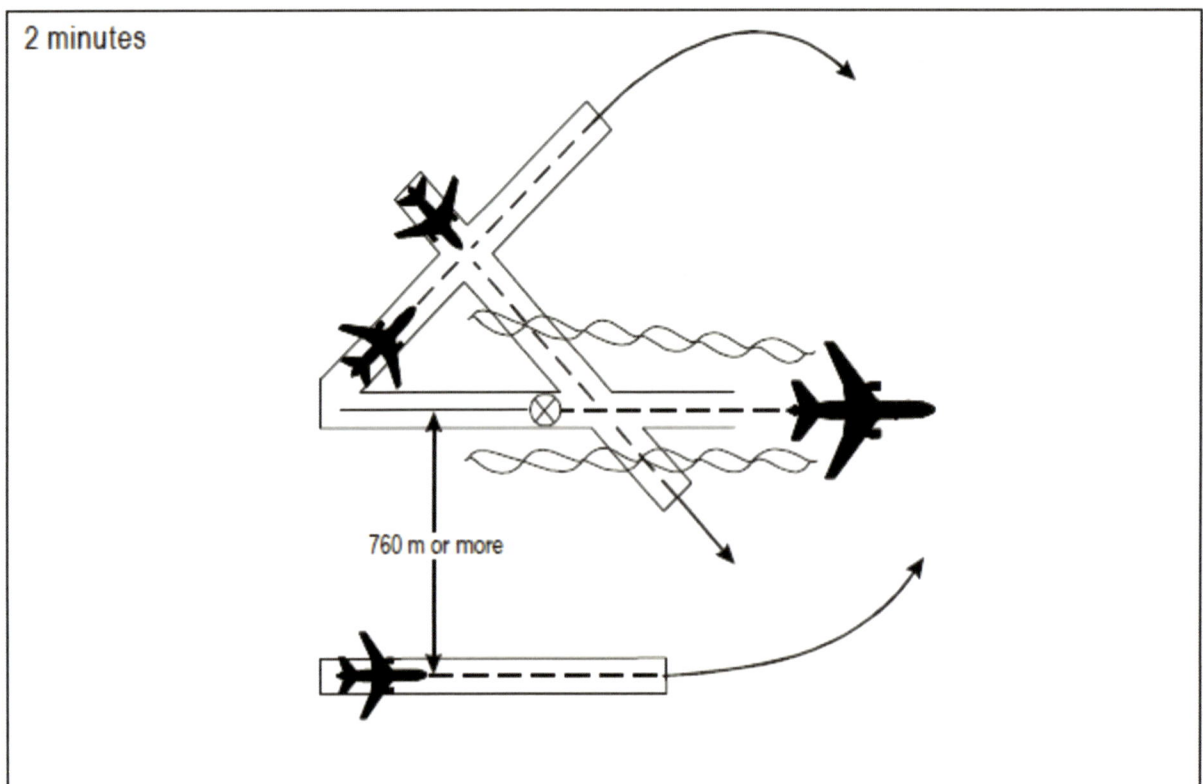

Figure 6.11 Two-minute wake turbulence separation for crossing aircraft

A separation minimum of 3 min is applied between a LIGHT and MEDIUM aeroplane when taking off behind a HEAVY aeroplane or a LIGHT aeroplane when taking off behind a MEDIUM aeroplane from:
a) An intermediate part of the same runway;
b) An intermediate part of a parallel runway separated by less than 760 m

.

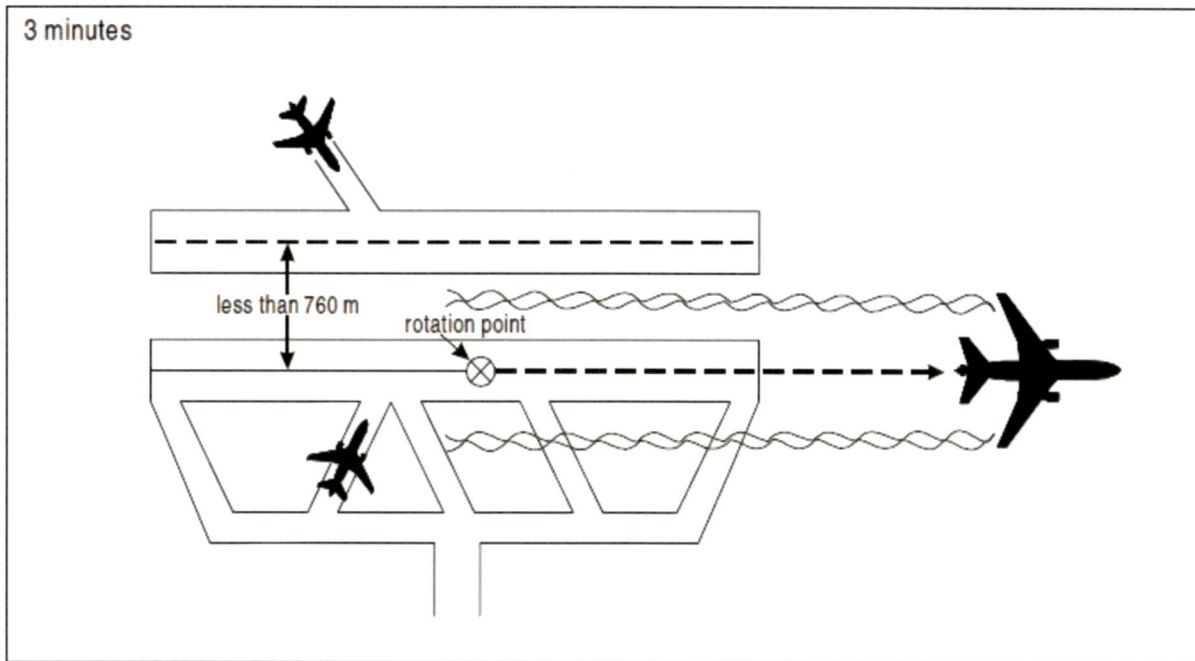

Figure 6.12 Three-minute wake turbulence separation for following aircraft

Intermediate takeoff

A separation minimum of 2 min is applied between a LIGHT or MEDIUM aeroplane and a HEAVY aeroplane and between a LIGHT aeroplane and a MEDIUM aeroplane when operating on a runway with a displaced landing threshold when:

a)   A departing LIGHT or MEDIUM aeroplane follows a HEAVY aeroplane arrival and a departing LIGHT aeroplane follows a MEDIUM aeroplane arrival; or

b)   An arriving LIGHT or MEDIUM aeroplane follows a HEAVY aeroplane departure and an arriving LIGHT aeroplane follows a MEDIUM aeroplane departure if the projected flight paths are expected to cross.

Opposite direction

A separation minimum of 2 min should be applied between a LIGHT or MEDIUM aeroplane and a HEAVY aeroplane, and between a LIGHT aeroplane and a MEDIUM aeroplane when the heavier aeroplane is making a low or miss approach and the lighter aeroplane is:

Utilising an opposite-direction runway for takeoff

Landing on the same runway in the opposite direction or on a parallel opposite direction runway separated by less than 760 m

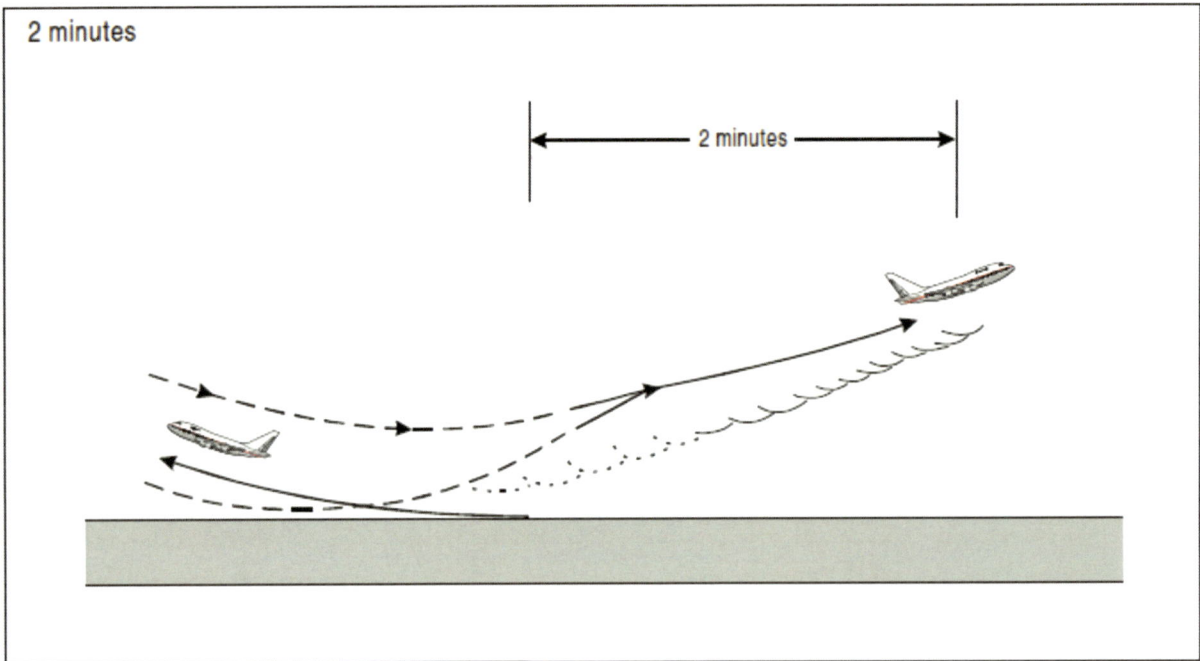

Figure 6.13 Two-minute wake turbulence separation for opposite direction take-off

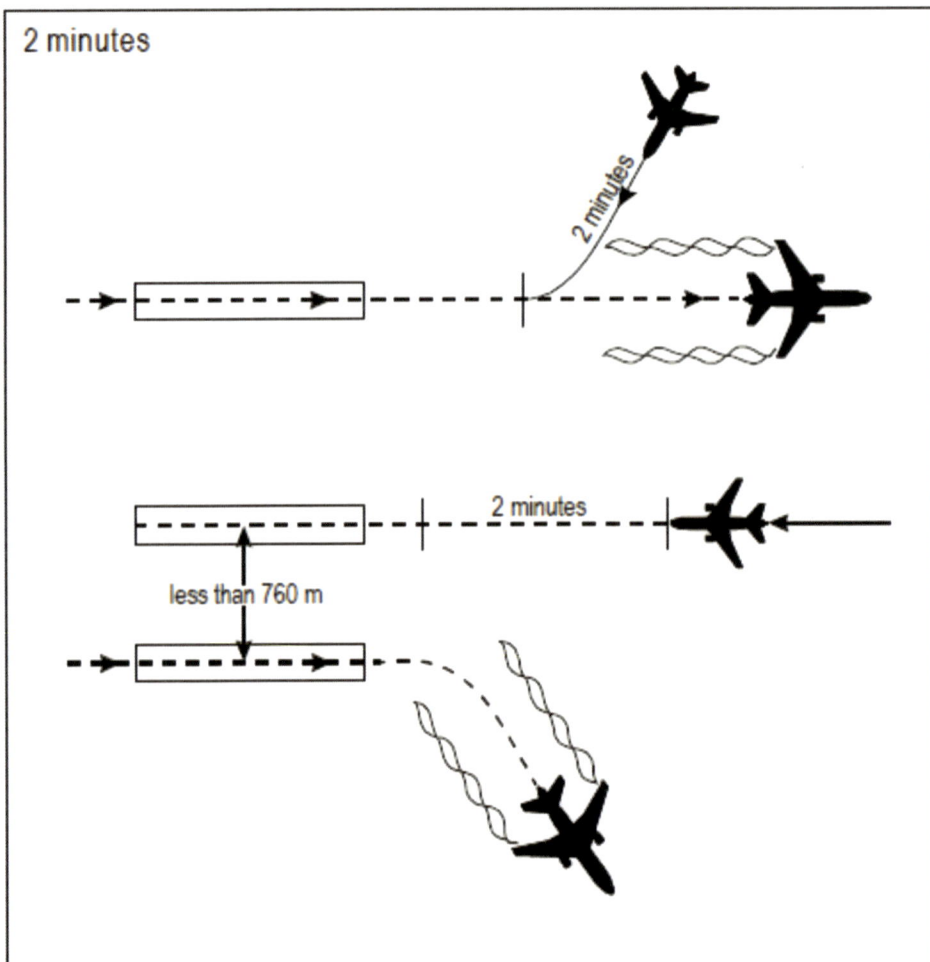

Figure 6.14 Two-minute wake turbulence separation for crossing aircraft

6.9   *Security*

6.9.1   *Requirements*

AMC1 ORO.AOC.100(a) Application for an air operator certificate OPERATOR SECURITY PROGRAMME

In accordance with Regulation (EC) No 300/2008, as part of granting the AOC, the CAT operator should provide the competent authority with the operator's security programme, including security training. The security programme should be adapted to the type and area of operation, as well as to the aircraft operated.

AMC1 ORO.GEN.110(a) Operator responsibilities SECURITY TRAINING PROGRAMME FOR CREW MEMBERS — CAT OPERATIONS

Without prejudice to Regulation (EC) No 300/2008, the CAT operator should establish and maintain a security training programme for crew members, including theoretical and practical elements. This training should be provided at the time of operator conversion training and thereafter at intervals not exceeding three years. The content and duration of the training should be adapted to the security threats of the individual operator and should ensure that crew members act in the most appropriate manner to minimise the consequences of acts of unlawful interference. This programme should include the following elements:

(a) determination of the seriousness of the occurrence;

(b) crew communication and coordination;

(c) appropriate self-defence responses;

(d) use of non-lethal protective devices assigned to crew members whose use is authorised by the Member State;

(e) understanding of behaviour of terrorists so as to facilitate the ability of crew members to cope with hijacker behaviour and passenger responses;

(f) in case where cabin crew are required, live situational training exercises regarding various threat conditions;

(g) flight crew compartment procedures to protect the aircraft;

(h) aircraft search procedures, in accordance with Regulation (EC) No 300/2008, including identification of prohibited articles; and

(i) guidance on the least risk bomb locations.

Reporting acts of unlawful interference
Following an act of unlawful interference on board an aeroplane the commander or, in his absence the operator, shall submit, without delay, a report of such an act to the designated local authority and the Authority in the State of the operator.

Aeroplane search procedure checklist
An operator shall ensure that all aeroplanes carry a checklist of the procedures to be followed for that type in searching for concealed weapons, explosives, or other dangerous devices.

ORO.SEC.100.A Flight crew compartment security

(a) In an aeroplane which is equipped with a flight crew compartment door, this door shall be capable of being locked, and means shall be provided by which the cabin crew can notify the flight crew in the event of suspicious activity or security breaches in the cabin.

(b) All passenger-carrying aeroplanes of a maximum certificated take-off mass exceeding 45500 kg, or with a MOPSC of more than 60 engaged in the commercial transportation of passengers, shall be equipped with an approved flight crew compartment door that is capable of being locked and unlocked from either pilot's station and designed to meet the applicable airworthiness requirements.

(c) In all aeroplanes which are equipped with a flight crew compartment door in accordance with point (b) above:

(1) this door shall be closed prior to engine start for take-off and will be locked when required by security procedures or by the pilot-in-command until engine shut down after landing, except when deemed necessary for authorised persons to access or egress in compliance with national civil aviation security programmes; and

(2) means shall be provided for monitoring from either pilot's station the entire door area outside the flight crew compartment to identify persons requesting entry and to detect suspicious behaviour or potential threat.

ORO.SEC.100.H Flight crew compartment security

If installed, the flight crew compartment door on a helicopter operated for the purpose of carrying passengers shall be capable of being locked from within the flight crew compartment in order to prevent unauthorised access.

Unlawful interference / hi-jacking

An aeroplane, which is being subjected to unlawful interference, shall endeavour to notify the appropriate ATS unit of this fact, any significant circumstances associated therewith and any deviation from the current flight plan necessitated by the circumstances. This will enable the ATS unit to give priority to the aeroplane and to minimise conflict with other aeroplanes.

6.9.2 Procedures

Unless considerations aboard the aeroplane dictate otherwise, the pilot-in-command should attempt to continue flying on the assigned track and at the assigned cruising level at least until able to notify an ATS unit or within radar coverage.

When an aeroplane subjected to an act of unlawful interference must depart from its assigned track or its assigned cruising level without being able to make radiotelephony contact with ATS, the pilot-in-command should, whenever possible:

1. Attempt to broadcast warnings on the VHF emergency frequency and other appropriate frequencies, unless considerations aboard the aircraft dictate otherwise. Other equipment such as on-board transponders, data links, etc., should also be used when it is advantageous to do so and circumstances permit.
2. Proceed in accordance with applicable special procedures for in-flight contingencies, where such procedures have been established.
3. If no applicable regional procedures have been established, proceed at a level which differs from the cruising levels normally used for IFR flight in the area by 300 m (1000') if above FL 290 or by 150 m (500') if below FL 290

Note: The unlawful interference (hi-jack) transponder code (Squawk) is 7500.

6.9.2.1 Selection of cruising level

Where no applicable regional procedures have been established it becomes the responsibility of the commander to select a cruising level appropriate to the circumstances existing on board the aeroplane. If he / she suspects that it may become difficult to navigate the aeroplane in accordance with the standard separation and along the cleared route or if forced to depart from the cleared route over which the aeroplane was operating, the commander should, attempt to do one or more of the following actions:

1. Maintain a true airspeed of no more than 400 KT and preferably an altitude of between 10000' and 25000'.
2. fly a course toward the destination which the hi-jacker has announced

These actions should be followed only if circumstances permit and providing it is possible to do so without jeopardising the safety of the flight

If these procedures result in either radio contact or air intercept the commander will attempt to comply with any instructions received which may direct the aeroplane to an appropriate landing field.

Should the commander suspect that the use of firearms might occur within the cabin it then becomes imperative to descend the aeroplane to at least 14000' in order to reduce the risk of an explosive decompression and resultant structural damage to the airframe.

6.9.2.2 Confirmation of hijack SSR Code

In addition to "squawking" 7500, the commander may actually use the words "Transponder Seven Five Zero Zero" meaning "I am being hijacked / forced to a new destination'.

ATS will acknowledge and confirm receipt of the Transponder Code 7500 by asking the commander to verify it. If the commander replies in the affirmative or does not reply the controller will not ask any further questions but will maintain a listening watch, respond to any request from the commander, and notify appropriate authorities.

6.9.3   Measures to be taken by the State regarding unlawful interference

Each Contracting State shall take adequate measures for the safety of passengers and crew of an aeroplane, which is subjected to an act of unlawful interference until their journey can be continued.

Each Contracting State responsible for providing air traffic services for an aircraft which is the subject of an act of unlawful interference shall collect all pertinent information on the flight of that aircraft and transmit that information to all other States responsible for the Air Traffic Services units concerned. This shall include those at the airport of known or presumed destination, so that timely and appropriate safeguarding action may be taken en-route and at the aircraft's known, likely or possible destination.

Each Contracting State should ensure that information received as a consequence of action taken in accordance with paragraph above is distributed locally to the Air Traffic Services units concerned, the appropriate airport administrations, the operator and others concerned as soon as practicable.

Each Contracting State shall provide such assistance to an aircraft subjected to an act of unlawful seizure, including the provision of navigation aids, air traffic services and permission to land as may be necessitated by the circumstances

Each Contracting State shall take measures, as it may find practicable, to ensure that an aircraft subjected to an act of unlawful seizure which has landed in its territory is detained on the ground unless its departure is necessitated by the overriding duty to protect human life.   States must recognise the importance of consultations, wherever practicable, between the State where that aircraft has landed and the State of the operator of the aircraft. Where a hijacked aeroplane is forced to depart (after a landing), the State where the aircraft has landed must notify the Authorities at the assumed or stated destination.

6.9.4   Flight-deck door precautions

The flight crew compartment door on all aeroplanes operated for the purpose of carrying passengers shall be capable of being locked from within the compartment in order to prevent unauthorised access.

6.9.5   *Carriage of weapons on board an aeroplane*

Contracting States should ensure that the carriage of weapons on board the aeroplane, by law enforcement officers and other authorised persons, acting in the performance of their duties, requires special authorisation in accordance with the laws of the States involved.

Contracting States should ensure that the carriage of weapons in other cases is allowed only when an authorised and duly qualified person has determined that they are not loaded, if applicable, and then only if stowed in a place inaccessible to any person during flight time.

Contracting States should ensure that the commander is notified as to the number of armed persons and their seat locations.

6.9.6   *Bomb warnings*

Here again there are two possibilities:
a) Aeroplane on the ground
b) Aeroplane in the air

Situation (a)
This is a situation likely to involve ground personnel and the Airport Authority mainly.

Due to the high level of screening at airports for the prevention of weapons or bombs being carried on board by passengers, the explosive device will usually have been placed in a piece of checked-in baggage or amongst the cargo, or mail. The notification therefore of the "bomb" will normally come by way of a telephone call to the airline or airport. This call will then be prioritised under the following categories:

Red - a specific threat to a specifically identified flight or in a specific area of the airport
Green - an airline, destination or in a particular terminal without specific details
Orange - a vague or generalised type of warning.

All operators and airports have in place procedures and personnel to deal with these threats and this machinery will be automatically activated depending upon the "colour" of the warning.

Situation (b)
If the bomb is actually in the possession of a passenger then we are looking at a version of the hijacking scenario. If however the device has been placed somewhere in the aeroplane and a thorough search of the cabin or cockpit does not reveal it then, unless informed to the contrary in the bomb warning, it must be assumed to be inaccessible in the baggage or cargo compartments.

6.9.7   *Actions by the commander*

a) While endeavouring to avoid antagonising the hijacker or if the device is remotely located, a slow, surreptitious and steady descent should be initiated to place the aeroplane, at least, below 14000' to reduce the potential structural damage in the event of an explosion. This action should be accompanied by a "mayday" call along with, if possible, a 7500 SSR "squawk', or only transmitting this code and no "mayday" along with speaking the code on the working frequency or on 121.5 MHz, depending upon the existing circumstances on board the aeroplane.
b)   If possible prepare the crew and passengers for a "crash landing'.
c)   Set course for the nearest aerodrome.
Request an airborne intercept and escort.

6.10   *Emergency and precautionary landings*

6.10.1   *Introduction*

'Flight 123 is coming back" is always guaranteed to cause a ripple of concern amongst the staff of the operations control / flight dispatch department. Such a message conveys the fact that this particular flight has encountered some sort of problem or potential emergency of sufficient gravity to cause the commander to decide to return to the point of departure.

6.10.1.1   *Precautionary landing*

It may be a genuine emergency but more often than not it is purely a precautionary landing due to some apparent equipment unserviceability or spurious warning alert. Upon receipt of such a warning, prudence would dictate that to return (to base) and have the apparent problem resolved is a better course of action than to continue flight.

6.10.1.2   *Emergency landing*

There are many potential causes for the flight crew to have to make an "emergency landing'. However, our modern day commercial aeroplane is of such a high standard of manufacture that fortunately actual emergency landings are a very infrequent event.
Some obvious causes would be:
a) uncontrollable cabin fire
b) uncontrollable engine fire
c) loss of all hydraulic pressure
d) loss of more than one engine on a multi-engine aeroplane

6.10.1.2.1   *On water landing - ditching*

A ditching similar to an emergency landing might arise where, due to an uncontrollable fire, multi-engine malfunction or severe control difficulties, the commander is forced to terminate the flight by making an over water emergency landing instead of making a successful landing at the nearest en-route alternate.

6.10.1.3   *Factors with regard to emergency landings / ditchings*

An emergency landing occurred at Sioux City in the State of Iowa, USA. The United Airlines, McDonnell Douglas DC1O was en-route from San Francisco to the Chicago O'Hare Airport in the State of Illinois. While at cruising altitude approximately mid-way in the flight the number 2 (tail) engine suffered a catastrophic main engine fan disc failure which resulted in an uncontained explosion during which the piping serving all three hydraulic systems was fractured and all the hydraulic fluid was lost. The aeroplane became essentially uncontrollable leaving the commander in no doubt that continued flight to final destination was impossible and that it was now necessary to land the aeroplane at the nearest airport.

Another emergency occurred to an El Al B747 cargo aeroplane en-route from Schipol Airport, Amsterdam in the Netherlands to David Ben Gurion Airport at Tel Aviv in Israel. Shortly after takeoff number 3 engine failed and in the process of failing actually became detached from the wing whereupon half the hydraulic fluid was lost and the slats on the leading edge of that wing were damaged rendering further flight virtually impossible. The commander chose to return to Schipol but unfortunately was unable to succeed in landing the aeroplane before all control was lost and the aeroplane crashed into a residential area.

More recently a US Airways airbus aircraft was ditched successfully into the Hudson River after a birdstrike caused all engines to fail.

6.10.1.4   *Ditching procedures*

Ditching a large aeroplane in the sea requires an appreciation of the interaction between the surface wind and the sea swell in the area. Another factor is the directions of these relative to one another and the height of any wave activity. As a general rule it is recommended that the aeroplane be land parallel to the sea swell rather than the into wind, but the actual technique used must be adjusted according to the circumstances prevailing. It is emphasised that these are general principles and that you must consult the Aeroplane Operating Manual (AOM) for detailed procedures relevant to the type being flown. It is recommended that the aeroplane weight be reduced as much as is practicable before ditching. If possible the C of G should be adjusted rearwards to reduce the degree to which the aeroplane will pitch forward onto the nose after touchdown. Maintain sufficient reserve of fuel to enable power to be used throughout the approach. The landing gear should be retracted. Obtain an approximate QNH for the alighting area from the nearest control station or from the meteorological documentation if no communication is possible. If your aeroplane is fitted with a radio altimeter then use that as an important source of vertical guidance. Select the direction giving the minimum relative speed between the aeroplane and the sea swell. The best heading is parallel to the primary swell either downwind and down the secondary swell or upwind and into the secondary swell. An attempt to land into a primary swell would be extremely hazardous.

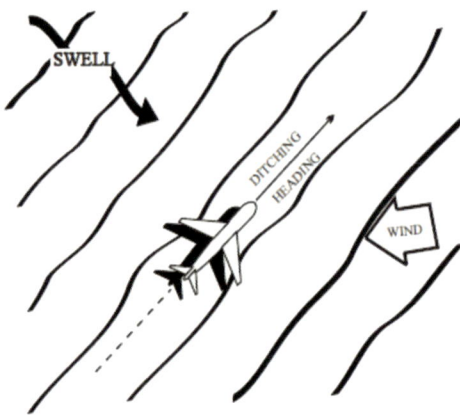

Single swell 15 KT wind

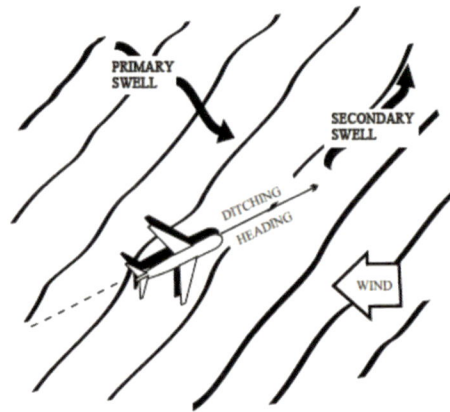

Double swell 30 KT wind

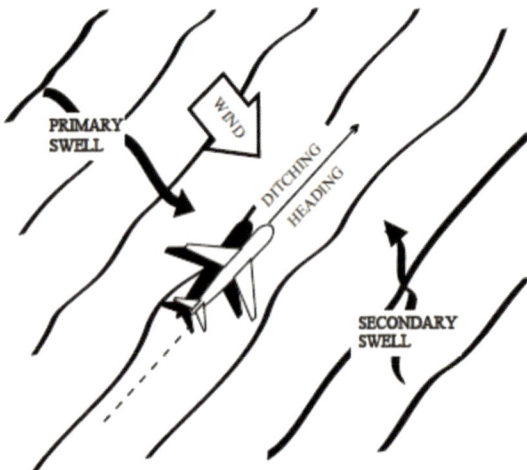

Double swell 15 KT wind

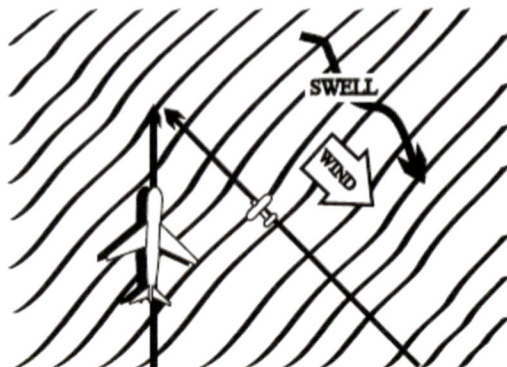

50 KT wind

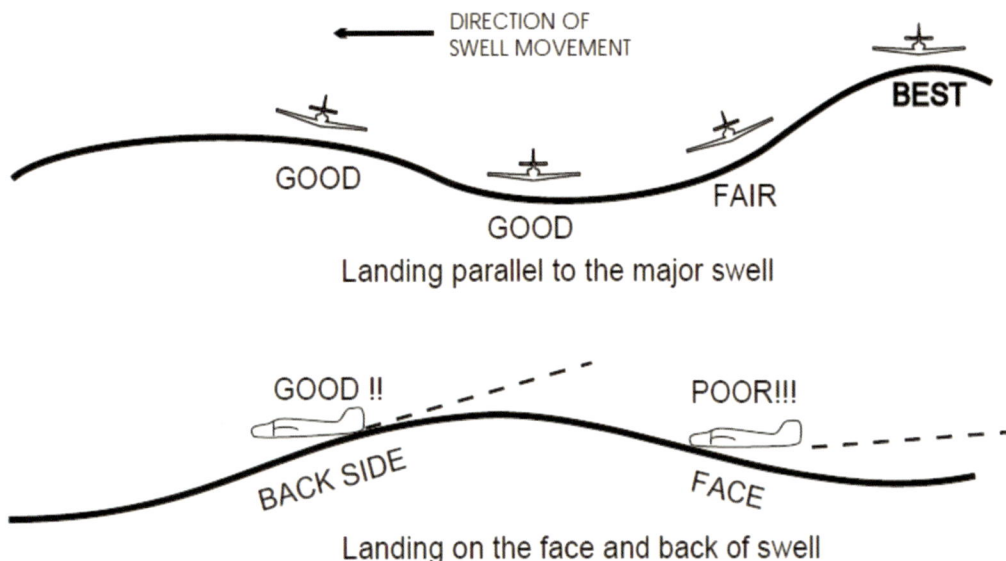

Figure 6.15 Ditching

The final approach should be made at normal approach speed, reducing to threshold speed and using full flap and slots. The rate of descent should be kept to a minimum. For night touchdowns landing lights should be used in the normal manner. At approximately 10' above the crest of the swell level off and rotate the aeroplane to the normal landing altitude. Do not attempt to stall the aeroplane onto the surface at angles greater than the normal landing as this will result in a severe impact, probably followed by a violent pitching down of the nose. Keep the aeroplane wings level with the surface and not the horizon. Contact the water at minimum forward speed and sink rate prior to contact. Close the throttle immediately prior to contact.

6.10.1.5   *Passenger briefing*

It is a matter of legal requirement that a passenger briefing be given prior to the start of every commercial aeroplane flight which must include a reference to the possibility of a "landing on water" and the use of the lifejacket and flotation equipment. The "card in the seat pocket in front of you contains additional information on emergency exits and escape slides" and by use of this technique it is brought to the attention of the passengers the availability and location of the emergency equipment. Should an actual emergency or precautionary landing, or a ditching, become likely then the cabin staff must ensure that the passengers take up the "crash position" upon receipt of the words "Brace, Brace" from the commander.

6.10.1.6   *Evacuation procedures*

The bottom line here is to have the aeroplane totally vacated of all passengers and crewmembers within 90 seconds of the aeroplane coming to a final stop. This is a legal requirement and the operator must demonstrate by means of simulated emergencies that both the cabin and flight deck crew are capable of achieving this with a full passenger load

The methods used will obviously depend upon the aeroplane type, location of emergency exits, number of cabin attendants available, and the type of "landing" experienced. In addition, the cabin crew is directed to select some able-bodied male passengers to supplement the number of personnel available to open the exits/doors in the event of some of the cabin attendants becoming incapacitated in the landing. Once the aeroplane has come to a complete stop the emergency exits and doors must be opened as quickly as possible, the slide rafts deployed and the passenger evacuation begun. Some of the aforementioned able-bodied males should be sent down the slide raft first. They can secure it at the bottom and assist the remaining evacuating passengers to clear the area. They should also prevent any gathering of people in this area and thereby slowing down the rate of evacuation and distancing from the aeroplane.

6.11   *Fuel Jettisoning*

6.11.1   *Fuel jettisoning scenario*

An aeroplane is dispatched at the maximum structural or performance limited takeoff mass at the start of a long-range flight. Within a very short time interval, after takeoff, some event occurs on board the aeroplane, engine failure, fire warning or some such similarly serious occurrence and the commander decides the correct action in the circumstances is to return to the point of departure and land. It is certain that the aeroplane will now arrive overhead the departure airport several tonnes heavier than the maximum permitted structural landing mass. If the runway is not long enough for an "overweight landing" to be attempted then the excess weight must be disposed of. The only way in which this can be done is to reduce the amount of fuel onboard in one of two ways:

- Continue to fly at low level at maximum cruising thrust to "burn-off" the excess fuel down to a weight commensurate with the maximum structural landing mass
- Jettison the excess fuel by use of the "fuel jettisoning)

As we have predicted this scenario on the aeroplane suffering a significant unserviceability the first of these two options is not really practical or indeed safe so the second (that of fuel jettisoning) becomes the required procedure. The required data and procedures for this will be contained in the AFM of the AOM. The two significant items are:

- The procedure for extending the "fuel jettisoning" chutes
- The rate of fuel jettisoning per minute at maximum pressure

Either the second pilot, systems panel operator or flight engineer will be tasked with these two jobs, and once the system is functioning then he / she must monitor the rate of fuel jettisoning down to that amount required to now have the aeroplane mass at the required maximum landing figure.

6.11.2   *CS 25 requirements*

CS 25 requires that:

- the fuel jettisoning system must be installed on aircraft unless it is shown that the aircraft meets the "landing climb: all engines operating" and "climb: one engine inoperative" (from go-around) requirements at maximum takeoff weight less the fuel necessary for 15 min of flight
- the jettisoning system must be capable of dumping enough fuel within 15 min to meet the climb requirements (starting at the weight given above)
- the system and operation must be free from fire hazard
- the fuel must discharge clear of any part of the aircraft
- the fumes or fuel must not enter any part of the aircraft
- jettisoning must not adversely affect controllability of the aircraft
- means must be provided to prevent jettisoning of fuel in tanks used for takeoff and landing below the level which allows climb from sea level to 10000' and thereafter to fly for 45 min cruise at speed for maximum range
- the jettisoning valve be designed to be closed during any part of the jettisoning operation

6.11.3   *Legal Requirements*

Nothing should be dropped / sprayed from aircraft unless cleared by ATS, therefore, ATS should be informed of the need to dump fuel and a clearance received.

Although the jettisoned fuel evaporates almost instantaneously upon leaving the "dump" chute being heavier than air it will gradually descend towards the surface of the earth while in its dissipating state. Consequently fuel jettisoning / dumping is prohibited over highly populated or built-up areas. Once notified that fuel dumping is necessary, ATC will usually give a clearance to an area / altitude where it can be done. If necessary, the commander may decide otherwise due to the nature of the emergency.

6.11.4   *Safety precautions*

Aviation fuel, indeed any propulsion fuel, is highly inflammable and therefore highly dangerous. Therefore precautions must be taken to ensure that any risks of ignition and the lighting of the fuel must be strictly controlled and eliminated.

There are certain activities where this possibly might occur and the following is a list of the major potentially hazardous circumstances:

- The first and most obvious is - no smoking.
- No use or limited use of the High-Frequency (HF) radio as this equipment emits an electric current, which could introduce a spark into the surrounding atmosphere that is full of vaporising fuel.
- Use of electrical equipment such as navigation lights, strobe beacons or landing lights to be avoided.
- The flight pattern to be flown in such a way that the aeroplane does not fly "back or through" the area containing the vaporising fuel.
- Operation of flaps slots / slats must be avoided lest there be some friction and a "spark" generated.
- Fuel jettisoning is not to take place in areas where a "lightning strike" from a thunderstorm or cumulonimbus cloud in the vicinity might take place

6.12   *Transport of Dangerous Goods*

6.12.1   *Introduction*

With the progressive development of airline commercial cargo and freight operations, the Authorities and operators became aware that it was necessary to develop rules and procedures for the carriage of certain goods and materials, the nature of which posed a hazard to the aeroplane in which they were being transported. There have been several incidents and a number of major accidents arising from the improper carriage of dangerous goods, which exploded or ignited and caused structural failure. The leakage of toxic material into the aeroplane has also resulted in incidents / accidents causing either, loss of consciousness on the part of the flight crew or worse. Under the auspices of ICAO internationally agreed procedures were drawn up under what is now known as "The Carriage of Dangerous Goods" and all flight crew and ground personnel are given special training with regard to the handling, boarding and carriage of dangerous goods. A special "dangerous goods" cargo manifest must be prepared and given to the commander to advise him/her that these hazardous materials are on board and the nature of them. The relevant ICAO Annex lays down the types of dangerous goods that may be carried subject to certain strict precautions and those that may not be carried under any circumstances. A specific labelling procedure is also included whereby the flight crew and ground staff can immediately recognise from the symbology; the type of goods concerned, no matter where in the world they are being shipped.

The most common terms are as follows:

Acceptance Check List.
A document used to assist in carrying out a check on the external appearance of packages of dangerous goods and their associated documents to determine that all appropriate requirements have been met.

Cargo Aircraft.
Any aircraft which is carrying goods or property but not passengers. In this context the following are not considered to be passengers:

A crew member.
An operator's employee permitted by, and carried in accordance with, the instructions contained in the Operations Manual;
An authorised representative of an Authority; or
A person with duties in respect of a particular shipment on board.

Dangerous Goods *Accident.*
An occurrence associated with and related to the transport of dangerous goods, which results in fatal or serious injury to a person or major property damage.

Dangerous Goods Incident.
An occurrence, other than a dangerous goods accident, associated with and related to the transport of dangerous goods. This may not necessarily occur on board the aircraft, but results in injury to a person, property damage, fire, breakage, spillage, leakage of fluid or radiation or other evidence that the integrity of the packaging has not been maintained. Any occurrence relating to the transport of dangerous goods which seriously jeopardises the aircraft or its occupants is also deemed to constitute a dangerous goods incident.

Dangerous Goods Transport Document.
A document which is specified by the Technical Instructions. It must be completed by the person who offers dangerous goods for air transport and shall contain information about those dangerous goods. The document must bear a signed declaration stating that the dangerous goods are fully and accurately described by their proper shipping names and UN numbers (if assigned) and that they are correctly classified, packed, marked, labelled and in a proper condition for transport.

Freight Container.
A freight container is an article of transport equipment for radioactive materials, designed to facilitate the transport of such materials (either packaged or unpackaged) by one or more modes of transport. (Note: see Unit Load Device where the dangerous goods are not radioactive materials.)

Handling Agent.
An agency performing, on behalf of the operator, some or all of the latter's functions including receiving, loading, unloading, transferring or other processing of passengers or cargo.

Overpack.
An enclosure used by a single shipper to contain one or more packages and to form one handling unit for convenience of handling and stowage. (Note: a unit load device is not included in this definition.)

Package.
The complete product of the packing operation consisting of the packaging and its contents prepared for transport.

Packaging.
Receptacles and any other components or materials necessary for the receptacle to perform its containment function and to ensure compliance with the packing requirements.

Proper Shipping Name.
The name to be used to describe a particular article or substance in all shipping documents and notifications and, where appropriate, to be displayed on packaging.

Serious Injury.
An injury which is sustained by a person in an accident and which:

Requires hospitalisation for more than 48 h, commencing within seven days from the date the injury was received; or
Results in a fracture of any bone (except simple fractures of fingers, toes or nose); or
Involves lacerations which cause severe haemorrhage, nerve, muscle or tendon damage; or
Involves injury to any internal organ, or
Involves second or third degree burns, or any burns affecting more than 5% of the body surface; or
Involves verified exposure to infectious substances or injurious radiation.

State of Origin.
The Authority in whose territory the dangerous goods were first loaded on an aircraft.

Technical Instructions.
The latest effective edition of the Technical Instructions for the Safe Transport of Dangerous Goods by Air (ICAO Doc 9284-AN/905), including the Supplement and any Addendum, approved and published by decision of the Council of the International Civil Aviation Organisation.

UN Number.
The four-digit number assigned by the United Nations Committee of Experts on the Transport of Dangerous Goods to identify a substance or a particular group of substances.

Unit Load Device.
Any type of aircraft container, aircraft pallet with a net, or aircraft pallet with a net over an igloo. (Note: an overpack is not included in this definition; for a container containing radioactive materials see the definition for freight container.)

6.12.2   *Approval to Transport Dangerous Goods*

An operator shall not transport dangerous goods unless approved to do so by the Authority.
In addition the following rules apply:
An operator shall comply with the provisions contained in the Technical Instructions on all occasions when dangerous goods are carried, irrespective of whether the flight is wholly or partly within or wholly outside the territory of a State. Articles and substances which would otherwise be classed as dangerous goods are excluded from the provisions of this Subpart, to the extent specified in the Technical Instructions, provided:
They are required to be aboard the aeroplane in accordance with the relevant regulations or for operating reasons
They are carried as catering or cabin service supplies;
They are carried for use in flight as veterinary aid or as a humane killer for an animal
They are carried for use in flight for medical aid for a patient, provided that:
Gas cylinders have been manufactured specifically for the purpose of containing and transporting that particular gas;
Drugs, medicines and other medical matter are under the control of trained personnel during the time when they are in use in the aeroplane;
Equipment containing wet cell batteries is kept and, when necessary secured, in an upright position to prevent spillage of the electrolyte; and
Proper provision is made to stow and secure all the equipment during takeoff and landing and at all other times when deemed necessary by the commander in the interests of safety; or
They are carried by passengers or crewmembers.
Articles and substances, intended as replacements for those in (b)(1) above, shall be transported on an aeroplane as specified in the Technical Instructions.

6.12.3   *Limitations on the Transport of Dangerous Goods*

The following rules govern the limitations on the carriage of dangerous goods.
An operator shall take all reasonable measures to ensure that articles and substances that are specifically identified by name or generic description in the Technical Instructions as being forbidden for transport under any circumstances are not carried on any aeroplane. An operator shall take all reasonable measures to ensure that articles and substances or other goods that are identified in the Technical Instructions as being forbidden for transport in normal circumstances are only transported when:
They are exempted by the States concerned under the provisions of the Technical Instructions or,
The Technical Instructions indicate they may be transported under an approval issued by the State of Origin.

6.12.4   *Additional responsibilities of operators*

Classification
An operator shall take all reasonable measures to ensure that articles and substances are classified as dangerous goods as specified in the Technical Instructions.

Packing
An operator shall take all reasonable measures to ensure that dangerous goods are packed as specified in the Technical Instructions.

Labelling and Marking
An operator shall take all reasonable measures to ensure that packages, overpacks and freight containers are labelled and marked as specified in the Technical Instructions.

Where dangerous goods are carried on a flight, which takes place wholly or partly outside the territory of a State, labelling and marking must be in the English language in addition to any other language requirements.

Dangerous Goods Transport Document
An operator shall ensure that, except when otherwise specified in the Technical Instructions, dangerous goods are accompanied by a dangerous goods transport document.

Where dangerous goods are carried on a flight, which takes place wholly or partly outside the territory of a State, the English language must be used for the dangerous goods transport document in addition to any other language requirements.

Acceptance of Dangerous Goods
An operator shall not accept dangerous goods for transport until the package, overpack or freight container has been inspected in accordance with the acceptance procedures in the Technical Instructions.

An operator or his handling agent shall use an acceptance checklist. The acceptance check list shall allow for all relevant details to be checked and shall be in such form as will allow for the recording of the results of the acceptance check by manual, mechanical or computerised means.

Inspection for Damage, Leakage or Contamination
An operator shall ensure that:
Packages, overpacks and freight containers are inspected for evidence of leakage or damage immediately prior to loading on an aeroplane or into a unit load device, as specified in the Technical Instructions;
A unit load device is not loaded on an aeroplane unless it has been inspected as required by the Technical Instructions and found free from any evidence of leakage from, or damage to, the dangerous goods contained therein;
Leaking or damaged packages, overpacks or freight containers are not loaded on an aeroplane;
Any package of dangerous goods found on an aeroplane and which appears to be damaged or leaking is removed or arrangements made for its removal by an appropriate authority or organisation. In this case the remainder of the consignment shall be inspected to ensure it is in a proper condition for transport and that no damage or contamination has occurred to the aeroplane or its load; and
Packages, overpacks and freight containers are inspected for signs of damage or leakage upon unloading from an aeroplane or from a unit load device and, if there is evidence of damage or leakage, the area where the dangerous goods were stowed is inspected for damage or contamination.

Removal of Contamination
An operator shall ensure that:
Any contamination found as a result of the leakage or damage of dangerous goods is removed without delay; and

An aeroplane which has been contaminated by radioactive materials is immediately taken out of service and not returned until the radiation level at any accessible surface and the non-fixed contamination are not more than the values specified in the Technical Instructions.

Loading Restrictions
Passenger Cabin and Flight Deck. An operator shall ensure that dangerous goods are not carried in an aeroplane cabin occupied by passengers or on the flight deck, unless otherwise specified in the Technical Instructions.

Cargo Compartments. An operator shall ensure that dangerous goods are loaded, segregated, stowed and secured on an aeroplane as specified in the Technical Instructions.

Dangerous Goods Designated for Carriage Only on Cargo Aircraft. An operator shall ensure that packages of dangerous goods bearing the "Cargo Aircraft Only" label are carried on a cargo aircraft and loaded as specified in the Technical Instructions.

Provision of Information
Information to Ground Staff. An operator shall ensure that:
Information is provided to enable ground staff to carry out their duties with regard to the transport of dangerous goods, including the actions to be taken in the event of incidents and accidents involving dangerous goods; and
Where applicable, the information referred to in (I) above is also provided to his handling agent.

Information to Passengers and Other Persons
An operator shall ensure that information is promulgated as required by the Technical Instructions so that passengers are warned as to the types of goods which they are forbidden from transporting aboard an aeroplane; and

An operator and, where applicable, his handling agent shall ensure that notices are provided at acceptance points for cargo giving information about the transport of dangerous goods.

Information to Crew Members. An operator shall ensure that information is provided in the Operations Manual to enable crew members to carry out their responsibilities in regard to the transport of dangerous goods, including the actions to be taken in the event of emergencies arising involving dangerous goods.

Information to the Commander. An operator shall ensure that the commander is provided with written information, as specified in the Technical Instructions.

Information in the Event of an Aeroplane Incident or Accident

The operator of an aeroplane, which is involved in an aeroplane incident, shall on request, provide any information required minimising the hazards created by any dangerous goods carried.

The operator of an aeroplane, which is involved in an aeroplane accident, shall as soon as possible, inform the appropriate authority of the State in which the aeroplane accident occurred of any dangerous goods carried.

Training programmes
An operator shall establish and maintain staff training programmes, as required by the Technical Instructions, which must be approved by the Authority.

Operators not holding a permanent approval to carry dangerous goods. An operator shall ensure that the following personnel:

Crew members;

Passenger handling staff; and

Security staff employed by the operator who deal with the screening of passengers and their baggage, have received training which, as a minimum, must cover the areas listed below and be to a depth sufficient to ensure that an awareness is gained of the hazards associated with dangerous goods, how to identify them and what requirements apply to the carriage of such goods by passengers.

AREAS OF TRAINING

General philosophy

Limitations on Dangerous Goods in air transport

Package marking and labelling

Dangerous Goods in passengers' baggage

Emergency procedures

Operators holding a permanent approval to carry dangerous goods. An operator shall ensure that:

Staff who are engaged in the acceptance of dangerous goods have received training and are qualified to carry out their duties. As a minimum this training must cover the following areas to a depth sufficient to ensure the staff can take decisions on the acceptance or refusal of dangerous goods offered for carriage by air;

AREAS OF TRAINING

General philosophy

Limitations on Dangerous Goods in air transport

Classification and list of Dangerous Goods

General packing requirements and Packing Instructions

Packaging specifications markings

Package marking and labelling

Documentation from the shipper

Acceptance of Dangerous Goods, including the use of a checklist

Loading, restrictions on loading and segregation

Inspections for damage or leakage and decontamination procedures

Provision of information to commander

Dangerous Goods in passengers' baggage

Emergency procedures

Flight crewmembers have received training that, as a minimum, must cover the areas listed below. Training must be to a depth sufficient to ensure that an awareness is gained of the hazards associated with dangerous goods and how they should be carried on an aeroplane;

AREAS OF TRAINING

General philosophy

Limitations on Dangerous Goods in air transport

Classification and list of Dangerous Goods

Package marking and labelling

Loading, restrictions on loading and segregation

Provision of information to commander

Dangerous Goods in passengers' baggage

Emergency procedures

The following personnel:

Passenger handling staff;

Security staff employed by the operator who deal with the screening of passengers and their baggage; and

CRANFIELD AVIATION TRAINING SCHOOL LTD. PART-FCL GBR.ATO-0136

CATS CATS INNOVATION CENTRE, LUTON, Bedfordshire LU2 8DL U.K.

www.catsaviation.com

6-42

Operational Procedures

Crewmembers, other than flight crew members, have received training which, as a minimum, must cover the following areas to a depth sufficient to ensure that an awareness is gained of the hazards associated with dangerous goods and what requirements apply to the carriage of such goods by passengers or, more generally, their carriage on an aeroplane.

AREAS OF TRAINING
General philosophy
Limitations on Dangerous Goods in air transport
Package marking and labelling
Dangerous Goods in passengers' baggage
Emergency procedures

An operator shall ensure that all staff requiring dangerous goods training receive recurrent training at intervals of not longer than 2 years.

An operator shall ensure that records of dangerous goods training are maintained for all staff trained in accordance with sub-paragraph (d) above.

6.12.5   *Dangerous Goods Incident and Accident Reports*

An operator shall report dangerous goods incidents and accidents to the Authority. An initial report shall be despatched within 72 h of the event unless exceptional circumstances prevent this

6.13   *Contaminated Runways*

6.13.1   *Definitions*

Contaminated runway - more than 25% of the surface area (whether in isolated areas or not) within required length and width being used is covered by:-

- surface water more than 3mm deep; or slush or loose snow equivalent to more than 3mm of water
- snow compressed into a solid mass (i.e. compacted snow)
- ice, including wet ice

Damp runway - surface not dry but moisture on it does *not* give it a shiny appearance

Wet runway - sufficient water on surface to give it a shiny appearance but no significant standing water *or* covered with water, or equivalent, less than that specified for a contaminated runway (i.e. less than 3mm deep)

Dry runway - neither wet nor contaminated (includes paved runways with grooves or porous pavement which retain effectively dry braking action even with moisture present)

6.13.2   *Hydroplaning*

Hydroplaning may be described as a substantial reduction in friction between tyres and surface due to a thin layer of water that separates the tyres from the runway. It is more likely at high speeds on wet, slushy or snow-covered runways, which have smooth textures. The types of hydroplaning which may be encountered are dynamic, viscous and reverted rubber.

6.13.2.1   *Dynamic hydroplaning*

This occurs in standing water or slush about 3 mm or more deep (e.g. contaminated surface) when a wedge of water builds up and lifts tyre away from surface. The greater the aircraft speed, depth of water and pressure in the tyres, the more likely it is to take place.

When dynamic hydroplaning occurs water depth is greater tyre tread depth

6.13.2.2 Viscous hydroplaning

Viscous hydroplaning occurs when the tyre slips on a thin film. It can occur on a very thin film of water (or heavy dew) not more than one-thousandth of an inch deep if it covers a smooth surface. Textured surfaces (e.g. grooves) alleviate the condition

6.13.2.3 Reverted rubber hydroplaning

This is caused by a prolonged locked wheel skid where reverted rubber acts as a seal between tyre and runway. Water gets trapped, heats up and forms steam, which lifts the tyre off the surface. Grooves on the runway alleviate the condition.

6.13.2.4 Minimum dynamic hydroplaning speed

The minimum speed for dynamic hydroplaning may be calculated as follows:

Minimum hydroplaning speed	$= 9 \sqrt{\text{tyre pressure (psi)}}$ KT
	$= 34 \sqrt{\text{tyre pressure (bar)}}$ KT

Note: Viscous hydroplaning can occur at speeds less than those for dynamic hydroplaning

6.13.2.4.1 Techniques to reduce hydroplaning effect

The following techniques are recommended to reduce the effects of hydroplaning:
- approach to land at slowest possible airspeed
- land firmly
- lower nose wheel as soon as main wheels are firmly on the surface
- avoid heavy braking above minimum hydroplaning speed; use aerodynamic braking

6.13.3 Braking Action

Braking action may be measured / calculated or estimated friction coefficients and are used to provide indications of surface friction characteristics. The following table shows classifications in use.

Measured / calculated coefficient	or	Estimated surface friction
0.40 and above		GOOD – 5
0.39 to 0.36		GOOD / MEDIUM- 4
0.35 to 0.30		MEDIUM – 3
0.29 to 0.26		MEDIUM / POOR – 2
0.25 and below		POOR – 1
9 – unreliable		UNRELIABLE – 9

6.13.3.1 Effect of contamination on performance

The coefficient of rolling resistance increases with contamination therefore a longer ground run is needed for takeoff. The coefficient of friction reduces with contamination therefore there is a reduced braking effect. Heavy rain destroys the boundary layer and results in an increased stalling speed.

6.13.3.2 SNOWTAM

SNOWTAM FORMAT

(COM heading)	(PRIORITY INDICATOR)	(ADDRESSES)		
	(DATE AND TIME OF FILING)		(ORIGINATOR'S INDICATOR)	
(Abbreviated heading)	(SERIAL NUMBER) S W E G	(LOCATION INDICATOR) E G	DATE/TIME OF OBSERVATION	(OPTIONAL GROUP)

SNOWTAM (Serial number)			
(AERODROME LOCATION INDICATOR)	**A)** E G		
(DATE/TIME OF OBSERVATION *(Time of completion of measurement in UTC)*)	**B)**		
(RUNWAY DESIGNATORS)	**C)**		
(CLEARED RUNWAY LENGTH, IF LESS THAN PUBLISHED LENGTH *(m)*	**D)**		
(CLEARED RUNWAY WIDTH, IF LESS THAN PUBLISHED WIDTH *(m; if offset left or right of centre-line add 'L' or 'R')*)	**E)**		
(DEPOSITS OVER TOTAL RUNWAY LENGTH *(Observed on each third of the runway, starting from threshold having the lower runway designation number)*) NIL – CLEAR AND DRY 1 – DAMP 2 – WET or water patches 3 – RIME OR FROST COVERED *(depth normally less than 1 mm)* 4 – DRY SNOW 5 – WET SNOW 6 – SLUSH 7 – ICE 8 – COMPACTED OR ROLLED SNOW 9 – FROZEN RUTS OR RIDGES)	**F)**		
(MEAN DEPTH *(mm)* FOR EACH THIRD OF TOTAL RUNWAY LENGTH)	**G)**		
(FRICTION MEASUREMENT ON EACH THIRD OF RUNWAY AND FRICTION MEASURING DEVICE MEASURED OR CALCULATED COEFFICIENT or ESTIMATED BRAKING ACTION 0.40 and above GOOD - 5 0.39 to 0.36 MEDIUM/GOOD - 4 0.35 to 0.30 MEDIUM - 3 0.29 to 0.26 MEDIUM/POOR - 2 0.25 and below POOR - 1 9 - unreliable UNRELIABLE - 9 *(When quoting a measured coefficient use the observed two figures, followed by the abbreviation of the friction measuring device used. When quoting an estimate use single digits)*	**H)**		
(CRITICAL SNOWBANKS *(If present, insert height (cm)/distance from the edge of runway (m) followed by 'L', 'R' or 'LR' if applicable)*)	**J)**		
(RUNWAY LIGHTS *(If obscured, insert 'YES' followed by 'L', 'R' or both 'LR' if applicable)*)	**K)**		
(FURTHER CLEARANCE *(If planned, insert length (m)/width (m) to be cleared or if to full dimensions, insert 'TOTAL')*)	**L)**		
(FURTHER CLEARANCE EXPECTED TO BE COMPLETED BY *(UTC)*)	**M)**		
(TAXIWAY *(If no appropriate taxiway is available, insert 'NO')*)	**N)**		
TAXIWAY SNOWBANKS *(If more than 60 cm, insert 'YES' followed by distance apart, m)*)	**P)**		
(APRON *(If unusable insert 'NO')*)	**R)**		
(NEXT PLANNED OBSERVATION/MEASUREMENT IS FOR) *(month/day/hour in UTC)*	**S)**		
(PLAIN LANGUAGE REMARKS *(including contaminant coverage and other operationally significant information, e.g. sanding, deicing)*)	**T)**		

NOTES   1 Information on other runways, repeat from C to P
                2 Words in brackets ( ) not to be transmitted

Figure 6.16 SNOWTAM format

Significant points to note are:

- metric units used and units of measurement not reported
- maximum validity = 24 h
- new SNOWTAM must be issued whenever there is a significant change in conditions (e.g. change in μ (friction co-efficient) of about 0.05, change in available length/width of runway of 10% or more, ...)
- cleared runway length in metres (if less than published length) placed in main body of SNOWTAM; uncleared length reported in plain language at the end of the main body
- cleared width (if less than published) placed in the main body

CRANFIELD AVIATION TRAINING SCHOOL LTD. PART-FCL GBR.ATO-0136
CATS INNOVATION CENTRE, LUTON, Bedfordshire LU2 8DL U.K.   www.catsaviation.com
6-45   Operational Procedures

CHAPTER 7

Abbreviations

ACAS	Airborne Collision Avoidance System		HIALS	High Intensity Approach Lighting System
AD	Aerodrome		HLA	High Level Airspace
AFM	Aeroplane Flight Manual		HOT	Hold-Over Time
AIP	Aeronautical Information Publication		HUD	Head-Up Display
ALS	Approach Light System		HUDLS	Head-Up guidance Landing System
AMC	Acceptable Means of Compliance		IALS	Intermediate Approach Light System
AOC	Air Operator Certificate		ICAO	International Civil Aviation Organisation
APU	Auxiliary Power Unit		IEM	Interpretative and Explanatory Material
APV	Approach procedure with Vertical guidance		IFR	Instrument Flight Rules
ATC	Air Traffic Control		ILS	Instrument Landing System
ATPL	Airline Transport Pilot's Licence		INS	Inertial Navigation System
ATS	Air Traffic Services		IRS	Inertial Reference System
BALS	Basic Approach Light System		JAA	Joint Aviation Authority
C of A	Certificate of Airworthiness		JAR	Joint Aviation Regulations
CAVOK	Ceiling and Visibility Okay		LDA	Landing Distance Available
CAT	Category		LIFUS	Line Flying Under Supervision
CAT	Clear Air Turbulence		LLZ	Localizer
CDFA	Continuous Descent Final Approach		LNAV	Lateral Navigation
CDL	Configuration Deviation List		LRNS	Long Range Navigation System
CMV	Converted Meteorological Visibility		LVP	Low Visibility Procedures
CS 25	Certification Specification 25		LVTO	Low Visibility Takeoff
CTA	Control Area		MAPt	Missed Approach Point
CVR	Cockpit Voice Recorders		MASPS	Minimum Aircraft System Performance Specification
DA	Decision Altitude			
DH	Decision Height		MEL	Minimum Equipment List
DME	Distance Measuring Equipment		MMEL	Master Minimum Equipment List
DR	Dead Reckoning		MET	Meteorological
EASA	European Aviation Safety Agency		MIALS	Medium Intensity Approach Light System
EEC	European Economic Community		MLS	Microwave Landing System
ELT	Emergency Locator Transmitter		MNPS	Minimum Navigation Performance Specification
ENR	Enroute		MNPSA	MNPS Airspace
ETA	Estimated Time of Arrival		MNT	Mach Number Technique
ETOPS	Extended range Twin Operations		MSL	Mean Sea Level
EVS	Enhanced Vision System		MTOM	Maximum Takeoff Mass
EZFM	Estimated Zero Fuel Mass		MTR	Minimum Time Route
FAF	Final Approach Fix		NADP1	Noise Abatement Departure Procedure 1
FALS	Full Approach Light System		NADP2	Noise Abatement Departure Procedure 2
FCL	Flight Crew Licensing		NALS	No Approach Light System
FDR	Flight Data Recorder		NAR	North American Route
FMS	Flight Management System		NAT	North Atlantic
FGS	Flight control Guidance System		NM	Nautical Miles
FL	Flight Level		NDB	Non-Directional Beacon
FOO	Flight Operations Officer		NOTAM	Notice to Airmen
GBAS	Ground-Based Augmentation System		OAC	Oceanic Area Control Centre
GLS	GPS Landing System		OCA	Obstacle Clearing Altitude
GNE	Gross Navigation Error		OCA	Oceanic Control Area
GNSS	Global Navigation Satellite System		OCH	Obstacle Clearing Height
GPS	Global Positioning System		OPS	Operational Procedures
GPWS	Ground Proximity Warning System		OTS	Organised Track System
HF	High Frequency		PANS	Procedures for Air Navigation Services

PAR	Precision Approach Radar		RVR	Runway Visual Range
PBE	Portable Breathing Equipment		RVSM	Reduced Vertical Separation Airspace
PIC	Pilot In Command		TCAS	Traffic Collision Avoidance System
PPL	Private Pilot's Licence		THR	Threshold
PRM	Preferred Route Message		VFR	Visual Flight Rules
PTS	Polar Track Structure		VASI	Visual Approach Slope Indicator
RAC	Regulation And Control		V_2	Velocity at screen height 1 engine out
RCLL	Runway Centre Line Lights		V_{AT}	Velocity At Threshold
RNP	Required Navigation Performance		V_{MO}	Maximum Operating speed
RTZL	Runway Touchdown Zone Light		V_{ZF}	Velocity zero flap
SATCOM	Satellite Communication		VDF	VHF Direction Finding
SELCAL	Selective Calling		VHF	Very High Frequency
SLOP	Strategic Lateral Offset Procedure		VOR	VHF Omnidirectional Range
SSR	Secondary Surveillance Radar		WATRS	Western Atlantic Route System
SRA	Surveillance Radar Approach		ZFT	Zero Flight Time
RNAV	Area Navigation			

CRANFIELD AVIATION TRAINING SCHOOL LTD. PART-FCL GBR.ATO-0136
CATS INNOVATION CENTRE, LUTON, Bedfordshire LU2 8DL U.K.   www.catsaviation.com

7-2

Operational Procedures